Wisdom About Wisdom

Wisdom About Wisdom

How the Bible Defines and Redefines Wisdom

Greg Giles

WIPF & STOCK · Eugene, Oregon

WISDOM ABOUT WISDOM
How the Bible Defines and Redefines Wisdom

Copyright © 2025 Greg Giles. All rights reserved. Except for brief quotations in critical publications or reviews, no part of this book may be reproduced in any manner without prior written permission from the publisher. Write: Permissions, Wipf and Stock Publishers, 199 W. 8th Ave., Suite 3, Eugene, OR 97401.

Wipf & Stock
An Imprint of Wipf and Stock Publishers
199 W. 8th Ave., Suite 3
Eugene, OR 97401

www.wipfandstock.com

PAPERBACK ISBN: 979-8-3852-3870-5
HARDCOVER ISBN: 979-8-3852-3871-2
EBOOK ISBN: 979-8-3852-3872-9

VERSION NUMBER 04/28/25

Unless otherwise indicated, all Scripture quotations are from the ESV® Bible (The Holy Bible, English Standard Version®), copyright©2001 by Crossway, a publishing ministry of Good News Publishers. Used by permission. All rights reserved.

Scripture quotations marked (TEV) are taken from Good News Bible: The Bible in Today's English Version. Old Testament: © American Bible Society, 1976. New Testament: © American Bible Society, 1966, 1971, 1976.

Scripture quotations marked (HCSB) are taken from the Holman Christian Standard Bible®. Copyright©1999, 2000, 2002, 2003 by Holman Bible Publishers. Used by permission. Holman Christian Standard Bible®, Holman CSB®, and HCSB® are federally registered trademarks of Holman Bible Publishers.

Scripture quotations marked (NASB) are taken from the New American Standard Bible. Copyright©The Lockman Foundation 1960, 1962, 1963, 1968, 1971, 1972, 1975. Chicago, Moody Press. All rights reserved.

Scripture quotations marked (NIV) are taken from the The Holy Bible, New International Version®, NIV® Copyright©1973, 1978, 1984, 2011 by Biblica, Inc.® Used by permission. All rights reserved.

Scripture quotations marked (TLB) are taken from The Living Bible copyright © 1971 by Tyndale House Foundation. Used by permission of Tyndale House Publishers Inc., Carol Stream, Illinois 60188. All rights reserved.

Dedicated to those who encouraged me to keep going
and helped me along the way:

David Grier—good friend and my look-alike colleague.
Sulia Mason—once my student, now my mentor.
Christy Haman, Cheri Mullet, and Heidi Holland—wonderful
daughters who made this book their own project.
Jean Giles—beloved wife and constant encouragement.

Contents

Preface | xi
List of Abbreviations | xvi

Part One: Defining Wisdom | 1
    1 Getting Guidance | 3
    2 Who Is Wise? | 8
    3 The Spectrum of Wisdoms | 12
    4 Does Wisdom Work? | 24

Part Two: Defining Biblical Wisdom | 29
    5 Introducing the Wisdom Literature | 31
    6 The Worldview of Biblical Wisdom | 33
    7 Wisdom and Moral Judgment | 44
    8 Becoming Wise | 63
    9 Thinking About Wisdom | 77

Part Three: Studies in the Book of Proverbs | 81
    10 Introducing the Book of Proverbs | 83
    11 Learning from Proverbs (Small *p*) | 90
    12 Four Kinds of Wisdom in Proverbs | 96
    13 "Get Wisdom" | 106
    14 Don't Be a Fool! | 115
    15 Every Good Path | 126
    16 Four Character Traits of the Righteous | 132

- 17 The Worldview of Proverbs | 145
- 18 The Wisdom of Proverbs for Today | 152

Part Four: Studies in Ecclesiastes | 155
- 19 What Is an Ecclesiastes? | 157
- 20 The Investigation Begins | 162
- 21 Vanity Fair | 166
- 22 "Wisdom Without Wisdom" | 173
- 23 "Round and Round It Goes . . ." | 177
- 24 Wisdom for an Uncertain World | 183
- 25 The Gifts of God | 189
- 26 The Two Conclusions of Ecclesiastes | 194
- 27 The Theology of Ecclesiastes | 198
- 28 The Wisdom of Ecclesiastes for Today | 203

Part Five: Studies in the Book of Job | 209
- 29 A Drama in Five Acts | 211
- 30 "Have You Considered My Servant Job?" | 217
- 31 With Friends Like These . . . | 221
- 32 Job's Defense | 229
- 33 Job's Paradox | 232
- 34 God Breaks His Silence | 237
- 35 Vindication! | 244
- 36 Wisdom in the Book of Job | 247
- 37 The Wisdom of Job for Today | 251

Part Six: The New Testament: Redefining Wisdom | 255
- 38 The Turning Point in Biblical Wisdom | 257
- 39 Wisdom Incarnate | 260
- 40 God's Mysteries Revealed | 270
- 41 James and the Prayer for Wisdom | 287
- 42 James and the Two Wisdoms | 293

Part Seven: Refining Wisdom | 305
- 43 Truth Applied to Life | 307
- 44 The Inauspicious Record of Wisdom | 314

45 No One Is Smart Enough to Be Wise | 321
46 Restoring Wisdom | 325
47 Wisdom for the Rest of Us | 336

Bibliography | 339

Preface

THIS IS A BOOK about wisdom: what it is, how it works, and how to use it to make our lives better. To be more precise, this is a book about biblical wisdom, the wisdom we learn about in Scripture. And, as we shall see, biblical wisdom is often not what we normally expect from a book about wisdom!

We might expect wisdom to be the same everywhere, but that is clearly not true. Go to a library or a bookstore—if you can still find one—or go online and look for books about wisdom as a topic, and there are not many. But if you look for books offering advice about how to improve your career, your wealth, your health, or your relationships, you will find hundreds of thousands. Those books of advice are wisdom books. And if you search for books that teach a skill, such as how to play the piano, play pickleball, fix up your house, care for your pets, cook pasta, maintain your vehicles, make a productive garden, plan a trip, and so forth, you will find a seemingly endless number of such how-to books. They are also a form of wisdom.

There are many kinds of wisdom out there! Perhaps we would expect that the Bible would offer a single, simple view of wisdom, but that is also not true. While there are common themes within the wisdom writings in the Bible—we will call that commonality *biblical wisdom*—each of the Bible's wisdom books presents a different perspective on wisdom—sometimes very different. We find one perspective in Proverbs and a very different perspective in the book of Job. And when we get to the New Testament we find a third, totally new perspective on wisdom. A common theme in all of these scriptural passages about wisdom is that wisdom is less about smarts and more about hearts; that is, character formation is one goal of biblical wisdom. So, to understand biblical wisdom, we will need to learn from each of these distinct perspectives. This book,

Wisdom About Wisdom, will try to sort out the different varieties and the qualities of biblical wisdom.

There is, however, one view shared by all of Scripture: wisdom is a highly valued trait, one that everyone should seek:

> Wisdom is supreme—so get wisdom. (Prov 4:7 HCSB)

But to "get wisdom" assumes that we first understand wisdom. What is wisdom? What is biblical wisdom? Both generic wisdom and biblical wisdom share the belief that wisdom can make a person's life better—better for themselves and better for those around them. This book shares that goal: to make life better for anyone who seeks wisdom.

This book is similar to most other books on wisdom in one way: it draws on personal experiences and studies. This book draws on my experiences as an international traveler and as a missionary who has served in cultures around the world. Many of the illustrations in the book have come from that background. This range of experiences at home and abroad has added to my understanding of wisdom. It is my hope that readers will also learn from the insights I have gained along the way.

But the chief difference in this book is that it is based on my study of the Bible, particularly the biblical books known as the wisdom literature. My goal has been to understand wisdom from God's perspective. This book does not try to cover all 461 Bible verses that use the words "wisdom" or "wise,"[1] but it does try to cover the major themes relating to wisdom that emerge in the wisdom literature. The goal is to understand what the Bible means when it tells us to "get wisdom."

I have long enjoyed reading the Old Testament wisdom books: Proverbs, Ecclesiastes, and Job. These books offer wisdom about how to become better people with better relationships, and they provide insight into making sense of the difficult questions of life. And when we turn the page in our Bibles, entering the New Testament, we learn a whole new perspective on wisdom: God's plan from the beginning to bring salvation through the Messiah. And, finally, the book of James tells how God-given wisdom can make a Christian's faith complete.

This book will study wisdom through both topical studies and book studies. It is divided into seven parts: (1) a general introduction to the topic of wisdom, (2) an introduction to biblical wisdom through topical studies, (3) studies in the book of Proverbs, (4) studies in Ecclesiastes,

---

1. There are 461 verses in the King James Version. The word count in other translations may vary.

(5) studies in Job, (6) studies in the New Testament wisdom passages, including the Gospels, Paul's epistles, and the book of James, and (7) my conclusion, refining and restoring wisdom.

Part 1 is a general introduction to wisdom. What is wisdom? How does it improve our lives? Of course, this subject has inspired countless books from different perspectives in almost every culture throughout time. So, part 1 is a very general summary of both generic wisdom and biblical wisdom.

Part 2 is an introduction to the themes common to biblical wisdom. It is divided into brief topical studies: the worldview of biblical wisdom, moral judgment, the means of attaining wisdom, and a brief introduction to the wisdom books.

Parts 3 through 6 contain studies of each of the wisdom books or writings. These studies are essays, not commentaries. There is no attempt to go verse by verse or chapter by chapter. They don't cover every important topic found in those books; rather they focus on the teachings about wisdom. Each of the wisdom books teaches wisdom and becoming wise in its own way—sometimes they are surprisingly different from one another. Together they provide a multifaceted picture of what wisdom is and what its role is in everyday life. Through these studies we will define and redefine wisdom several times!

Part 7 summarizes my quest for understanding wisdom, including wisdom's shortcomings, and my attempt to restore the kind of wisdom that the world needs now.

WHAT ARE THE BENEFITS OF STUDYING BIBLICAL WISDOM?

Missing from most books on wisdom is God's perspective. That perspective is the goal of *Wisdom About Wisdom*. The following list is a preview of the things we will learn by studying the wisdom literature. These are among the chief benefits to expect as we "get wisdom":

- One primary purpose of wisdom is to clarify our understanding of moral truth: What is right and what is wrong? Which paths are straight and which are crooked? Wisdom tells us.

- Wisdom shows us the good path leading to righteousness, leading to God's blessings. Thus, wisdom becomes "the missing link" to gaining God's blessings!
- Making right choices in daily life results in internalizing moral principles that become the basis of good character. So, wisdom is the path to character transformation.
- The Holy Spirit within a believer's heart gives him or her access to the mind of Christ. This super wisdom enables that believer to live wisely among nonbelievers.
- Wisdom completes what is lacking in the Christian's growth toward maturity. A wise Christian will be a complete Christian.
- Wisdom produces better people, which will result in better marriages, better families, better neighborhoods, better communities, and better nations.
- "Righteousness exalts a nation" (Prov 14:34). Wisdom and righteousness are partners in this.
- And we shouldn't underestimate the difference that acquiring wisdom can make in a person's life.

Perhaps you noticed that one of the most common expectations about wisdom is missing from the above list of benefits: there is no mention of a "how to" for making good decisions or solving personal problems. That is because the Bible's wisdom books don't ever lay out a standard procedure for decision making or problem solving. That is not the purpose of biblical wisdom.

So, what is the real purpose of biblical wisdom? Read on. And as you read, get used to finding more things that are different from what you have assumed about wisdom.

I should explain my use of different Bible versions for quoting Scripture. The majority of quotations have been taken from the English Standard Version (ESV). If no other version is identified after a Bible quotation, it is from the ESV. But sometimes I have opted to quote from other versions, maybe because that version stated the verse more clearly, but sometimes my choice is just due to a personal preference: I like the way another version stated the verse. (For example, I chose the Holman translation of Prov 4:7 at the beginning of this preface—"Wisdom is supreme—so get wisdom"—because I like it better than any other version!) There are a few places in which the translation of the Hebrew or Greek text is debated, and I quote the version that I think got it right. Whenever I quote from versions other than the ESV, I cite the source. A list of all the versions I used is on the page of abbreviations. By using different sources my goal was to help the reader to better understand the meaning of each Scripture.

List of Abbreviations

BIBLE VERSIONS

ESV—English Standard Version

HCSB—Holman Christian Standard Bible

KJV—King James Version

NASB—New American Standard Bible

NET—The NET Bible

NIV—New International Version

NKJV—New King James Version

TEV—Good News Bible: The Bible in Today's English Version

TLB—The Living Bible, Paraphrased

REFERENCE BOOKS

NBD—*New Bible Dictionary*. 3rd ed. Edited by D. R. W. Wood et al. Downers Grove, IL: InterVarsity, 1996.

NIDNTT—*New International Dictionary of New Testament Theology*. 3 vols. Edited by Colin Brown et al. Grand Rapids: Zondervan, 1978.

NIDOTTE—*New International Dictionary of Old Testament Theology and Exegesis*. 5 vols. Edited by Willem VanGemeren et al. Grand Rapids: Zondervan, 1997.

PART ONE

Defining Wisdom

Basically, wisdom is the art of being successful, of forming the correct plan to gain the desired results.
—David Hubbard

This is true—until it isn't.

1

Getting Guidance

Life doesn't come with a GPS. That's a good thing because GPSs have at times led me astray.

I remember the time—true story—my wife Jean and I were driving to a wildlife refuge in south Texas. We were using our iPhone Maps app to guide us to the visitors center. Three roads led onto the refuge, but the GPS sent us down the wrong one. A few miles down that road the GPS told us to turn onto a side road, which would bring us to the visitors center. That side road was a single lane running along the top of a levee, meaning there were steep slopes dropping down about fifteen feet on both sides. About a mile down that road we encountered a locked gate, blocking our path. There was no way to go forward and not enough room to turn around, so our only option was to back up for a mile, hoping we didn't go off the edge on either side. My wife watched the edge on her side, and I watched the edge on mine as I cautiously drove backward. It was a stressful drive! Fortunately, we didn't meet any other cars until we reached the intersection where we had turned onto that side road. There we encountered another car that was about to turn onto this road because their GPS had sent them this way to the visitors center. We warned them to turn around and find a different route, which they did. It seems that a GPS is a real blessing—except when it's wrong.

This true story is a parable about wisdom. We often depend on wisdom to give us guidance. When we face a problem or an opportunity, we must decide what to do next. Perhaps we will rely on our own knowledge and resources to plan the best route forward. Or perhaps we will seek advice from a trusted friend or recommendations from a mentor or professional counselor. Both of these methods of deciding what to do next are good—except when they lead us to choose the wrong path.

Guidance is good only if it's right. Even an allegedly *smart* phone can send us down the wrong road, leaving us trapped at a dead end—and, unlike the story above, many times it may be impossible to reverse course and get back to where we started. We're stuck. Even "expert" advice can turn out to be bad advice. Our search for wisdom may sometimes turn out like that!

A different option is to ask God for wisdom. Praying for wisdom is popular among religious people, but I have even known nonreligious people to call out to God for guidance when they are in trouble. It seems that desperation can lead anybody to pray! This book, *Wisdom About Wisdom*, is a survey of wisdom in general and biblical wisdom in particular, and so we will look at what Scripture says about the prayer for wisdom. As we consider what the Bible says about this, we may find that it differs from our usual understanding of wisdom and how to obtain it.

There is another lesson about wisdom I learned from the parable above: a parable is a story. Stories, especially true stories, teach wisdom. Using life stories to illustrate wisdom assures that it is practical. In other words, to be wise, advice should actually work in real life.

DEFINING WISDOM

Wisdom is truth applied to life.

We can diagram this statement as the connection between three keywords:

Wisdom is the bridge connecting two important contexts: our personal situation (perhaps a life problem, a dilemma, or an opportunity, but something involving a choice to be made) and the truth (knowledge or understanding) that relates to that situation. Wisdom applies truth in the form of guidance regarding the choice to be made.

Another way to state this definition is

> wisdom is the link between the theoretical and the practical.

To be wise one must understand how theory and practice fit together.

The first word in the diagram above is *truth*. Truth is a quality of knowledge, either factual accuracy or trustworthy principles. The iPhone GPS in my parable did not have accurate information about the route to the visitors center, therefore its directions were wrong—and dangerous. They did not qualify as wisdom. The world is full of "GPSs" giving advice about how to reach a personal goal or how to avoid a serious problem. Each of these guidance systems claims to be based on truth, on an accurate knowledge base, but not all actually are based on truth. Maybe the first task of wisdom is knowing which source of truth can be trusted. Perhaps knowing who to trust may be the biggest challenge in getting good advice.

The third word in the diagram is *life*. To be practical, wise advice must be useful in real circumstances. We typically seek advice when we are making plans or facing problems. Life problems include things like getting lost on the way to the visitors center, a sickness to be treated, a breakdown to be repaired on a car or a computer, a relationship to be developed or restored, finances to be invested, or a career to be planned. Those are times we need to know what to do next and we seek practical advice. Typically, we seek help from someone whom we believe to be wiser than we are.

Sometimes the wisdom we seek is more abstract; sometimes we are seeking answers to questions about the incongruities or mysteries of life—big questions like, How does one be a good person? What gives meaning to a person's life? How does one give and receive love? Why do good people suffer? And why do some seem to suffer more than others? What happens to us after we die? Is there a God and what does he expect of me? And, coming full circle, What is truth? What is wisdom? These last two questions show us that wisdom also has to answer questions about itself: we need wisdom about wisdom. Maybe what we often call wisdom is, in fact, not very wise!

The middle word in the diagram is *wisdom*, the bridge connecting truth to life. So, what is wisdom? How does it help to improve our lives? Wisdom is a quality of thinking, thinking carefully about life. It is aware of both the *truth* side and the *life* side of the diagram above. It can offer guidance, solve problems, plan strategically, develop better relationships, and much more. Of course, we can download apps that supposedly do that kind of thinking for us, but, as we have said, such apps can be wrong. Wisdom offers more reliable guidance than any app can generate!

The book of Proverbs uses several synonyms for wisdom: insight, prudence, knowledge, and understanding. But none of those synonyms are the same as wisdom. It requires relevant knowledge, understanding, and morality. Clearly there is a lot to be mindful of in getting wisdom!

Maybe the closest synonym for wisdom is understanding. Our English word "understanding" has an intellectual side, an empathy side, and a moral side. To understand something is different than to understand someone, and both are different than understanding why a decision may be right or wrong.

The intellectual side of understanding means having a comprehension of how something works and using that understanding to pick the best path forward. Intellectually, wisdom can be summarized as insight and foresight: understanding where we are now, where we want to be or ought to be, and the steps to get there. Insight and foresight are both required for making effective plans. As the quote by David Hubbard on the opening page of part 1 said, wisdom is "forming the correct plan to gain the desired result."[1]

Just as important as the intellectual side of understanding is the empathy side: understanding others' perspectives, feelings, needs, and rights. It may be possible to have generic wisdom without empathy for others, but it is not possible to have biblical wisdom without such understanding, or to have biblical wisdom without compassion and the deeds that flow from it.

Empathy is closely related to the moral side of wisdom. Moral wisdom is much more than a code of rules to be obeyed; it is judgment based upon a system of ethical principles. These principles become an inner compass that guides us on the straight path. Empathy plus morality lead us toward righteousness, justice, and fairness. Fairness leads us to treat others with kindness and respect. Biblically speaking, the best measure of wisdom is not personal success but how we treat one another.

But the most important aspect of wisdom and the primary perspective of biblical wisdom is having understanding, empathy, and morality

---

1. Hubbard, "Wisdom," 1244.

according to God's perspective. He cares more about who we are than how smart we are.

So wisdom is a way of thinking about life—thinking carefully, thinking morally—based on knowledge and understanding, leading to wise plans and actions. And during this process of thinking and acting, wisdom is becoming the kind of person that God approves.

We all seek wisdom—or we should—when we encounter a problem or a new opportunity along the path we are walking. The guidance we seek may be just for ourselves, or for our family or our community, or even for all mankind, but we must make a decision on how best to move forward. Bad advice and wrong guidance can leave us more lost than we already were. And even the iPhone Maps app makes mistakes. We want guidance from trustworthy sources, and we need advice that is practical.

After all, wisdom is only wisdom if it works in real life.

2

Who Is Wise?

PERHAPS WHEN WE THINK of wisdom, we think of a genius detective like Sherlock Holmes. He supposedly knew the science of criminology as well as the other sciences; he understood human psychology so well that he could read people; but most of all, he was very observant of detail: he looked at the facts of a crime as a big picture in which he could see links connecting the dots other detectives didn't see. Holmes was brilliant, but was he wise?

What about Professor Moriarty, evil genius, master criminal, and Holmes' archenemy? In terms of what we call intelligence—which often passes for wisdom—the two men were equals. They faced off in two stories, and in the story "The Adventure of the Final Problem" the two men ultimately fought in hand-to-hand combat on the edge of a cliff, culminating in both men plunging to their deaths.[1]

Did either of these geniuses have wisdom? Ignoring that they are both fictional, the fact that their mutual brilliance canceled each other out in the end is evidence that neither of them was truly wise. Wisdom cannot be reduced to being smart or even being the smartest. It is not a strategy for winning on Jeopardy or for solving riddles (although the book of Proverbs lists riddles as one type of wisdom literature). Wisdom is less about smarts and more about hearts.

---

1. In a later story, the author, Arthur Conan Doyle, responded to public demand for more stories and resurrected Sherlock Holmes, but he left Moriarty dead—thus Holmes won in the end. Wikipedia, "Arthur Conan Doyle."

WHO HAS WISDOM?

One challenge of understanding wisdom is that the word is used in so many ways. Consider these common uses of the words "wisdom" and "wise" from cultures around the world:

- Wisdom may be found among philosophers and theologians: big picture thinkers such as Socrates—though he denied that he had wisdom[2]—or the apostle Paul. Philosophers and theologians may see the interconnectedness of all reality, enabling them to discern truth that is both theoretical and practical.

    I am blessed to have known a few philosophically minded individuals. These men and women are all smart, and I trust them to give careful thought to any question I might ask them. But one interesting observation about my wise friends is that their answers to my questions are rarely the same. They often disagree with one another. This reminds us that famous philosophers like Plato and his pupil Aristotle often did not agree, and it is also the case that intelligent, biblically grounded theologians often disagree. Having wisdom does not guarantee that there is only one answer to any question.

- Wisdom may also be found among experts, specialists, and skilled workers, those with in-depth knowledge or experience in a particular field—like the car mechanic who can repair anything or the fishing guide who knows where and how to catch bass or an accomplished surgeon or a quality contractor or the IT nerd who can recover my lost files (another true story). In times of need, we depend on doctors, lawyers, financial advisors, marriage counselors, and others who have expertise.

    Perhaps we are not used to thinking of a mechanic or a contractor as having wisdom, but in Exodus God told Moses that he had chosen and gifted Bezalel with "the Spirit of God, with ability and intelligence, with knowledge, and all craftsmanship, to devise artistic designs" for the tabernacle and its furnishings. God also gave "to all able men ability, that they may make all that I have commanded you" (Exod 31:3, 6). It seems that wisdom includes many sorts of expertise—with the mind and with the hands.

---

2. Dutra, "What Did Socrates."

- The word "wisdom" is often applied to those who have learned lessons from life experience—sometimes through the school of hard knocks. They become mentors to the next generation, passing along their practical insights. Parents are both mentors and role models for their children, sometimes in surprising ways: my daughter taught her sons how to do quilting, and my son-in-law taught his daughters how to knit. We hire teachers to pass on knowledge and the practical application of knowledge to their classes. But the best teachers and coaches also share life lessons that they have learned.

  I have had several teachers who greatly impacted my life. One example of this was when I was going through a faith crisis. I was pastoring a church in Liberia, West Africa, and I had taken a capable young man under my wing to train him to become a church leader. I trusted and defended him even when rumors surfaced that he was actually a criminal running from the law. When the rumors turned out to be true and he took off for another city, seeking others he could con, I began to doubt my discernment and my faith. I had been gullible. I began to wonder if others I was working with were conning me. During that time of doubting myself and my faith, I went back to graduate school where I studied under some great teachers, each of whom had served overseas, and each of whom understood the challenges of working with real people and their problems. Their faith sustained me through my time of doubting, and their teachings carried me on to a better understanding of how to serve Christ in the real world. Their wisdom helped me become slightly wiser.

- Wisdom may supposedly be found among fortune tellers, gurus, and astrologers who claim to understand the spirit world, reveal secrets, and tell the future. These sorcerers are believed to be able to access hidden knowledge or the mysteries of the universe through magic or through personal connections with deities. They may give cryptic messages to lead or mislead those who seek their guidance.

  Examples of such fortune tellers are the famous Oracle of Delphi who advised the ancient Greeks based on her supposed status as the priestess of the god Apollo, or tribal witch doctors who claim to interpret divine messages received in dreams or in signs they see in the entrails of sacrificed animals, or the stereotypical hermit sitting cross-legged inside a mountaintop cave meditating on the unity of everything.

In every country of the world, there are "oracles" who claim to know the unknowable, and many people seek wisdom from them—but I don't.

- Wisdom may be found among those who use common sense to understand how we should act in daily life situations. Sometimes their life principles have been reduced to pithy sayings, proverbs, or rules of thumb which have been attributed to Confucius, Solomon, or Poor Richard: "If you lie down with dogs, you will rise up with fleas."[3] Many books of advice and internet memes are filled with such gems (or junk) of wisdom.
- In a similar way wisdom may be found among the little old ladies who live down the street, who are observant and perceptive regarding human character. I am thinking of Agatha Christie's Miss Marple, but I suspect almost every neighborhood has a person like her who understands human character and gives good advice.

In summary, we perceive that a person is wise if they seem to be above average in discerning a path to make life better for themselves and for those around them. But the short list above shows there are many varieties of wisdoms. The world is filled with wisdoms, and they're not all the same.

---

3. Franklin, *Wit and Wisdom*, 42.

3

The Spectrum of Wisdoms

Is wisdom an aptitude, a trait, or a skill? However we think about it, clearly it is not a single thing. It comes in various forms and degrees. This chapter will survey the range of wisdoms from commonplace to complex to mysterious. The word "wisdom" can include thinking, based on common knowledge, and reasoning, based on tradition, based on technical expertise, based on big-picture perceptiveness, and based on intuition about the mysteries of life. Many of these kinds of wisdom will be important to our understanding of biblical wisdom. We will start our survey with the commonplace.

COMMON SENSE

Perhaps everyone has some degree of the wisdom known as common sense—at least that is our normal assumption, though it also seems that we frequently doubt that assumption.

Wisdom and common sense are alike—but not identical. Perhaps common sense is entry-level wisdom. As we commonly use the phrase, "common sense" is a way of thinking about doing ordinary tasks: What does normal experience or simple logic suggest is the best way to do something? There are generally accepted ways of reasoning and generally known facts and beliefs everyone can make use of in making ordinary decisions. The phrase "common sense" suggests one doesn't have to be "a rocket scientist" to do things that are "not brain surgery"; anyone with common sense can do them.

Some writers have taken this positive view of common sense to a deeper level. They suggest that there are basic, verifiable principles inherent in nature or in human nature that provide the basis for common sense reasoning. These foundational principles are sometimes called natural law theory. An example of this view is the pamphlet entitled *Common Sense* published by Thomas Paine in 1776. In this pamphlet Paine lays out arguments based on his observations of the social order in Europe for why the American colonists ought to unite in the cause of independence from British rule. His common-sense arguments were persuasive: many colonists read the pamphlet and joined the American Revolution.[1]

On the other hand, many times when the phrase "common sense" is used, the implication is that not everybody uses common sense. We often say that common sense is not common. We often criticize others for seeming to lack common sense: "He/she doesn't have common sense." This may be the most common way we hear the phrase used.

We may criticize anyone who disagrees with our view on some topic as lacking common sense—and they, in turn, may say the same thing about us! Thus, common sense may mean no more than that which makes sense to me!

Albert Einstein was a critic of the whole concept of common sense: "Common sense is actually nothing more than a deposit of prejudices laid down in the mind prior to the age of eighteen."[2] He was suggesting that what we call common sense is based on culture-specific biases and not on a universal way of thinking. Other critics have said that common sense, because it is common, is mediocre and needs to be improved upon. Nowadays there are various books entitled *Uncommon Sense* suggesting that they offer upgrades on common sense.

So, which is it? Is common sense the best way of thinking about how to do something, is it a mediocre way of thinking about doing things, or, as Einstein suggested, is it just a bunch of cultural biases we have each internalized during childhood? Whatever the phrase "common sense" means, there is no commonly accepted definition of the term.

The most widely held view of common sense is that there are better ways of thinking about or better ways of doing most things and that the

---

1. Wood, *American Revolution*, 55. *Common Sense* was "the most incendiary and popular pamphlet of the entire revolutionary era."

2. Albert Einstein, quoted by Barnett, *Universe and Dr. Einstein*, 52.

majority of people in a community will agree on those better ways. The weakness of this view is that in any community most people don't agree on what is the common-sense way of doing things. But despite its weaknesses, most people agree that there is such a thing as common sense—and most people wish that more people used their common sense!

My own view is that common sense is wisdom-lite. This minimalist view of common sense does not mean that it is unreliable. Many times, wisdom and common sense will give the same advice, but we expect a more serious, reasoned, and enduring response from wisdom, and we may reserve the word "wisdom" for the more complex or profound issues of life. But for most ordinary problems, common sense solutions will be good enough.

FOLK WISDOM

We can assume that many traditional forms of wisdom probably started out as common-sense solutions to ordinary problems, remembered and passed along from generation to generation. These traditional "truths" were first preserved as oral traditions, and in literate societies they were written down. Whether oral or written, all societies possess traditional wisdom, sometimes called folk wisdom.

Folk wisdom refers to a social group's traditional wisdom about how to live morally and effectively. Folk wisdom, like folklore, is often associated with tribal or peasant societies, but folk wisdom occurs in every kind of social group, modern as well as ancient, large and small, educated and illiterate, including various ethnic groups, regional groups, clubs, vocational associations, and sports teams. To possess a folk wisdom the social group must have existed long enough to develop traditions to be passed along from one generation to the next. Such traditions provide a sense of group identity, of history, and of the right way to do things. They preserve a culture's beliefs, morals, and myths. As "Tradition," the theme song of the musical *Fiddler on the Roof*, states, tradition enables a society to keep its balance in an unstable world.[3]

Some folk traditions are simply instructions on the "right" way to do ordinary things, perhaps expressed in idioms, proverbs, folk songs, or folk tales. The examples of such traditions are numerous. In China, children are taught the "right way" to write the characters of the Chinese

---

3. Harnick, "Tradition."

alphabet—and any other way of writing is wrong, as I learned when my students always corrected my way of writing, even if my writing looked the same as their own to my eye. In Australia there are numerous idioms, words, and phrases that express ideas unique to their dialect, such as "barbie," which is a local idiom for a barbecue. In most cultures there are proverbs that teach traditional precepts or maxims, such as this one from *Poor Richard's Almanack* (1733): "Be civil to all; sociable to many; familiar with few; friend to one; enemy to none." And in most cultures there are folk songs that teach the history or values of the group, such as the American folk song "Where Have All the Flowers Gone?"[4] Every society develops oral or written folktales, such as the stories of Br'er Rabbit, supposedly told by Uncle Remus from the American South; the story of Hansel and Gretel, one of the Grimm brothers' fairy tales from Germany; or the Mr. Spider stories from West Africa. Thousands of such folk traditions have been collected and catalogued for folk societies around the world.

My wife and I used to live in Liberia, West Africa, where we heard many local proverbs. Here is a sample of traditional African proverbs:

- "Man passed man"—meaning, no matter how smart or successful a person is, there is always someone better.
- "Nothing for nothing"—meaning, the witch doctor expects to be paid for his services.
- "Do not eat your chicken and then throw its feathers in the front yard"—meaning, don't show off your wealth.
- "No one tests the depth of the river with both feet"—meaning, to be safe keep one foot securely on dry ground.
- "The best time to plant a tree is twenty years ago. The second-best time is today"—meaning, instead of regretting what you didn't do yesterday, do it today.
- "Do not look where you fell but where you slipped"—meaning, every fall began with earlier carelessness.
- "The goat's luck is different from the sheep's luck"—meaning, every one's luck is different. Some have good luck, and some who do the same thing have bad luck. Nobody knows in advance if their luck will be that of a goat or a sheep.

---

4. Seeger, "Where Have All the Flowers Gone."

Some African proverbs are quite humorous:

- "If you think small things don't matter, you've never spent the night with a mosquito."
- "Marry a wife and buy clothes."

The best way to understand any culture is to be born and raised there, but for a newcomer one of the best ways to learn a new culture is to study the idioms and proverbs the locals use. Learning local proverbs not only helps with learning vocabulary, but they are a window into the belief and value systems of the culture—a way to understand its wisdom. As we shall see, the proverbs in the book of Proverbs are a window into the biblical belief system.

COUNSELORS

When we face difficult choices, we often seek advice. Perhaps we ask our parents, our teachers, our clergy, or our best friends what they think we should do. Nowadays many people go to advisors found on social media or television programs. Those who are more serious may go to licensed professionals who, for a fee, offer counsel regarding physical health, mental health, financial health, legal advice, or personal relationships. In our careers we seek out mentors who pass along practical advice based on their years of experience. Kings, presidents, and business CEOs surround themselves with boards or cabinets—experts who offer their advice. Politicians, business managers, and advertisers may rely on statisticians who give advice based on research data. And bookstores are filled with how-to books ranging from popular to highly technical instructions. All around us are counselors who claim to know the best path forward for whatever problem we may be facing, and they share their advice—often for a price. As the African proverb in the previous section said, "Nothing for nothing."

Elders

One of the oldest forms of counselors are village elders who offer their traditional wisdom to tribal chiefs. This system is still common in many parts of the world. I recall when two colleagues and I wanted permission to hold evangelistic meetings in an African village. We were taken to the town chief's hut inside of which was a circle of log benches. We were seated as part of the circle along with the town elders. Our request and their response were carried out with friendly formality, and the result was that we were officially welcomed to hold meetings in that town. The elders decided for the town.

The role of elders was very important in Israel's early history. The Hebrew word for elder is derived from the word "beard,"[5] implying both gender and age.

> The Hebrews accorded honor to the person who attained old age (an idea relatively foreign to today's Western culture) for the following reasons: (a) their belief that God granted long life as a sign of his blessing to people who were righteous and pleasing to him; (b) their belief that persons of greater age had acquired knowledge and wisdom from which others could benefit; and (c) if the Israelite culture was largely illiterate, as some have suggested, older people were the main source of oral history and tradition.[6]

The gray hair of an old man was a mark of respect (Prov 16:31; 20:29). "Elder" was more than an adjective meaning old; it was a title, an official position as leader or counselor. The elders had an official role associated with wisdom; they were the patriarchs of a family, a clan, or a city.[7]

In ancient Israel the town elders met informally at the city gate where they conducted official business (Ruth 4:1–12; Prov 31:23). The elders of the clans would sometimes gather to serve as leaders of the nation (Lev 4:15; Ps 107:32). God instructed Moses to meet with the elders of Israel when he first returned to Egypt to assume the role as their prophet-leader (Exod 3:16). Later this group of leaders was called the "seventy elders," who were the heads of the clans of Israel (Num 11:16).

Court Advisors

Over time the title of elder became more selective for a group of men recognized as leaders of the nation. The council of the elders became known as "the wise" and were viewed as one of the three pillars of Israel's society: the law as taught by the priests, the prophets who spoke for God, and

---

5. Aitken, "זקן," 1137–39.
6. Wegner, "זקן," 1136.
7. Aitken, "זקן," 1137–39.

the wise who gave counsel (Jer 18:18).[8] An official advisor gave guidance based on his understanding of the path forward. Because the wise understood such things their advice could ensure success for the king's plans.

The council of the elders advised the king (1 Kgs 12:6–11)—though he might not listen—and should they ever stop giving him counsel, it was a sign of impending disaster and of God's judgment on the land (Ezek 7:26–27).

Good court advisors could make the difference between a prosperous reign and ruin. Unfortunately, kings who were not themselves wise often chose advisors who gave bad advice. For example, young King Rehoboam, Solomon's son, was confronted by protestors demanding he reduce their forced labor. He consulted the elders who advised him to grant the people's wish, but Rehoboam also asked his youthful friends who told him to increase the required labor. Rehoboam chose the foolish advice of his friends, resulting in over half of his kingdom seceding and forming their own country (1 Kgs 12:1–24). It seems that a foolish king chooses foolish advisors.

This is still true: foolish rulers choose advisors who only tell them what they want to hear. As Solomon once wrote, "There is nothing new under the sun" (Eccl 1:9).

Diviners

There is one more ancient category of court advisors to consider: the forbidden one. In many cultures court advisors were believed to be able to foretell the future or reveal secrets by interpreting omens and dreams. Conjurers and magicians claimed to be able to communicate with spirits and to reveal secret knowledge. Such spiritistic practices were used throughout the ancient Near East and the court advisors to the kings of Egypt and Babylon used divination and practiced magic.

The Old Testament law prohibited the practices of contacting spirits, divination, and magic (Deut 18:10–12; Ezek 13:20–23). Despite these restrictions, it is not surprising that the Israelites often adopted the spiritistic practices of the surrounding nations. There are two primary reasons for forbidding these practices: they involve communication with

---

8. Aitken, "זקן," 1137–39.

spirits other than God, and their transactional purpose was for humans to manipulate the spirit world for their own ends.[9]

There were seeming parallels to spiritism within scriptural religion, which makes the prohibition seem confusing. One such parallel was the practice of interpreting dreams. Both the ancient Egyptian and Babylonian kings expected their court advisors to be able to interpret dreams (Gen 41; Dan 2, 4)—even dreams they had forgotten! When those advisors failed, Joseph and Daniel succeeded by relying on God's wisdom.

As a missionary in West Africa, I learned that many Africans still believe that dreams are communications sent from the spirit realm and a remembered dream was always considered significant. One time, an African high school student came to ask me to interpret something he had dreamt. He assumed that, as a Bible teacher, I would know. I was dumbfounded. My seminary training had not prepared me for a request like this! As I recall, I stumbled badly, saying something like, "Your dream was probably the result of indigestion from whatever you ate the previous day." That was hardly a culturally sensitive response! The truth was that I could not interpret his dream, but I should have followed Daniel's example and prayed before I answered. Daniel understood monotheism better than I do.

SPECIALISTS AND EXPERTS

In the previous chapter we listed expertise as one form of wisdom: the expertise of artists and artisans, musicians and writers, mechanics and carpenters, doctors and scientists, and the list goes on. They each have wisdom in one or more specialties.

---

9. The biblical worldview of monotheism acknowledges the reality of other spiritual beings but asserts that they are either servants of or rebels against the one true God. He is supreme and people must trust only him. In the Old Testament, idolatry was the chief sin, and divination and magic were perceived as a gateway into idolatry.

Part of the difficulty in forbidding spiritism is that there were legitimate biblical practices that resembled the forbidden ones. The practice of animal and grain sacrifices as offerings to God resembled the sacrifices in the temples of the surrounding pagan religions. The high priest carried the Urim and Thummin, two objects which were consulted to seek God's guidance for specific questions (e.g., 1 Sam 14:41). The exact nature and use of these objects is uncertain, but the practice resembled the pagan art of divination. The difference between the practices of pagan spiritism and the practices of the Hebrew religion was that the religion of Yahweh always focused on the one God and led to submission and obedience to him.

I know some mechanics whose sense of car repair goes beyond learned skills; it is based on an understanding of the principles of how engines work or don't work and on the science that underlies the mechanics. I have known many good doctors, but I have known a few, not many, who understand physiology and chemistry well enough that, when they encounter a novel health problem, can imagine why it is happening and what might be done to treat it. Good technicians are common, but wise specialists who understand the underlying principles, who can connect the dots that were not connected before and can even envision new connections, those individuals are rare. The ability to encounter a new problem and fix it just by thinking it through is one mark of wisdom.

For those of us who may not be experts in one area much less in multiple areas, there is still hope that we can become wise. We do not have to be a "know-it-all"; there is an alternate path to wisdom, which is available to everybody. Wisdom is learned by relying on others who possess the expertise I may lack. For me, it is wise to trust others to fix my car or to treat my diseases. I don't know much about those things, but I know and trust some who do. I don't expect the American president to be an expert on everything; in the midst of a pandemic, for example, I don't expect the president to be an expert in epidemiology, but for him/her to be wise, I expect them to listen to the doctors who do have that specialty. As we shall see in later chapters, listening to others who possess wisdom is a mark of wisdom.

Sages

Another mark of wisdom is the ability to see connections between very different realms of knowledge: seeing how art relates to science, or how math relates to theology; these rare individuals can do synthesis across the traditional boundaries of expertise. I have known a few such big-picture thinkers—and if I labeled them as wise, they would deny it, proving that they are the wisest of the wise.

Are there any individuals who possess wisdom about everything? Are there actually "sages" with super wisdom? Personally, I am skeptical that people with super wisdom exist. If anyone claims to have unmatched wisdom, I take that as *prima facie* evidence they don't. Socrates, the Greek philosopher (ca. 400 BC), tested the men of Athens who were reputed to be wise and found that none of them were truly wise. In fact, they were doubly unwise because not only were they not wise, but they did not know they were not wise. Socrates concluded that the only reason that he had an advantage over them was because he knew that he wasn't wise.[10]

However, according to many traditions from around the world, extraordinary wise men and women do exist. In many cultures, there have been legendary sages who are widely revered for their wide-ranging wisdom—for example, Lao Tzu, Confucius, Socrates, Gandhi, Deborah, and Solomon. The founders of religions are often thought to possess super wisdom. Moses, Jesus, Mohammed, the Buddha, and Bahá'u'lláh, for example, are often regarded as sages. But such super sages are more likely the stuff of fiction—for example, Yoda of *Star Wars*, Spock of *Star Trek*, or Winston, the wise next-door neighbor in the TV series *Home Improvement*. These fictional sages possess wisdom in multiple areas of life.

WISDOM AT THE EDGES OF HUMAN KNOWLEDGE

The normal role of wisdom is to discern the best path forward when we are facing common sorts of decisions. But another role of wisdom is to explore the realms of knowledge beyond the ordinary—the uncertain, the controversial, and the puzzling areas that appear past the edges of normalcy, and the paradoxes and mysteries that intrigue us or frighten us. Perhaps everybody speculates about these big questions, but understanding them requires deeper wisdom.

We may associate seeking answers to the mysteries of life with cartoons of people consulting hermits living in mountaintop caves, or, more humorously, with consulting Deep Thought, a fictional supercomputer that, when asked the meaning of life, calculated for 7.5 million years before concluding that the meaning of life is "forty-two."[11]

On a more serious note, philosophers and oracles have sought answers to the apparent imponderables and mysteries that sometimes reside in the back of our minds and at other times are staring us uncomfortably in the face so that we can't ignore them. Indeed, all of life is sprinkled with intriguing paradoxes. The wise know this and some even seek them out. As M. Scott Peck wrote,

---

10. Plato, *Apology* 3:20c–24e.
11. Adams, *Hitchhiker's Guide*, 120.

> For me, the capacity to embrace paradox—to perceive the validity of opposites, such as tolerance and intolerance, each in its own season—is a key to wisdom.[12]

I believe this second role of wisdom—wrestling with the contradictions and uncertainties of life—is also a purpose of the biblical wisdom literature. For example, the book of Job tells the story of a man whose entire life became a paradox. Though he was both intelligent and faithful, Job could not understand the incongruities that suddenly overwhelmed him.

The book of Job is more than a paradoxical story; it is also a textbook case study of some of the biggest questions of life: Why do bad things happen to good people? What does justice mean? Does God deal fairly with all people? Why do some people seem to suffer much more than others? And, ironically, in view of the claims to wisdom by both Job and his accusers, who is truly wise? And what is wisdom? The story of Job is regarded highly not because it resolves the mystery of suffering—it doesn't—but because it provides a basis for faith for all of us who likewise become overwhelmed by incongruities in our own lives. Though the book answers few of the big questions we ask, it provides wisdom and guidance for the unknown path ahead. (We will consider the book of Job in part 5.)

Authors of wisdom literature from many cultures, as well as the authors of biblical wisdom writings have pondered many of life's biggest questions: What is the meaning of life? Is the world designed? Why is the future so unpredictable? Why do good people behave so badly? And why do smart people act so foolishly? Wisdom literature from cultures around the world ponders these mysteries.

Here is a quote, attributed to Oliver Wendell Holmes, that expresses my ideal of wisdom:

> I would not give a fig for the simplicity on this side of complexity; but I would give my life for the simplicity on the other side of complexity.[13]

I have heard this three-stage model of knowing explained in this way: When we first enter any area of study it may seem simple, but if we press on, it always becomes complicated. At this point, some people revert to the simple form they knew before, but that reversal is being simplistic

---

12. Peck, *Abounding Grace*, 11.
13. Oliver Wendell Holmes, quoted in O'Toole, *Executive's Compass*, 5.

because it ignores the complexity. But if a person pushes on through the complexity, he or she will reach a simplicity on the other side of the complexity: an understanding that makes sense of the complexity without denying it. It enables the person to navigate through the complexity without being stymied by it. That simplicity beyond the complexity is a vantage point from which one can comprehend the big picture. We call that vantage point wisdom.

I am sure that there are many examples of individuals who have persevered through the complexity to find simplicity in the fields of philosophy, science, math, or theology. One lesson to be learned in the search for wisdom is not to jump too quickly for a simple answer, no matter how attractive it seems. Press on, and when you find the complexity, still press on. Wisdom is on the other side.

4

Does Wisdom Work?

Do you ever pray for wisdom? I do. When I face a big decision, whether a problem or an opportunity, I pray for guidance. When a friend or relative faces such a decision, I pray for them to have wisdom. When I know someone who is seriously ill or injured, I pray for wisdom for the doctors treating them. And when there is conflict between friends or relatives, arguing or being unkind, I pray for them to learn how they ought to treat one another. One of the surprises in the study of wisdom is that learning how to treat one another is critical to becoming wise.

I also pray for wisdom for government leaders. When we think of the major issues our national leaders face—international wars abroad and culture wars at home, economic instability, global pandemics and global warming, wildfires, floods, drought, and famine—it is clear they need wisdom! On the one hand, these major crises are not new. Similar crises are the stuff of human history and have been ongoing since our ancestors left the garden of Eden. The teacher of Ecclesiastes tells us, "There is nothing new under the sun" (Eccl 1:9). One important lesson from studying wisdom is that, though the details of history seem to change over time, the essence doesn't. Human nature and human history are, according to Ecclesiastes, cycles of events that repeat time after time. The reason I write this book is because I am convinced that the solution to these numerous crises is not better politics but better wisdom. I believe that, contrary to the popular folk song of the sixties,[1] what the world needs now is wisdom! (Though I agree with that song that we need more love as well.)

The Brits are lucky. They can pray for their king (or queen) just by singing their national anthem, "God Save the King." The British Commonwealth countries also sing that hymn as a prayer. But we Americans, because we fought to be free of their king, have no such shortcut. To pray for our leaders, we actually have to pray. Here is the prayer I often pray for America's president and other national and state officials:

> God bless them, protect them, and give them wisdom.

I pray that same prayer for our leaders no matter who the person is or which party they represent. No matter who is in power, they face the same major problems, and they need wisdom.

In my prayer, the request for God to give leaders wisdom means to give them guidance as to which paths to take and insight into how to fix the things that are broken. I also hope that they will have the wisdom to seek righteousness because "righteousness exalts a nation, but sin is a reproach to any people" (Prov 14:34).

That prayer expresses my hope for my country's leaders. But there are three concerns that I have regarding my prayers or anybody else's prayers for wisdom, whether regarding small personal problems or large national and global crises: (1) The people I pray for, including myself, do not actually seem to become wiser, and the problems they face often don't get solved. Does praying for wisdom work? (2) "When elephants fight, grass gets hurt" (an African proverb). Political fights always cause collateral damage, usually to the most vulnerable. Perhaps our prayers are complicit in this! And (3) the same sorts of problems we see in the world we also see in the church. In fact, the church does not just reflect the troubles in society, it often contributes to the crises that trouble our world! We will encounter these three concerns repeatedly throughout our studies of the biblical wisdom, so I will briefly introduce them now.

DOES PRAYING FOR WISDOM WORK?

My first concern is that I am not sure that my prayers for wisdom make anyone wiser. Perhaps this is not due to a problem with our prayers but

---

1. David, "What the World Needs Now."

with our understanding of wisdom itself. Biblical wisdom is not a fast track to problem solving. Don't get me wrong, wisdom, defined as insight and foresight, may sometimes help us to solve personal, national, or global problems, but that is not the primary task of biblical wisdom.

So, who knows how to fix these real and serious global problems? (I don't!) Perhaps the most useful verse in the Bible's wisdom writings is also found in Ecclesiastes:

> Whenever I tried to become wise and learn what goes on in the world, I realized that you could stay awake night and day and never be able to understand what God is doing. However hard you try, you will never find out. Wise men may claim to know, but they don't. (Eccl 8:16–17 TEV)

Profound! Not even the wise really understand what is going on! One of the biggest takeaways about wisdom according to Ecclesiastes is that those who claim to know how to fix the world's big problems don't really know! We could add that those who claim to know how to fix our smaller personal problems also don't know! We will return to this verse many times in our study of wisdom.

So, we may well wonder if wisdom is really up to the global-size expectations we may have for it. Why do I pray for wisdom for world leaders? Why do I pray for wisdom for myself? Perhaps we have all misunderstood wisdom. It is not just that we lack the wisdom to solve our problems, we lack wisdom about wisdom.

If the primary task of wisdom is not problem solving, then what is its purpose? The answer to that question was the focus of all the biblical wisdom writers.

"WHEN ELEPHANTS FIGHT, GRASS GETS HURT"

This bit of African folk wisdom is as true now as ever. When elephants fight, as elephants do, what is most likely to get hurt is the grass—collateral damage. This has always been true!

Elephants, representing the powerful rulers of the world—kings, presidents, politicians, generals, magistrates, and magnates—do indeed fight each other for dominance. Their battles fill our newscasts and podcasts every day. But when watching those fierce struggles, who pays attention to the grass getting trampled underfoot? Certainly the elephants don't care about the grass.

In this African proverb, the grass represents the little people, those without power or wealth to defend themselves, the poor and the vulnerable. In the midst of military or political campaigns, who notices the grass? The answer found in all of the biblical wisdom writings is that God cares about the grass. God pays as much attention to the grass as he does to the elephants—maybe more! And he expects his people, the ones with wisdom, to also care for the grass. King Lemuel, one of the authors of Proverbs, recalled the instruction he received from his mother:

> Speak up for those who cannot speak for themselves, for the rights of all who are destitute. Speak up and judge fairly; defend the rights of the poor and needy. (Prov 31:8–9 NIV)

This passage teaches that caring for the poor and needy is not just the responsibility of charitable individuals or organizations. It is the government's responsibility as well. To fail to do this is a sin. This strong emphasis on caring for the poor in the wisdom literature surprised me because my previous understanding of wisdom had focused on developing skills in strategic planning, not on social justice. But, as we shall see, justice—especially justice for the poor—is an essential part of biblical wisdom.

WHAT THE CHURCH NEEDS NOW

Would you be surprised to learn that wisdom often leads to bitter envy and selfish ambition, resulting in all kinds of evil, pride, quarrels, lust, and even murder? Wisdom can go bad! Perhaps you would think we were speaking about wisdom in pagan societies or in postmodern culture, but these descriptions of wisdom-gone-bad were written by James when writing to Christians and about Christians! He was concerned that these sins were already happening in the very first generation of churches (Jas 3:14–16; 4:1–6). He warned Christians about the dangers of wisdom being corrupted by sin.

Would James write such a warning to our churches today? Does envy and ambition produce every kind of evil in churches today? Sadly, our churches can become divided by the issues of culture wars that divide our country (and other Christianized countries as well). The quarrels and in-fighting that James observed in his day also divide our churches. Churches split over finances, ministry styles, and personality conflicts. None of this is new. Some churches care more about who is winning the current elephant battles than about involvement in serving Christ who is King of all kings. Throughout church history the church has often become bogged down in the politics of the day. The result has been a dismal record of excommunications, inquisitions, crusades, church splits, and nationalistic movements. As James observed in his day, churches can be part of the problem rather than part of the solution.

But, according to James, wisdom is not all bad. He also described a different kind of wisdom that Christians, especially Christian teachers, should seek. Understanding and acquiring this good wisdom is the purpose of our study in biblical wisdom. James quoted the book of Proverbs in his lecture on good wisdom, so that is where we begin.

PART TWO

Defining Biblical Wisdom

Wisdom has built her house and made seven columns for it. She has had an animal killed for a feast, mixed spices in the wine, and set the table. She has sent her servant girls to call out from the highest place in town: "Come in, ignorant people!" And to the foolish man she says, "Come, eat my food and drink the wine that I have mixed. Leave the company of ignorant people, and live. Follow the way of knowledge."

—Proverbs 9:1–6 TEV)

5

Introducing the Wisdom Literature

PART 1 OF THIS book dealt primarily with generic wisdom, the kind of wisdom that people in cultures around the world seek to make their lives better. In part 2 we will focus on the variety of wisdom we read about in the Bible, commonly referred to as biblical wisdom.

Over three-fourths of the Old Testament is about the nation of Israel and its relationship with God. It contains a record of the history of the nation of Israel, of the covenant between God and Israel, of the laws Israel was required to obey, and of the messages of the prophets, giving either hope or warnings to the people based on their obedience or disobedience to those laws.

The remaining fourth of the Old Testament contains books of poetry and wisdom. These writings fill in many of the gaps in the larger portion of the Old Testament. Here we find literature about worship, prayer, and daily life. The poetic books (Psalms, Lamentations, Song of Songs) use the genre of Hebrew poetry to express the emotional aspects of life: praise, prayer, grief, and love. The wisdom books (Job, Proverbs, Ecclesiastes) use the intellect to explore the practical and moral sides of life.

In the Old Testament the collection of wisdom writings is known as the wisdom literature. In addition to the three wisdom books listed above, there are various psalms and stories that are considered to be part of the wisdom writings.[1] The stories of Joseph in Genesis and Daniel also

---

1. Pss 1, 37, 49, 73, 111, 112, 127, 128, and 133 are considered to be wisdom psalms.

have wisdom themes. The New Testament does not have any books that are classified as wisdom books, but many passages in the gospels, in the writings of the apostle Paul, and in the book of James discuss themes typical of the wisdom literature. These writings will be the basis of our study of biblical wisdom.

The wisdom literature uses a distinctive style of writing consisting of lectures, speeches, debates, proverbs, poems, parables, and Q and A sessions. The wisdom literature contains unique content, focusing on practical instructions for daily life, on moral judgment, and on the search for answers for the hard questions as to why life does not always work out as expected. In particular, the wisdom literature is concerned with how God works behind the scenes of daily life to accomplish his plans for the world.

Hubbard, "Wisdom Literature," 1245–46.

6

The Worldview of Biblical Wisdom

THE BIBLICAL WRITERS WERE all in love with wisdom—literally, they loved wisdom[1] (at least the writers of the wisdom literature were so enamored). They considered wisdom to be more valuable than money, jewels, possessions, and political power! They taught that wisdom was the key to good health, long life with loving grandchildren, public respect, success in this life, as well as their hope for a positive future in the afterlife. But attaining health and wealth was not the goal of biblical wisdom but the by-products of something much more valuable that wisdom offered.

The biblical writers' love for wisdom was based on their view of God: God is wise—all wise. Wisdom is God's superpower. Wisdom is the capstone of his attributes. Therefore, for a person to become godly (like God) requires that they become wise.

These writers based their view of wisdom on God's role as Creator and Administrator of his universe and of the lives of people. God rules the world, including nature, animals, spirits, and humankind, by his knowledge and power, and, wonderfully, he rules the world with righteousness and justice. But God's ways of ruling his world are often incomprehensible to us. Many times, God's allegedly wise rule makes no sense to human observers, even to those who believe in him the most. As the wisdom writers sought to understand the meaning of life, they were often stymied at this point: God's wisdom was unknown and seemingly

---

1. For examples of their love for wisdom, see Prov 4:7–9 and 8:17.

unknowable. In order for our wisdom to "work," it has to adapt to living in God's world where his ways differ from our ways. All of the wisdom writers struggled with this contradiction, but they all found an answer, the same answer, for how to live wisely in this world.

So, biblically speaking, wisdom is both the best possible possession and it is inaccessible. This is the paradox of wisdom: to become godly requires that we become wise, but we don't know how. And, as Proverbs repeatedly warns, while walking the straight path, missteps into foolishness are always possible.

Worldviews and Wisdom

Earlier chapters have given several definitions of wisdom. Here is a comprehensive definition:

> Wisdom is understanding how the world works and choosing actions that will work in that world.

According to this definition, wisdom is based on an understanding of reality, what is real and how reality functions. Understanding how the world works is one meaning for the word "worldview." So, wisdom is closely linked with worldview.

Every culture in the world values wisdom—though, depending on the worldview, understandings of wisdom can be quite different. For example, a villager in a tribal society who believes he lives in a world populated by invisible ghosts and spirits and who depends on fortune tellers and witch doctors for success in life (the worldview of animism)[2] will understand wisdom in a very different way than a person who believes the world consists exclusively of combinations of matter and energy with no spirits or supernatural events (the worldview often called naturalism),[3] and who solely depends on science and technology for his success. Based on their different worldviews, these individuals will understand wisdom very differently from each other. And they will both understand wisdom differently from a monotheist who believes that there is one God who is the Creator of the universe and the Sustainer of life. For a monotheist,

---

2. Animism is also known as spiritism or spiritualism. It is the worldview that underlies many of the polytheistic religions of the world.

3. Naturalism is also called materialism or realism. It is the worldview most often associated with secularism.

God is the ultimate reality, and therefore to understand how the world works requires understanding his ways.

DEFINING MONOTHEISM[4]

> There is one and only one God who is the source of everything else.

This definition of monotheism could be expressed with a quote I once saw on a Christian poster:

> There are two foundational truths in life:
> There is a God, and I am not he.

God alone is God, and therefore, I am not God. Both sides of this truth are repeatedly expressed throughout Scripture. In the following verse God affirms the first half of that truth and its implications for us:

> Thus says the Lord, the King of Israel and his Redeemer, the Lord of hosts: "I am the first and I am the last; besides me there is no god." (Isa 44:6)

In this single verse God declared himself to be the King, Redeemer, and Lord, titles which express his relationship to his creatures. He is supreme, above us, and our only hope of rescue from our enemies and from our sin. He is the first and the last—meaning he has always existed, even prior to creation, and will always exist, even after the end of the universe. Being first and last means he is alone; there are no rival gods. But God is much more than these titles express: he is the source of all truth, beauty, morality, justice, love, and wisdom. To the extent that humans have any vague sense of truth, beauty, morality, justice, love, or wisdom—and I think that we all have an inherent sense of these things—we are, in fact, sensing the reality of God!

This is the worldview of monotheism. Those who have biblical wisdom know these things and live their lives accordingly.

On the other hand, a working definition of foolishness is believing oneself to be equal or superior to God in regard to truth, beauty, morality, justice, love, or wisdom. Sadly, the foolish belief in the superiority of one's own wisdom is common to people in every culture around the

---

4. There are various forms of monotheism found in other cultures and religions, but for our study in this book, we will only consider biblical monotheism.

world—and doubly sad, it is even common within Christian churches. Christians often seem to think that our ways are wiser than God's ways. In our prayers we often offer advice to God about what he ought to do to make things better. Christians, like people everywhere, forget that we are not God, nor are we qualified to be his counselor (Isa 40:13–14, 18, 25; Rom 11:33–36). The second certainty of monotheism is that I am not God, nor am I God's equal in any respect.

The word "monotheism" is often shortened to "theism," which simply means the belief in God.

Ethical Monotheism

A more complete name of the biblical worldview is "ethical monotheism," which has a definition derived from the basic definition of monotheism:

> There is one God who is good and who expects his people to be good.

As simple as that definition of ethical monotheism is, it seems difficult for any one of us to live it out appropriately. Can people be expected to be as good as God? That sounds ridiculous! But the expectation that we be good as God is good is stated in many ways throughout Scripture. The tenets of ethical monotheism can be summarized as follows:

1. God is the only wise God, with unsearchable judgments and inscrutable ways (Rom 16:27). His wisdom is superior to all forms of human wisdom.

2. God is the Righteous One (Prov 21:12) whose character defines morality—the knowledge of good and evil, which was desired by our mother, Eve.

3. While human wisdom is a gift of God and is useful in many ways, it is very limited in its ability to understand the things that God has done from the beginning of time until the end of time and all that happens in between (Eccl 3:11; 8:17).

4. Even at its best, human wisdom shares all the limitations, biases, and moral flaws of human nature, and when it is corrupted by "jealousy and selfish ambition," wisdom produces disorder and every vile practice (Jas 3:16).

Biblical wisdom contrasts the righteousness of God with the unrighteousness of humankind. All of us have chosen crooked paths that turn away from God, morality, and wisdom. Each in our own way have become fools. Teaching humanity the path back to God and his righteousness is a central purpose of the wisdom literature. Biblical wisdom does not provide a simple answer to every question or a solution for every problem, but it provides a secure place upon which a believer can stand to choose the best path for his or her life.

Human wisdom has limits as to what problems it can solve. An important part of being wise is recognizing those limitations. The wisest of the wise know that wisdom is still far beyond them. As the apostle Paul (quoting Job and Isaiah)[5] wrote,

> Oh, the depth of the riches of wisdom and knowledge of God!
> How unsearchable are his judgments and how inscrutable his ways!
>
> "For who has known the mind of the Lord,
>   or who has been his counselor?
> "Or who has given a gift to him
>   that he might be repaid?"
>
> For from him and through him and to him are all things. To him be glory forever! Amen. (Rom 11:33–36)

This New Testament affirmation is based squarely on the Old Testament understanding of wisdom, and it reveals a direct link between monotheism and wisdom: God alone is all wise. And it confirms the basic truth from the wisdom literature: God's wisdom is far beyond our abilities to discover.

Biblical wisdom begins by acknowledging that there is a God and that I am not God. It recognizes that he is the source of wisdom and that even the wisest among us are at best still learning his wisdom.

WISDOM AND GOD'S SOVEREIGNTY

God's wisdom would not be possible without his sovereignty—the two are linked.

---

5. In this passage Paul quotes Isa 40:13 and Job 41:11.

We often use the English word "sovereign" to refer to a monarch, a king or queen, the highest ranked leader of a nation. God, however, is higher: he is the singular King of kings and Lord of lords (1 Tim 6:15–16). We see his sovereignty in that he can and does do whatever his wisdom determines. In the whole universe, he is the ultimate doer.

> I perceived that whatever God does endures forever; nothing can be added to it, nor anything taken from it. God has done it so that people fear before him. (Eccl 3:14)

This verse links God's sovereign deeds with his purpose for those deeds: for people to fear him—a reference to the fear of the Lord as the first step in human wisdom. Human wisdom begins by recognizing God's sovereign rule. He is the chief actor in the cosmos, in human history, and in every human life. In some parts of the Bible, God's actions are revealed and explained, but in the wisdom literature his activities are often concealed in the background. But there would be no wisdom in the wisdom literature without God working.

The following list shows how God's sovereignty is seen in his actions:[6]

- God is a God who acts and brings his plans to realization.
- So God is the Creator of both the first heavens and earth and the final eschatological heavens and earth.
- God creates not only physical light and darkness (Gen 1:3) but also good and evil in the historical and suprahistorical realms.
- God brings forth all the bountifulness of nature (Gen 1:11; Ps 107:37; Jer 12:2).
- God brings to pass whatever he will in his role as judge and Lord of the government of the world.
- In general, he does great things (Ps 71:19; 106:21) in creation (Ps 104) and in history (Ps 136). He brings about righteousness and justice (Ps 103:6).
- He makes the poor and the rich, all classes of people (Prov 22:2). Therefore, anyone who oppresses a poor person shames his Creator (14:31; 17:5).
- In sum, the Lord is the doer of all things and proper subject of the verb "to do" in the Old Testament.

---

6. The list was adapted from Carpenter, "עשה," 547–49.

THE WORLDVIEW OF BIBLICAL WISDOM

Perhaps Job summarized God's ultimate sovereignty over human life and circumstances most succinctly when speaking after the tragic loss of his wealth and his children:

> Naked I came from my mother's womb, and naked I shall return. The Lord gave, and the Lord has taken away; blessed be the name of the Lord. (Job 1:21)

Job did not condemn God for the tragedies that had struck his life. Bringing troubles was God's right. And God's right is always right. (As we shall see in our studies of the book of Job, he did at times question God's right as right, but he ultimately repented of those doubts.)

Two passages regarding Job's life reveal the irony of God's sovereign control of his life: At the beginning of his story, Satan complained that God had placed a hedge around Job, shielding him from affliction. But Job would soon complain that God had hedged him in, preventing him from escaping the afflictions that had overtaken him (Job 1:10; 3:23). From either perspective, God was sovereignly watching over Job.

In the New Testament, God's sovereignty is revealed in the completion of his eternal plan for redemption by the incarnation and atoning sacrifice of his Son, uniting all the nations of the world into one family of faith. In both testaments God has a plan for all he does—though we usually don't know the details of that plan (Job 42:1–3; Rom 11:33–36).

We should not, however, understand God's sovereign deeds in relation to humankind as one-sided. The wisdom literature makes clear that there is an interaction between God and each person. People get to make choices that seem good to them, but God judges them based on those choices. Based on his evaluation of our thoughts and deeds, our motives, and our plans for future actions, God determines the outcome of our plans. As we say, "Man proposes, but God disposes."[7]

If wisdom is defined as understanding how the world works and choosing actions accordingly, then biblical wisdom begins with the knowledge that God is sovereign over his world and over our lives and choosing to live accordingly.

> The fear of the Lord is the beginning of wisdom;
> All those who practice it have a good understanding.
> His praise endures forever! (Ps 111:10)

---

7. Thomas á Kempis, *Imitation*, bk 1, 19:2.

WISDOM AND CREATION

The biblical wisdom books all understand wisdom to be based on God having created the universe. Creation is not just a historical event or an answer to a child's question, Who made this? The doctrine of creation is not just about origins; the universe was not simply made; it was designed. And without the assumption of design, wisdom itself would not be possible.

Biblical wisdom is grounded on the knowledge that God created the world to be orderly and therefore somewhat predictable. The wise are those who discern the orderly patterns in nature and in human nature and use that understanding to predict what will happen next in life, making possible rational decisions and good advice. Therefore, the logic flows as follows:

> God → wise design → created order → predictability → wise decision making

But the biblical understanding of the relationship of wisdom to creation goes even deeper than this. A major theme in the biblical literature is that wisdom is connected with creation, both in the sense that God made the world with wisdom and also, in a strange sense, that wisdom was an active participant in the activity of creating. The wisdom writings portray wisdom as an active cocreator of the universe and of humankind. Is this just poetry, or does it suggest that wisdom is more than a cognitive skill? Is it actually a person?

Let's examine three creation texts, each of which is marked by its use of the word "beginning":

- "In the beginning, God created the heavens and the earth" (Gen 1:1).
- "The Lord made me [Wisdom] as the beginning of his creation, before his works of long ago" (Prov 8:22 HCSB).
- "In the beginning was the Word, and the Word was with God, and the Word was God. He was in the beginning with God. All things were made through him, and without him was not anything made that was made" (John 1:1–3).

These three references expand our understanding of the creation event: the Creator was God, the cocreator was Wisdom, and the personal

Creator was the Word, Jesus. Creation was clearly much more complex than we often imagine.

Both Proverbs and Job (Prov 8:22–31; Job 28) describe wisdom as the first thing God created. Using poetic imagery, these two passages create surprising images of wisdom's role in creation. Proverbs 8 personifies wisdom as Lady Wisdom,[8] who describes herself either as a craftsman actively involved in creating or as a child frolicking with delight[9] as she observed creation in progress. Job 28 describes God making, testing, and confirming wisdom as a tool—a tool he then used in creating the world. Such poetry is difficult to interpret: was wisdom a standard of quality control, a tool which God used, a craftsman cocreating, or a young child spectator celebrating the whole event? Whichever way we understand this poetry, the clear meaning is that the world and mankind were made wisely, and therefore, the proper way to live in the world is to live in accordance with that wisdom.

The Old Testament uses poetry to describe wisdom's role as cocreator, but the New Testament took this idea literally and identified it with the preincarnate Christ. Jesus Christ was the eternal Word (the *Logos*) by whom all things were created (John 1:1–3) In Hebrew thought, the word "Word" refers to God who spoke the world into existence. In his epistles, Paul identifies the Creator as Christ himself (Col 1:15–16; 2:3). Once again, we can say that God is the Creator who created wisely; wisdom is the cocreator acting alongside of God; and Jesus, the eternal Word, was the personal Creator.

The biblical creation texts give us a picture of God, the Creator, as intimately involved with his creation. Not only did he make the world but he continues to maintain and sustain it. He knows and cares about the lives of his creatures: all the people, the animals, and even the sparrows. We see God's personal care for the humans he made in his image in his concern that Adam might be lonely; and so he created Eve to be his wife. After they disobeyed him and tried to hide, he walked about the

---

8. In Prov 1–9, wisdom is personified as a female who both speaks for God and recruits young people to follow the path of wisdom. Her role within the book of Proverbs will be discussed further in part 3. Because she is female, I call her Lady Wisdom.

9. The Hebrew word can be translated either as "child" or as "craftsman." Though most translators choose the common translation of "craftsman," NET Bible Translator footnote (Prov 8 n52) lists several possible translations and why "child" may be correct in this context. See also NIV fn. for 8:30. The two words suggest a different role for Wisdom alongside God during creation. Was wisdom a spectator or a coworker in creation?

garden seeking them. He had already made plans to restore them. Ultimately, he became humanity's Kinsman-Redeemer who, at personal cost, brought his lost children home. This understanding of the Creator being continually active in caring for his creation is crucial in understanding both wisdom and salvation.

But, first, there is one more link between creation and wisdom.

Innate Wisdom

In the book of Job, chapters 38–39, God responds to Job's accusations that he had been treating Job unjustly. He did this by asking Job a series of questions to demonstrate how little Job knew about administering the world. God not only created a whole universe, but he runs it on a daily basis. His response includes everything God made: the stars, the oceans, the clouds, day and night, the weather, droughts, and floods, and all kinds of living creatures, including the dreaded Behemoth and Leviathan. In the midst of this passage is a verse that reveals how God has given wisdom to all his creatures.

There are two possible translations of the Hebrew text, each of which reveal different senses of the same truth. The first translation from the NIV emphasizes God creating different species with wisdom for their particular needs:

> Who gives the ibis wisdom or gives the rooster understanding?
> (Job 38:36 NIV)

The ibis and the rooster each have been given an innate sense, perhaps what we call instinct, that tells them how to behave in order to survive in their very different environments. God also asserts that it was he who taught lions to hunt, ravens to feed, and mountain goats and deer to give birth and raise their young (38:39—39:30). It is unthinkable that any living creature could survive a single day without some degree of innate wisdom. In his speech to Job, God asserts that he created all creatures with the knowledge they need to live—including humans.

Proverbs acknowledged the wisdom of animals when it instructed sluggards to learn from the industrious ant or when it contrasted the recklessness of criminals with the caution of birds, which avoid a snare set out in the open. It seems that animals, each in their own way, are wiser than humans! We can and should learn from them.

However, the other possible translation of Job 38:36 emphasizes God giving wisdom to humans:

> Who has put wisdom in the inward parts or given understanding to the mind? (ESV)

God has given innate wisdom to humans. Like other species, we are born with instinctual knowledge of how to feed and how to bear and raise our young, but this verse suggests more than basic instinct. God gives every human a degree of wisdom and understanding. Perhaps this innate wisdom is a partial definition of the image of God in mankind.

God's fingerprint in the form of innate wisdom is found in every human being. Because it is common to us all, it may be the basis of what we call common sense and common grace. Common sense refers to basic human rationality and common grace to basic human morality. Both common sense and grace are often criticized for being inadequate—and rightly so—but it seems there is an inherent ability to reason and an inherent capacity for love and goodness within the human heart. Job 38:36 tells us that human wisdom may be an ID marker, pointing Job and the rest of us back to our Maker.

When we say that God created his world wisely, we mean more than it was designed well; we mean he placed some wisdom into each of his creatures. Each species of animal was given the kind of wisdom it would need to survive and thrive. And people, made in the image of God, received a portion of wisdom both for survival and as a basis for living in community. This innate sense is grounded both in the natural order and in the moral order, which God designed into his creation.

But properly applying this God-endowed reason and morality requires a deeper kind of wisdom: moral judgment. We will continue that thought in the next chapter.

7

Wisdom and Moral Judgment

God is good and expects his people to be good.
—THE WORLDVIEW OF ETHICAL MONOTHEISM

THIS DEFINITION OF THE biblical worldview affirms both God's morality and his expectation that his human creations, made in his image, will also be moral. This is the biblical standard, repeated and reinforced in every book of the Bible. And every book also declares humanity's failure to achieve this standard of godlike morality; nobody achieves godliness.

Wisdom and moral judgment, while distinct, are inseparable. God created the world with both a natural order and a moral order. True wisdom understands the moral order and chooses actions that fit within that order. One can't be wise without also being righteous. The wisdom books assume the possibility of human moral improvement through wisdom, and they assume human responsibility for the choices we make. Of course, the human problem is that none of us practices justice and righteousness well enough to satisfy God's expectations. That is why wisdom is necessary.

How does morality relate to wisdom? On the one hand, experience shows that smarter people are not necessarily more moral. There are evil geniuses and corrupt theologians. Even Solomon, who was revered as the wisest man of his day, struggled with living out his own moral teachings in his personal life (1 Kgs 11:1–11). The supposed link between wisdom and morality is not very evident in the real world. This apparent failure of wisdom to bring about righteousness is a chief concern of the wisdom literature.

The wisdom literature not only teaches correct moral behavior, but it wrestles with the problems that arise in applying those standards to real people living in the real world. Teaching people to be moral is the challenge facing wisdom in every culture. The biblical answer to that challenge takes us down some unexpected paths!

THE KNOWLEDGE OF GOOD AND EVIL

The first reference to wisdom in the Bible does not portend a promising future for human wisdom! We read about it during Eve's encounter with the serpent:

> So when the woman saw that the tree [of the knowledge of good and evil] was good for food, and that it was a delight to the eyes, and that *the tree was to be desired to make one wise*, she took of its fruit and ate, and she also gave some to her husband who was with her, and he ate. (Gen 3:6, emphasis added)

Thus, in Eve and Adam's search for wisdom, they foolishly chose the wrong path to becoming wise. Contrary to the serpent's promise, when they ate the forbidden fruit they did not become like God—quite the opposite—they lost the moral innocence which had been the sole basis of their righteousness and the basis of their fellowship with God. They died that day, not physically, but they lost their direct connection with the source of all life and the source of wisdom.

The "wisdom" that the serpent offered Eve and Adam actually turned them away from God and his wisdom. In the instant that they gained the knowledge of good and evil, they also lost it. Hereafter mankind would not be able to clearly distinguish good and evil, right and wrong, truth and error, wisdom and foolishness. What could have become clear to Eve, if she had recognized the serpent's lie as a lie, instead became confusing. And that is how history went wrong.

Eve and Adam made three mistakes in their pursuit of wisdom: First, they sought wisdom apart from God. That resulted in a broken relationship with God who is the source of wisdom. Eve seemed to think that wisdom was just an add-on to her existing knowledge base. In her quest for a quick wisdom upgrade, she damaged her relationships with God, with others, and with herself. Thus, she became less wise.

Eve and Adam's second error was that they sought moral knowledge by breaking the only rule that they had been given to obey. They accepted the serpent's lie that moral understanding could be gained through an act of disobedience. The tempter's falsehood was that the best way to learn about something is to try it for yourself, trial and error. That may work for learning about eating green eggs and ham, but it is a foolhardy way to learn about eating poisonous mushrooms! In the garden of Eden, the forbidden fruit was more like a poisonous mushroom than a nutritious apple; and Eve, Adam, and all of us, have suffered the consequences of Eve's taste test.

Eve's third error was accepting the serpent's suggestion that she had the right to decide matters of good and evil for herself. God had told Adam that the fruit was deadly, but Eve chose to decide for herself. She looked closely at the fruit and saw that it looked good, was seemingly tasty, and might make her wise. (How could she tell that?) Adam and Eve's sin was not just disobeying a rule but rejecting God's right to make the rules. First, Eve doubted God, then she defied God, and then she assumed that she knew better than God did.

Those errors—seeking wisdom as though it was simply an intellectual trait to be acquired, seeking moral understanding by disobeying a moral rule, and doubting God's determination of right and wrong—have led to the moral confusion in the world today. What is good? What is evil? It seems we still don't know.

There was, however, one thing that Eve got right in her encounter with the serpent: she recognized that wisdom and moral knowledge are closely connected. But it would be centuries before the connection of wisdom and morality could be adequately explained by the wisdom writers.

A Corrected Knowledge of Good and Evil

Are "good" and "evil" opposites? It is common to think of them as a matched set of opposites, like black and white or hot and cold.[1] Good and evil are often used as synonyms for right and wrong, but the meaning

---

1. Technically, neither "black and white" nor "hot and cold" are actually opposites. Though they appear to be opposites, in reality they are not. The same is true for "good and evil."

of both words is much broader than morally good (right) and morally bad (wrong). Actually good and evil are not opposites; rather, they are contradictions of each other.

First, we should note that both "good" and "evil" can be used in a nonmoral sense. A delicious dish tastes good, a talented singer sounds good, a skilled carpenter can do a good job on a project, an idea that I like is a good idea, and happiness can be described as feeling good. Likewise, "evil" can refer to a natural disaster like an earthquake, tornado, famine, or a life-threatening disease. None of these uses of "good" or "evil" has the moral sense of right or wrong, and we wouldn't say that a good cook is necessarily a good person, or that the victim of a disease is an evil person (though Job's "friends" made this mistake—see Job 31). A good singer might be called a virtuoso, suggesting that good singing is a virtue, which makes no sense.

In their moral sense, however, "good" and "evil" describe attitudes or behaviors that conform to moral standards or fail to do so. And, by association, people who have good behavior can be called "good," and those who have evil behavior can be called "evil." But what determines whether an act is deemed morally good or evil? It is possible to create lists of good deeds and of bad deeds (and every religion and culture creates such lists) but understanding good and evil goes much deeper than following lists or obeying rules. Ethicists have published volumes trying to identify when a deed is considered good or evil—and their analyses are not simple or straightforward.

What is "good"? Biblically speaking, God is good (Ps 100:5). Goodness is his nature (see, e.g., Exod 33:19; Ps 34:8), and his character defines goodness, rather than the other way around. Good describes his treatment of his creatures, and his blessings bring goodness to people's lives. His laws express morally correct behaviors. For humans to become good means for them to become more like God (godly).

A second use of "good" is for life itself. Just being alive and enjoying the blessings of life are goods. Scripture says that when a person enjoys an abundance, has a life free from misfortune, and lives until old age so that he or she can enjoy children and grandchildren, that is a good life. For Israel, life in the promised land was a special good made available through its covenant relationship with God (Deut 8:1).

A third sense of goodness is moral purity. Morality is defined both by God's laws and by social norms that teach us prone-to-sin humans how we should think and act. These moral standards define goodness, and humans who obey those standards are called good. In the Old Testament the most common standard of morality was God's law, such as the Ten Commandments, which God revealed as part of the covenant. The law identifies specific moral behaviors, religious practices, and social norms that are good. The prophets, Proverbs, and Jesus offered commentaries on how these laws apply in daily life.

Jesus answered the question about which was the greatest commandment by saying that loving God wholeheartedly and loving your neighbor unselfishly are the two greatest commandments (Matt 22:38–39). The apostle Paul taught that loving others is the fulfillment of the whole law (Rom 13:8–10). These verses suggest that love is the greatest moral good. Paul taught that a seemingly good deed not motivated by love is worthless (1 Cor 13:1–3). Thus, the motive for a deed is an essential component in identifying whether or not it is good.

So, in Scripture, goodness is associated with God and godliness, with life and those things which preserve and enhance life, and with moral attitudes and behaviors—especially those motivated by love. In the biblical worldview, these three forms of good are distinct but may be linked. According to the book of Proverbs, good people who have good hearts and make good choices in their daily lives will be blessed by the good God with long life and success, thus receiving the good life people desire. The wise know this and live accordingly.

By contrast, the biblical use of the word "evil" is more than just a synonym for "very bad"—though it is that. The Hebrew word for "evil" is derived from a root meaning "to spoil" or "break in pieces."[2] "Evil" implies a contradiction of "good" in all its forms. Whatever opposes or contradicts God is evil. Whatever devalues or damages life, including natural disasters, diseases, murder, and human conflict, is evil. Thus, death itself is an evil. And whatever contradicts moral goodness is evil. All sin is evil. Evil describes any person, event, or action that contradicts God, life, or moral purity.[3]

Jesus called human nature evil (Matt 7:11); it's not that we are all as bad as Cruella Deville or the Riddler but that we are all sinners by nature. Thus, we all fall short of meeting the expectation in ethical monotheism that because God is good, we should also be good. Jesus divided the

---

2. Howley, "Evil," 348.
3. Baker, "רעע," 1156.

world's peoples into categories of good and evil, a distinction he based on the fruit we bear and on the way we talk.

> Either make the tree good and its fruit good, or make the tree bad and its fruit bad, for the tree is known by its fruit. You brood of vipers! How can you speak good, when you are evil? For out of the abundance of the heart the mouth speaks. The good person out of his good treasure brings forth good, and the evil person out of his evil treasure brings forth evil. (Matt 12:33–35)

The wisdom books use the words "good" and "evil" in the same way as Jesus did in the quote above. Good and evil are found in the heart and made visible in behavior, especially in how we use words. A good or an evil person is known by the fruit they bear. According to Proverbs, good people walk good paths and wicked people walk crooked paths (Prov 2:9, 12–15). We each choose our path, and God watches the choices we make:

> The eyes of the Lord are in every place, keeping watch on the evil and the good. (15:3)

> Whoever diligently seeks good seeks favor, but evil comes to him who searches for it. (11:27)

According to the biblical worldview, the conflict between good and evil is the root metaphor for all of life. This is not just a conflict between God and his angels and the devil and his demons but a conflict within each heart: a person battling himself or herself to make good or evil choices, each of which forms their character in one direction or the other. In this conflict we all get to choose which side we are on.

WISDOM AND RIGHTEOUSNESS

The most common word in Scripture for "goodness" or "morality" is "righteousness." It is impossible to understand Hebrew thought from its beginnings in the Pentateuch through its development in both testaments without understanding the concept of "righteousness" and the related words "righteous," "upright," and "right." With the exception of the doctrines of God and humans, the concept of righteousness may be the central concept in the Hebrew worldview.

Basically, righteousness means right-ness. Righteousness relates to right behavior, right character, right relationships, and a right attitude toward God. Living in the right way, the way God approves, is key to receiving his blessings. We can define righteousness in three distinct forms: moral right-ness, loving relationships, and a right relationship with God.

The word "righteous" is derived from the Hebrew word for "straight," such as a line drawn with a straight edge.[4] To be straight assumes conformity with an agreed upon moral standard, such as the law of God, the laws of society (civil law), or group norms (commonly accepted behaviors). However, a complete understanding of righteousness requires more than correct deeds based on conformity to rules; it also requires the correct motives associated with those deeds. Together deeds and motives become internalized as values within each heart, equaling righteousness. For example, for a person to be righteous, their good deed, such as giving to the poor, should be based on a heart value of caring for others, and should be motivated by love (1 Cor 13:3). If any of these three components is missing—the deed, the value it is based on, and its motivation—the righteousness of the deed is incomplete and may even be judged as unrighteousness! Incomplete righteousness will not be approved by God.

The second meaning of the word "righteousness" refers to how we should treat others—that is, with justice, equity (fairness), generosity, love, and kindness. In the words of Jesus, the standard for right relationships is to love one's neighbor as oneself—where "neighbor" includes strangers, foreigners, and even enemies (Matt 5:43–48; 19:19; Luke 10:25–37).

The third and most important meaning of righteousness is maintaining a right relationship with God: fearing him, submitting to and obeying him, trusting him, and being humble before him. Being righteous before God, the Righteous One (Prov 21:12), the judge of righteousness, is the most important aspect of being righteous. It is God who ultimately decides who is and who isn't righteous (1 Chr 29:17; Pss 26:1–2, 50:6; Eccl 12:14).

> The Lord's curse is on the house of the wicked, but he blesses the dwelling of the righteous. Towards the scorners, he is scornful, but to the humble he gives favor. (Prov 3:33–34)

> The sacrifice of the wicked is an abomination to the Lord, but the prayer of the upright is acceptable to him. The way of the wicked is an abomination to the Lord, but he loves him who pursues righteousness. (15:8–9)

---

4. Milne, "Righteousness," 1020.

The standards for right-ness are derived from God's character. Remembering the definition of ethical monotheism, that God is good and expects his people to be good, the righteous should seek to develop a godly character. The book of Proverbs calls those with righteous character "upright" or "blameless."

An upright character does not mean sinlessness, but sin-*less*-ness. The righteous will sin less. Though the upright may stumble, they get up and move on. Their integrity guides and guards them.

> The integrity of the upright guides them, but the crookedness of the treacherous destroys them. Riches do not profit in the day of wrath, but righteousness delivers from death. The righteousness of the blameless keeps his way straight, but the wicked fall by his own wickedness. (11:3–5)

On the other hand, crooked deeds, wicked thoughts, or unloving motives; treating one's neighbor in an unjust or deceitful way; and choosing not to fear and obey God are marks of unrighteousness and sin. The correction for sin is repentance—a change of attitudes and behavior.

"No one living is righteous before you," and "surely there is not a righteous man on earth who does good and never sins" (Ps 143:2; Eccl 7:20), but God is gracious and forgiving (Jas 2:13; 1 John 1:9). God in his mercy can declare a sinner righteous (Rom 3:26; Eph 2:4–9). For all sinners, God's mercy is our only hope of being declared righteous.

Other Meanings of Righteousness

This basic definition of righteousness takes on additional meanings in each of the Bible's testaments.

In the Old Testament, righteousness is closely associated with faithfulness to the Sinai covenant. The evidence for such faithfulness was not just obedience to the covenant laws, but loving, trusting, and fearing God. Faithfulness implied being holy (set apart) as God's elect people.

But the chosen people—like all of us—failed to keep the laws of the covenant. And like all of us, they were unfaithful to God at times. The remedy for disobedience and unfaithfulness was/is repentance. Under the regulations of the covenant, repentance was expressed through animal sacrifices and offerings made in the tabernacle or temple. Such sacrifices were both a penalty for the wrongdoing and a symbolic offering of oneself, symbolizing the sinner's return to God. Sacrifices were God's appointed way of restoring the covenant relationship, making possible for an unrighteous person to again be declared righteous.

In the New Testament, however, we find an unexpected twist in the biblical understanding of righteousness: unearned righteousness could be credited by God to those who have faith. The background of this was in the story of Abram, also known as Abraham, who trusted God to keep his promise, even the humanly impossible promise of having a child in his old age. God accepted Abraham's faith and credited it to him as righteousness (Gen 15:6; Gal 3:6–9). This is the first biblical example of righteousness being based solely on faith, not works.

The apostle Paul used the Abraham story as the basis of his theology of salvation in which righteousness is the gift of God based on faith (Rom 1:17; 3:26; 4:13–16). The idea of righteousness based on faith became a new basis for entering into a relationship with God, replacing the former requirement of righteousness based on obedience to the law.

Righteousness by faith is a transaction requiring a balancing input on the divine side. Because Jesus Christ kept God's law, he was fully righteous. It is his righteousness that is credited to those who believe in him. On the cross he took our sin and made possible our receiving his righteousness (Rom 5:17; 2 Cor 5:21). Jesus said that he did not come for the sake of the righteous, who would not need salvation, but to save sinners (Matt 9:13). But since none are righteous and all are sinners, Jesus came for all.

There is however one more biblical usage of "righteousness" which is found in both testaments: the righteousness that describes an eschatological ideal, a future hope. "Righteousness," "peace," and "justice," describe a coming time when God and mankind will live together in a proper relationship with each other. God will be honored as God, people will love and respect one another, and God will restore his fallen world to its intended state (Isa 32:16–18; Rom 14:17; 2 Pet 3:13). This future time is associated with the expected messianic age, the kingdom of God.

Thus, righteousness, which is the basis of being approved by God, can either be DIY (do it yourself) by obedience to God's law, or it can be received as a gift by grace through faith. The first view dominates the old covenant; the second dominates the new covenant, made possible by the perfect righteousness of Christ. Though these two understandings of righteousness may seem to be opposites of each other, neither is complete without the other.

Connecting Wisdom and Righteousness

Righteousness is not exclusively a religious term. It is expected in how we live daily in every area of life, including marriage, family, business, work, neighborliness, community mindedness, compassion for the needy, love for enemies, care for animals, and even care for the land. This broader use of righteousness is found in the wisdom books, especially in Proverbs.

But in another sense, the meaning of righteousness is very religious: a righteous person is one who fears the Lord, trusts him, and abides by his covenant on a daily basis. The reward for righteous living is God's blessing of a long and full life.

The wisdom literature makes two connections between righteousness and wisdom. First, the more obvious connection is that wisdom defines which sort of thoughts and deeds are righteous. Righteousness defines which paths are wisest to walk. Wisdom and righteousness are partners, and living morally is always the wise choice. To paraphrase Ecclesiastes, to be unrighteous is both stupid and crazy (Eccl 7:25 NIV). Wisdom supports righteous living by providing knowledge of right and wrong behaviors, by enabling the internalization of right values, which result in good character.

The second connection between wisdom and righteousness, one that is not spelled out in Scripture outside of the wisdom writings, is that wisdom is an alternate path to righteousness and, therefore, is an alternate path to receiving God's approval and blessings. The promises of God's blessings for living wisely in Proverbs closely parallel the blessings promised to Israel for keeping his covenant commandments (Prov 2:20–22). And these covenant-level blessings were available to anyone, Jew or gentile, who followed the path of wisdom. Even a gentile could be blessed by God!

To summarize, righteousness could be achieved by obedience to the law, by faithfulness to the covenant, by making wise choices on a daily basis, by loving one another, by faith in God's ability to keep his promises, and by faith in Christ, the Righteous One (Acts 22:14). Throughout Scripture, righteousness is the primary word regarding God's approval and his blessings.

WISDOM AND JUSTICE

The concept of "justice" is closely related to righteousness. Both are partners of wisdom:

> [Wisdom says,] "I walk in the way of righteousness, in the paths of justice..." (Prov 8:20)

And God approves those who do both:

> To do righteousness and justice is more acceptable to the Lord than sacrifice. (Prov 21:3)

Justice is an expression of righteousness regarding how we treat others. A simple definition of justice is fairness to each person—which is more difficult than it sounds!

Biblical justice can be defined by two distinct standards: the absolute standard of divine justice and the relative standard of human equality. Human administration of justice is measured by how well it achieves both standards. Divine justice is sometimes pictured as God sitting on his throne, meting out just decisions to nations and to individuals, or Christ sitting in final judgment of the nations, dividing them into the categories sheep or goat based on their treatment of others (Ps 1:5–6; 96:13; Matt 25:31–46). This standard of divine justice means that human judges are expected to be as just and as fair as God is.

The other standard of justice is human equality. Jesus taught this in two famous passages which are called the Golden Rule, and the second greatest commandment:

> For whatever you wish that others would do to you, do also to them, for this is the Law and the Prophets. (Matt 7:12)

> You shall love your neighbor as yourself. (Matt 22:40b; see also Lev 19:18b)

Together these verses teach that human justice requires treating all people, including neighbors, the poor, and foreigners, as our equals who deserve treatment equivalent to what we want for ourselves.

In between these two standards are a range of applications of justice for the multiple forms of interactions in which we continually participate, including legal justice, social justice, and social norms. Legal justice is usually based on civil law. Social justice is defined by respecting equal rights for others without discrimination. Social norms, or interpersonal justice, involve the norms of etiquette—that is, treating others with kindness, respect, and honesty. The general standard for all of these interactions is fairness for all.

Divine justice. Scripture teaches that God's justice is perfect (Deut 32:4; Prov 29:26; Gen 18:25). While we understand God's justice in the Old Testament as primarily for the nation of Israel, his covenant people to whom he had given his laws, he rules the whole earth with justice (Ps 105:7). We see his justice both as he judges other nations (Jer 48–51); and, ultimately, we see his justice in his universal offer of mercy (Ps 96:10; Acts 10:34–36; Rom 2:6–11; 10:12).

Legal justice. We often think of justice in its legal context: police, judges, lawyers, and witnesses arguing cases in a courtroom. Scripture requires that legal justice be administered honestly and fairly, based on the same laws for all, including both the high and the lowly, and even for foreigners (Deut 27:19). We often depict Lady Justice as being blindfolded—without bias toward one side or the other. In this vein, kings and judges are to render honest determinations of guilt and innocence. Any false testimony or bribery is an abomination in the eyes of God (Prov 17:15; 18:5).

Social justice. Just as God does not show favoritism in judging the world's peoples, so he expects fairness for all in how we treat others in the community, in the marketplace, and in the neighborhood. God made every nation, tribe, people, and language, Jew and gentile, rich and poor, and male and female as equals in his eyes, and therefore as equals in our eyes (Rev 7:9; Gal 3:28; Prov 22:2). Just as his laws and his mercy are given to all, we must treat others in that way. Prejudice or discrimination based on human identity rather than on God's values is an injustice and is sin.

There is, however, one prominent exception to this rule of equal treatment for all. Social justice requires extra compassion for the most vulnerable in society: widows, the poor, strangers, and foreigners. It even includes love for one's enemies. We will discuss this exception in more detail in our study of Proverbs 15.

Interpersonal justice. Justice extends down into our personal lives and how we treat others on a daily basis. Every culture has its own social norms telling people how to treat one another. Biblically speaking, the standard is equality, treating others as we desire to be treated—whether we like them or not, whether they like us or not. The basic attitudes of this standard are meekness, love, faithfulness, honesty, and kindness. These norms forbid lying, cheating, bullying, and insulting. To take advantage of others for personal gain is injustice and sin.

According to the Bible, legal and social justice are to be given by all and to all. But there is a common—and controversial—standard for justice: retribution.

Retribution

The primary standard for justice in many cultures and religions is retribution. According to the retribution standard, everyone gets what they deserve as a consequence of their behaviors: Do good and be rewarded. Do bad and be punished. A related concept is retaliation, as expressed in the oft quoted rule of an "eye for eye, tooth for tooth" (Exod 21:24).[5]

In the Old Testament retribution was often believed to be God's sole standard for justice. God chose to give blessings or curses based on the faithfulness of his people as seen in their obedience or disobedience to his laws. This was clearly seen in the Sinai covenant in which Israel's right to live in the promised land, and their prosperity and safety within that land, was contingent on their faithfulness to their covenant with God (Lev 26; Deut 7). The prophets interpreted the ups and downs of Israel's history as the divine response to their current faithfulness to God as seen in their obedience to his laws. We see a similar understanding of the blessings and curses in daily life based on each person's righteousness in the book of Proverbs (2:21–22; 11:19). Throughout Scripture a common understanding of God's administration of justice was that people get exactly what they deserve—no more, no less, whether prosperity or suffering; and the common expectation was that this justice would occur within the time of one's life on earth.[6]

Though retribution justice could result in either punishment for sin or blessings for good behavior, it seems that the focus was more often on

---

5. This is called the *lex talionis*—the law of retaliation. This rule does not *require* an eye for an eye as a necessary punishment; rather it *limits* the punishment for one injured eye to no more than one eye and so forth. This standard of justice is that the punishment cannot exceed the crime. In the Sermon on the Mount, Jesus taught a better ethical standard than the *lex talionis*: turn the other cheek (Matt 5:38–42). Harman, "עין," 386.

6. The concept of an afterlife in which perfect justice would finally be administered did not occur until after the writing of the Old Testament, though intriguing suggestions about a resurrection, escape from Sheol, and being received into glory or heaven are present in the Old Testament.

the negative: curses and vengeance for the wicked. In modern English we have a similar tendency to refer to justice more in the negative sense: a criminal gets justice, meaning punishment for their wrongdoing.

Retribution is simple to understand, but its use is often simplistic and prone to error. There are many variables to be considered in administering justice, such that this one simple rule by itself can actually result in injustice. There are two significant problems with retribution as a standard for justice. First, at times people try to work backwards from someone's life circumstances: either financial success or a "miraculous" healing as evidence of having done good deeds; or, on the other hand, sickness, natural disaster, or even a life of poverty can be identified as evidence of some prior sin that earned this negative outcome. This karma-like belief is common in many cultures.[7] My wife and I have lived in another country where the birth of a deformed or disabled child is attributed to some sin the parents—particularly the mother—had committed. In a similar way American Christians sometimes attribute a major earthquake or other natural disaster at home or in some other country to God's judgment on the sin or pagan religion of that country. And Christians may blame an individual who has a serious disease for sin or for a lack of faith to be healed. This is the same error committed by Job's three friends who falsely accused him of sin based on his suffering. These examples are all a misapplication of retribution theology—and, as we shall see in our study of the wisdom books, the truth is that we don't know why God does what he does, whether we feel it is good or bad. When we judge others based on their circumstances, rarely do we actually know as much as we claim to know!

The other significant error that may occur within retribution justice is that it cannot account for the numerous exceptions to the rule that occur in real life. Why do good things often happen to bad people? Why do bad things often happen to good people? This error occurs because retribution theology doesn't consider other possible causes for either positive or negative circumstances that occur in everyone's life from time to time. Those circumstances may have nothing to do with justice. They are undeserved.

The wisdom literature wrestles with the exceptions to the rule of retribution justice: Why do the righteous sometimes suffer more than the wicked? (Eccl 7:15; 8:14). Why do the wicked sometimes prosper more than the righteous? (Ps 73). Why do the good die young? These

---

7. The traditional Hindu belief in karma is based on the idea that people get what they deserve for some prior act in this life or in a previous reincarnation. This belief has been used to justify the rich being rich and the poor being poor.

common contradictory experiences raise difficult questions about the nature of justice.

If retribution was God's sole standard for justice, why are there so many exceptions to the rule? In order to answer that question, we must recognize other variables that can influence the administration of justice. It is not simply guilt and innocence or "getting what one deserves." One variable is the personal motivation for someone's actions. What we deserve is not based solely on what we do but also on why we do it. For example, pious deeds motivated by enhancing one's reputation rather than on love may deserve condemnation rather than praise (Matt 6:1–2, 5, 16; 1 Cor 13:1–3).

Another variable is human corruption as the real cause of injustice—that is, human judgments by biased and greedy government officials seeking bribes or helping out their friends may override justice in court. The list of behaviors God hates includes "a lying tongue, and hands that shed innocent blood, a heart that devises wicked plans, . . . [and] a false witness that breathes out lies" (Prov 6:16–19). In other words, God hates corrupt justice.

Another variable that may affect the course of justice is the length of time required for justice to be meted out, making it less effective. The idea that "the millstones of God grind slowly but they grind very fine" can mean that both blessings and punishments will eventually come for all, but it may take time.

Another variable in the administration of justice is that totally unforeseen factors may enter in, such as Satan's proposal to test Job's faith with affliction even though he was not guilty of sin. Life's trials may be tests meant to prove and improve our faith (Jas 1:2–4).

The most hopeful variable in the administration of justice is the possibility of mercy. The Old Testament acknowledges that God's people don't get what they deserve, God's love and mercy overcome his justice (Ps 103:10–13). In the New Testament, the good news of the gospel is entirely based on mercy overcoming justice.[8] On the cross, Christ got

---

8. Fortunately for us all, God's justice can be mitigated through mercy, forgiveness, and atonement:

> Though justice be thy plea, consider this—
> That in the course of justice none of us
> Should see salvation. We do pray for mercy,
> And that same prayer doth teach us all to render
> The deeds of mercy. (Shakespeare, *Merchant of Venice*, I.VI)

what he didn't deserve so that by his mercy we get what we don't deserve (2 Cor 5:21)!

Thus, there are many variables that can affect the straightforward administration of justice. These variables create exceptions to the rule of retribution and therefore can overturn the expectation that everyone gets what they deserve.

Though there are many exceptions to the rule, this does not mean that retribution theology is always wrong. I suspect that most people in most cultures believe that goodness should be rewarded, and wickedness should be punished. I also prefer that kind of world—except perhaps when I am the guilty one. Most people favor retribution theology as the standard for divine justice, but the reality seems so inconsistent.

If people don't always get what they deserve, then what does justice mean? The answer in each of the wisdom books is that God can be trusted to do what is right. God's justice is believed to be perfect, based on his complete knowledge, without favoritism, and fair to all. God, as the judge of all the world, would never declare the innocent to be guilty, nor punish the innocent along with the guilty. But God's ways are often inscrutable, including his administration of justice. Therefore, humans can't know why life often seems unfair, but we are called to trust that God does know and that his judgments are wise.

It may be fair to say that if Israel had not held to an overly rigid view of retribution theology, the books of Ecclesiastes and Job might not have needed to be written!

WHAT GOD EXPECTS OF US

The simple definition of the worldview of ethical monotheism is God is good and expects his people to be good.

The first part of that definition is that God is good. That is the easy part. God's goodness includes his steadfast love, mercy, faithfulness, and compassion for all his creatures. His goodness is the sole basis for our forgiveness. Micah marveled that God's goodness and steadfast love led him to casting our sins into the depths of the sea—out of sight, out of mind, gone forever (Mic 7:18-20); this does not mean God forgets them, but it means we can. Due to God's goodness, our sins are no longer a barrier between God and us!

The second part of the definition of ethical monotheism is that the good God expects his people to also be good. This expectation was applied to Israel through their covenant with God, and it also applied (and still applies) to all mankind (Eccl 12:13–14). Perhaps the clearest statement of what God expects from his people is in this well-known verse from the book of Micah:

> He has told you, O man, what is good; and what does the Lord require of you but to do justice, and to love kindness, and to walk humbly with your God? (Mic 6:8)

What did Micah say that God requires of each of us? To be good, meaning to act with justice, kindness, and humility.

Though this expectation applies to all of us, Micah was specifically addressing the Jews of his day. In the verses prior to v. 8, Micah used exaggeration to draw a contrast between what God expected and what the Jews wrongly thought he expected:

> With what shall I come before the Lord,
>   and bow myself before God on high?
> Shall I come before him with burnt offerings,
>   with calves a year old?
> Will the Lord be pleased with thousands of rams,
>   with ten thousands of rivers of oil?
> Shall I give my firstborn for my transgression,
>   the fruit of my body for the sin of my soul? (6:6–7)

Micah's exaggerated description of the Jews in his day was to show that they thought God wanted them to be extra religious. His point was if a Jew were to sacrifice thousands of rams, or give ten thousand containers of oil, or, even, as a last resort, make the most extreme sacrifice possible, giving the life of his firstborn son (as pagans did) in order to gain forgiveness for his sin, not even these extreme acts of "worship" would qualify someone as being good in God's sight. In other words, being religious, even being excessively religious, was not the goodness that God expected.

The application of Micah's teaching for Christians today is that being excessively religious does not make us good and does not satisfy God. Suppose a Christian goes to every church meeting, serves in every ministry, and makes exorbitant donations to the church or to other ministries; none of these religious activities would make us good Christians. To understand goodness, Christians also need to pay attention to the words of Mic 6:8.

What did the Lord require of Israel—and what does he require of us? To be good means practicing justice, kindness, and humility. The verbs associated with those three expectations are "to do," "to love," and "to walk." What we do (our behavior), what we love (our attitudes), and how we walk (our consistent pattern of life)—how we treat others and how we relate to God—should demonstrate justice, kindness, and humility. This is what God expects for us to be good as he is good.

In a passage similar to the passage in Micah, Jeremiah spells out the meaning of justice:

> Thus says the Lord: Do justice and righteousness, and deliver from the hand of the oppressor him who has been robbed. And do no wrong or violence to the resident alien, the fatherless, and the widow, nor shed innocent blood in this place. (Jer 22:3)

Just as God cares about justice for the disadvantaged, for the victims of oppression, and for foreigners, God expects his people to care in this way. And, just as God shows mercy—kindness, faithfulness, compassion, forgiveness—toward his people, he expects us to be kind, compassionate, and forgiving toward others. Or, as Jesus expressed it, "I say to you, love your enemies and pray for those who persecute you, so that you may be sons of your Father in heaven" (Matt 5:44–45; see also 19:19). Jesus added that loving *all* others fulfills the law.

The third mark of goodness listed by Micah is walking humbly with our God. The verb "walk" suggests that humility is not a one-time response, a bowing down in church, or a bowing of our heads when we pray; it is a consistent pattern of life. To "walk with" someone is to be identified with them and to fellowship with them. Walking with God means consistent humility, an attitude of lowliness and submission.

While humbling ourselves before an Almighty God may seem like an obvious response, what makes this attitude more meaningful is that Jesus also did this; he humbled himself by becoming a servant (Phil 2:6–8). God does not just require humility, he models it for us! This demonstrates that he is good and how we are to be good.

Generic wisdom, the wisdom that people around the world seek, is not always linked to morality. There are evil geniuses. And, as we shall see in the book of James, a corrupted form of wisdom may sometimes be found within Christian churches (Jas 3:13–15). But biblical wisdom, the kind the Bible teaches, is always linked with morality. The book of Proverbs defines this wisdom as based upon righteousness, justice, and fairness (Prov 1:3; 2:9). God is good and expects his people to be righteous, just, and fair.

8

Becoming Wise

No one is born wise.

—AFRICAN PROVERB

THIS PROVERB IS CORRECT. Wisdom is not inborn; it must be acquired. The question is how to become wise.

In cultures around the world two normal paths to wisdom are recognized: the path of aging—the elderly are assumed to be wise—and the path of mentoring, or learning from those who already have wisdom. In addition, many cultures accept a supernatural path to wisdom through visions, dreams, or the study of Scripture. In particular Christians may cite prayer and Bible study as their source of wisdom. All four of these paths are mentioned in the Bible. The following is a brief survey:

1. In the Bible, as in most cultures, wisdom is expected to be found among the old. The elderly are thought to be wiser (Job 32:6–10). The advisors to the leaders of the tribes of Israel were older men called "elders." And woe to the king who ignored the advice of the elders (1 Kgs 12:8–11)!

    Young children, on the other hand, were thought to lack understanding (Isa 7:15–16; Jonah 4:11). Proverbs called youth "simple," meaning naïve and inexperienced. Even Jesus as a child had to grow in "wisdom, stature, in favor with God and man" (Luke 2:52). Aging is a natural process believed to bring wisdom—though elders are not guaranteed to be wiser. Sometimes a young fool grows up to be an old fool.

2. In every culture, wisdom may be learned from mentors who pass along their knowledge and understanding to the next generation. Such mentors include parents, teachers, and advisors. Perhaps these mentors gained their wisdom by learning from a previous generation of teachers or perhaps they gained it through a lifetime in the school of hard knocks.

A biblical example of such instruction in learning wisdom is the book of Proverbs, which offers case studies in wise decision making. Its proverbs teach prudence to youth or continuing education for adults. It also advises young people to gain wisdom by observing examples around them, either the good examples of wise adults or the bad examples of fools.

3. At the other extreme, biblical wisdom can be acquired supernaturally. Wise men like Joseph (the son of Jacob), Daniel, and the Magi (the so-called three wise men) are prime examples of wisdom as knowledge gained through supernatural means.

God gave Joseph and Daniel skill at interpreting dreams, which demonstrated the superiority of their wisdom to that of the pagan advisors to the kings of Egypt and Babylon. Due to their divinely given wisdom, Joseph and Daniel were selected by these kings to become chief advisors or, in Joseph's case, prime minister.

An unexpected instance of receiving divine wisdom is the story of the Magi (from which we get our word *magician*) who traveled to see Jesus around the time of his birth. They were gentile astrologers who followed a "star" to locate the child who had been born King of the Jews—clearly an example of divine guidance! However, the wisest thing these "wise men" did was to stop in Jerusalem to ask for directions. Their knowledge of astronomy was not enough to lead them to the child; they needed the Bible as well.

As we know, at the end of their story, God gave the Magi guidance through a dream. In both Old and New Testaments, God often used dreams to give supernatural guidance.

4. If we asked Christians how to acquire wisdom, the most common answer would be by prayer and Bible study. Those are good answers. As James wrote, "If any of you lacks wisdom, let him ask God, who gives generously to all without reproach, and it will be given to him" (Jas 1:5).

And as the apostle Paul wrote to Timothy,

> From childhood you have been acquainted with the sacred writings, which are able to make you wise for salvation through faith in Christ Jesus. All Scripture is breathed out by God and profitable for teaching, for reproof, for correction, and for training in righteousness, that the man of God may be complete, equipped for every good work. (2 Tim 3:15–17)

Paul said that Scripture gives wisdom for salvation, for righteousness, and for preparation for ministry. First, Scripture teaches us and then we use Scripture to teach others. Wisdom in, wisdom out.

So, there are four paths to biblical wisdom. But the Old Testament also gives us a case study in how to gain wisdom.

LEARNING FROM SOLOMON

When the people of Israel thought about wisdom, their first thought would have been of King Solomon, who was considered the wisest person of his time. He was so wise that kings—and one queen—from surrounding nations sent envoys to hear him teach. The wisdom highlights of his reign were his request for God to give him wisdom (1 Kgs 3), his beautiful prayer of dedication at the opening of the new temple (8:22–61), and his authorship of two wisdom books, Proverbs and Ecclesiastes; both are great resources of wisdom.

The source of Solomon's wisdom is recorded in the famous story from the early days of his reign when God appeared to him in a dream and offered to give him anything he requested. Solomon's response showed he already had some wisdom.

> Now, O Lord my God, you have made your servant king in place of David, my father, although I am but a little child. I do not know how to go out or come in. And your servant is in the midst of your people whom you have chosen, a great people, too many to be numbered or counted for multitude. Give your servant therefore an understanding mind to govern your people, that

I may discern between good and evil, for who is able to govern this your great people? (1 Kgs 3:7–9)

God was pleased with Solomon's request and assured him that he would give him "a wise and discerning heart," plus wealth and honor—provided that he would walk in obedience to God and keep his commandments (1 Kgs 3:10–15).

Note three elements in Solomon's request: (1) an admission that he was not yet wise, (2) a request to learn to distinguish right from wrong, and (3) a desire to understand how to make wise decisions in order to rule effectively. These three requests serve as a model for all of us on how to seek wisdom.

Solomon's First Request

We each need to acknowledge that we are not yet wise. It is a mark of a fool to believe that one is already wise and to have no desire for further instruction (Prov 26:12; 28:26; Rom 12:16). To boast of one's wisdom is the opposite of wisdom. As Jeremiah reminded us, there is really only one thing of which any person can boast:

> Thus says the Lord: "*Let not the wise man boast in his wisdom*, let not the mighty man boast in his might, let not the rich man boast in his riches, but let him who boasts boast in this, that he understands and knows me, that I am the Lord who practices steadfast love, justice, and righteousness in the earth. For in these things I delight," declares the Lord. (Jer 9:23–24, emphasis added)

Ironically, having wisdom excludes boasting of wisdom! Any claim of possessing "great and unmatched wisdom" is, according to James, a form of lying (Jas 3:14–15). Real wisdom begins with humility. This humility is not false humility; it is simple honesty: we all start life without wisdom.

Solomon's Second Request

Solomon asked that he might learn to distinguish right from wrong—that is, that he might develop moral judgment. This is the knowledge of good and evil that Eve sought in the garden but lost by doubting the only rule regarding food in the garden. So she lost her path to wisdom, and her understanding of right and wrong turned into moral confusion.

Solomon's request acknowledged that wisdom and righteousness are partners. One cannot become wise without moral understanding and moral behavior. As we shall see in the book of Proverbs, Solomon came to understand right and wrong as more than a set of rules to be obeyed; he came to see them as principles of righteous living based on God's character and resulting in treating one another with honesty, fairness, and kindness.

Solomon's Third Request

Solomon also asked that he might learn wise decision making in order to become an effective ruler. The best-known example of his making a wise decision was the incident of two prostitutes who both claimed to be the mother of one infant son. They each had given birth to a son but when one of the babies died, they both claimed the living one as their own. Nowadays a DNA test would have resolved the matter easily, but without that, Solomon used a maternal-love test. He ordered the baby to be cut in half and each mother to be given one half. One woman agreed to this deal but the other said, "Don't kill him. Let her take him." Based on his understanding of human nature, Solomon recognized that the loving response was that of the actual mother (1 Kgs 3:16–28).

Hopefully, none of us will ever face as uncertain a decision regarding life or death as this story contains, but in every life, there will be thousands of difficult decisions to make. We will need wisdom to face those decisions. Like Solomon we can ask God for wisdom—and we don't need to wait for a dream to prompt that request. In the book of Proverbs, Lady Wisdom assured her readers that this kind of wisdom is available not only for kings and judges but for all mankind (Prov 8:4, 15–16), for all who seek wisdom.

Solomon's instructions for gaining wisdom in Proverbs reflect these three requests he made in his prayer for wisdom. But he took his instructions a step further; wisdom must be taken into one's heart—that is, into one's character.

CHARACTER FORMATION

Though no one is born wise, some do become wise. And others become fools. Both of these labels describe a person's character. Such statements may seem offensive to those of us who have been taught not to label others, but these personal characterizations (note the root word "character" here) are considered appropriate by the authors of the wisdom literature. The wise, the fools, the upright, and the wicked are the main character types identified in the wisdom literature. And recognizing the distinctions between these four types is critical to living wisely. In Scripture, character counts!

Perhaps the most surprising takeaway for the modern reader is that the character type of "wise" is actually possible; therefore becoming wise ought to be a goal for each of us.

The word "character" doesn't actually appear in the Bible; the word "heart" is the closest equivalent. Wisdom and uprightness are located in a person's heart. The instruction Proverbs gives to those of us wanting to become wise is that there are two steps: First, we must allow wise teachings to enter our hearts—that is, to shape our character to become an internal compass to guide our steps. And, second, we must guard our heart—that is, protect our character—for the heart is the source of everything we do:

> Above all else, guard your heart, for everything you do flows from it. (4:23 NIV)

As we have said, wisdom is more about hearts than smarts.

What Is Character?

In the most general sense, everybody has character—meaning, everybody has a set of characteristics that are his or her normal. Are we patient or impatient? Honest or deceitful? Compassionate or selfish? We could consider many other traits. Each of us is known to our friends according to our individual set of traits. Those who know us well will recognize these attitudes and actions as typical and even predictable for us. In this general sense, everyone has character, maybe good or bad or in between.

Perhaps some will object to this statement by saying that character is never quite so clear cut. For example, I may be very patient and very impatient depending on the circumstances. I may be honest with some people and dishonest with others. Each person's attitudes and actions may seem to be unpredictable. Maybe there is no such thing as consistent character.

I disagree with that criticism. While people are never 100 percent predictable, there are tendencies in how people think and act. Therefore, we all know some people we trust and some people we don't trust based on our previous interactions with them. My assessment of a person's trustworthiness is based on my assessment of their character.

As Guy Woods wrote,

> A slanderer eventually exhibits the effects of his sin in his whole personality. His outlook on life becomes polluted, his confidence in his fellows vanishes, and his spiritual life dwarfs and dies. A mechanic may be capable of doing excellent work; but if we catch him lying to us, we immediately regard his work as untrustworthy. It is an ancient and true adage that one is no better than his word.[1]

Woods is right: words are a measure of the heart. As Jesus said, "Out of the abundance of the heart the mouth speaks. A good person out of his good treasure brings forth good, and the evil person out of his evil treasure brings forth evil" (Matt 12:34–35). Our words reveal our character!

While past performance is not a perfect predictor of future behavior, we depend, in our assessment of character, on past performance in all of our relationships. The heart is the center and the source of one's life. The heart can be good or evil, straight or crooked. In Proverbs, one with a wise heart heeds instruction and obeys commandments (Prov 4:1–6). But a wicked person has a perverted heart, which is always plotting evil (6:12–15).

In the preface I observed that solving problems is not the primary purpose of biblical wisdom, and I asked what that purpose might be. Character formation is a major part of that purpose. Good character starts with wise choices, which become good habits, which become the basis of character. A wise person has wisdom stored in their heart. Wisdom and good character go together.

But having good character is not yet having wisdom, at least not biblical wisdom. That requires dependence on the God who gives wisdom.

THE FEAR OF THE LORD

The Bible uses many phrases to describe a person's response to God: seek, love, believe, trust, obey, serve, follow, worship, praise, thank, hope,

---

1. Woods, *James*, 164–65.

confess, walk, and remember. But I suspect that for most Christians "fear" would not be near the top of their list of responses to God, yet it is one of the most common responses mentioned in the Bible. We can easily understand "trust God" or "love God," but what does "fear God" mean?

In the wisdom literature the "fear of the Lord" is specifically tied to gaining wisdom. Consider the following verses:

> And he [God] said to man, "Behold, the fear of the Lord, that is wisdom, and to turn away from evil is understanding." (Job 28:28)

> The fear of the Lord is the beginning of wisdom; all those who practice it have a good understanding. His praise endures forever! (Ps 111:10)

> The fear of the Lord is the beginning of wisdom,
> And the knowledge of the Holy One is insight. (Prov 9:10)

> The end of the matter; all has been heard. Fear God and keep his commandments, for this is the whole duty of man. For God will bring every deed into judgment, with every secret thing, whether good or evil. (Eccl 12:13–14)

Let's examine this important phrase within the context of Prov 9:10, the theme verse of the book of Proverbs. The key word in that verse is "fear." What does "fear" mean?

Anyone who was raised in Sunday school or has participated in Bible studies has probably been taught that the word "fear" in these verses doesn't mean "afraid." Other suggested meanings are "respect" or "revere," as if the verse we are studying might read, "Reverence for the Lord is the beginning of wisdom." While "reverence" is an appropriate attitude toward God, I disagree that "being afraid" is not. A word study of "fear" in Scripture shows it to have a stronger sense than "respect" or "revere." The meaning of "fear" in Scripture is somewhere in between "afraid" and "reverence":

> Being afraid of God ← "The fear of the Lord" → Reverence for God

This median meaning of "fear" was illustrated by C. S. Lewis in *The Lion, the Witch, and the Wardrobe*. In this story, four children from earth accidentally travel to the fantasy land of Narnia, a place populated by humans and talking animals. Aslan the lion (who represents Christ in these stories) is the rightful king of Narnia, though he had not been seen there for a long time. When Susan, one of the children, heard that Aslan the lion was coming, she became frightened. She asked if he was safe to be around. Mr. Beaver tried to explain to her what the lion Aslan is like, "Safe? Who said anything about safe? . . . 'Course he isn't safe. But he's good. He's the King, I tell you."[2] Susan's fear of encountering a lion, even a good lion, was understandable! What Mr. Beaver was really saying was that God isn't safe, but he is good. That is the double-sided meaning of the fear of the Lord.

The Bible uses several Hebrew and Greek words for fear. Each of these words can mean both the stronger sense of "afraid" and the lesser sense of "respect." They refer to fear/respect for God, fear/respect for kings, fear/respect for human masters, and fear/respect for parents (Prov 24:21; Lev 19:3). The word "fear" can be paired with "trembling" when it refers to service to God and to fellow believers (Phil 2:12; 2 Cor 7:15). The phrase "fear and trembling" implies a much stronger sense than just respect. The Corinthian believers treated their pastor, Titus, with "fear and trembling" (2 Cor 7:15). I wonder if we treat our pastors with such trembling!

Jesus taught his disciples not to fear humans "who kill the body but cannot kill the soul. Rather fear him who can destroy both soul and body in hell" (Matt 10:28). There is a genuine sense of "afraidness" in Jesus' statement—and rightly so. God is holy and we are not. God is mighty and we are not. Unless he shows mercy, we are all condemned to death and hell; therefore, fear him. Fortunately, as Mr. Beaver said, he is also good!

Both senses of fear can be found in one verse:

> Moses said to the people, "Do not fear, for God has come to test you, that the fear of him may be before you, that you may not sin." (Exod 20:20)

In other words, they should not be scared of God, but they should fear God (it is the same Hebrew word in both instances). Moses meant that God did not plan to kill them, but God did want to warn them to stop sinning. This conclusion that the fear of God should lead people to quit sinning occurs frequently in Scripture, as the following examples show:

- In Exodus, we read that the Egyptian midwives disobeyed the pharaoh's command to kill the Hebrew baby boys because they feared God; therefore God blessed them with their own children (Exod 1:17, 21).

2. Lewis, *Lion, Witch, Wardrobe,* 86.

- When Pharaoh and his officials, on the other hand, saw the plagues that God brought against Egypt, three times they feigned repentance and submission; yet Moses knew that they still did not fear the Lord God (Exod 9:30). Therefore, the plagues continued. Fearing God is more than lip service.

- In the same passage, during the plague of hail, there is an enlightening use of the word "fear": Moses warned Pharaoh that the worst hailstorm ever was coming. The Egyptian officials who "feared the word of the Lord" hurried off to get their slaves and livestock into shelter. But those who ignored the word of the Lord did not act to protect their property (Exod 9:20–21). Fearing God's word was evidenced by acting on it. Fear led to action.

- Moses instructed Israel just prior to his death, "And now, Israel, what does the Lord your God require of you but to fear the Lord your God, to walk in all his ways, to love him, to serve the Lord your God with all your heart and with all your soul, and to keep the commandments and statutes of the Lord, which I am commanding you today for your good?" (Deut 10:12–13)

The final passage above contains five verbs describing what God asked his people to do: fear, love, walk, serve, and keep his commands. "Fear the Lord your God" is the first on the list and suggests a wholehearted commitment to him. Having such fear leads to the other responses: love, service, and obedience.

Throughout the Old Testament, fearing God is associated with obedience to God's law and with turning away from sin. Such turning from sin is not due to a personal sense of morality, as important as that is. Rather it is because God has commanded moral behavior, and he is God.

The fear of God is also mentioned in the New Testament as an incentive for moral behavior:

> Since we have these promises, beloved, let us cleanse ourselves from all defilement of body and spirit, bringing holiness to completion in the fear of God. (2 Cor 7:1)

> And if you call on him as Father who judges impartially according to each one's deeds, conduct yourselves with fear throughout the time of your exile. (1 Pet 1:17)

> Honor everyone. Love the brotherhood. Fear God. Honor the emperor. (1 Pet 2:17)

> Submitting to one another out of reverence [fear] for Christ. (Eph 5:21)

This last reference speaks of the fear of Christ in the same way as the fear of God. Fearing Christ leads Christians to live morally, including in mutual submission to each other.

The fear of the Lord is not just an individual response to God, it is also an integral part of being in covenant with him. This was true both in the Sinai covenant—also called the old covenant—and in the new covenant prophesied by Jeremiah:

> They shall be my people, and I will be their God. I will give them one heart and one way, that they may fear me forever, for their own good and the good of their children after them. I will make with them an everlasting covenant, that I will not turn away from doing good to them. And *I will put the fear of me in their hearts*, that they may not turn from me. (Jer 32:38–40)

In this prophecy of a new covenant, God declared, "They will be my people, and I will be their God." God promised to do good to his people—in fact, to "never stop doing good to them." Their part is to always fear him, which suggests a never-ending, humble submission to him as their Lord and their God. What is new in this new covenant is that God will give them the singleness of heart and action to make fearing him possible. It is a mark of God's grace that he enables our fearing him.

Fearing God and Wisdom

In the wisdom literature, "fearing the Lord" has one additional association: it is the necessary first step in acquiring wisdom (Prov 9:10, Job 28:28). Fearing the Lord is required for wisdom because wisdom is a gift from God who gives it to those who humbly submit to him.

> This "fear" is no abject terror, nor is it simply reverential awe, but a deep-seated humility grounded in an abiding awareness of one's absolute dependence for existence on the undeserved mercy of Yahweh. Only through such humility and dependence

is the human heart prepared to perceive and receive the wisdom that God gives.[3]

To fear the Lord means to humbly submit myself to the Lord, to have a consistent commitment to him, which leads to obedience to his commands and wholehearted worship and service to him—because he is my God.

THE SPIRIT OF WISDOM

Wisdom is just as important in the New Testament as it was in the Old, but the means of attaining it have changed. This change is due to the arrival of the Messiah who is Wisdom incarnate, and to the indwelling of the Holy Spirit within each believer.

As Jesus told his disciples prior to his death,

> I will ask the Father, and he will give you another Helper, to be with you forever, even the Spirit of truth, whom the world cannot receive, because it neither sees him nor knows him. You know him, for he dwells with you and will be in you. (John 14:16–17)

This promise of a continuous divine presence within each believer is a preview of the New Testament teaching about wisdom. For Christians the Spirit has become our primary link to acquiring wisdom.

Four Forms of Wisdom for Christians

The *first form of wisdom* is a simple extension of wisdom as taught in the Old Testament. Wisdom is about knowledge and understanding applied to daily life. This is the kind of wisdom that King Solomon requested of God: to make good decisions. The apostle Paul chided the Corinthians for lacking this ordinary kind of wisdom which could be used to settle disputes among them.

> Can it be that there is no one among you wise enough to settle a dispute between the brothers? (1 Cor 6:5)

When a dispute about the distribution of food for widows arose between the Christians who spoke Greek and those who spoke Hebrew, the apostles told the church to choose leaders based on administrative wisdom to handle the matter:

---

3. Wilson, "Wisdom," 1283.

> Pick out from among you seven men of good repute, full of the Spirit and of wisdom, whom we will appoint to this duty. (Acts 6:3)

The apostles delegated responsibility to handle minor issues to Christians perceived to be wise.

The *second form of wisdom* is an extension of the first. Because of the indwelling Spirit, all Christians can live wisely in difficult days. Paul referred to his day as being both evil and an opportunity. We face similar times, and we need wisdom to negotiate such times.

> Look carefully then how you walk, not as unwise but as wise, making the best use of the time, because the days are evil. Therefore do not be foolish, but understand what the will of the Lord is. (Eph 5:15–17)

> Walk in wisdom toward outsiders, making the best use of the time. Let your speech always be gracious, seasoned with salt, so that you may know how you ought to answer each person. (Col 4:5–6)

Living wisely by using our time wisely requires living as children of the light: doing good and what's right and living in truth—things that please the Lord (Eph 5:10). And living wisely means interacting with nonbelievers with grace, attractive speech, and knowledge in order to answer their questions and charges and perhaps to win them to the faith.

The *third form of wisdom* is brand new in the New Testament. Believers have access to a much higher wisdom because they have the mind of Christ (1 Cor 9:16)—a result of the Holy Spirit within them. This enables them to understand the world, especially spiritual realities, as Christ did.

> "For who has understood the mind of the Lord, so as to instruct him?" But we have the mind of Christ. (1 Cor 2:16)

Christians, by the Spirit, have insight into the mind of God! Through the Spirit, the believer can understand spiritual realities that the wisest person without the Spirit cannot—as Jesus promised (John 14:17).

Paul saw worldly wisdom as counterproductive to receiving the gospel. The philosophers and rulers of that age mocked the gospel and mocked Christians for being foolish. Paul acknowledged that the level of human wisdom found among Christians was nothing to brag about, but that didn't matter because with the mind of Christ they were wiser than the philosophers.

A *fourth form of wisdom* was for a few believers (but not all) to have as a spiritual gift. The first of the gifts listed in 1 Cor 12 is "a message of wisdom." What is this wisdom? It probably refers to the understanding or guidance the church needs for knowing what to do, particularly in the start-up days of the church age.

Wisdom for Today

Wisdom is available to the church through leaders chosen for their wisdom and through the exercise of the spiritual gift of wisdom given by the Spirit. In addition, there is a general wisdom available to all Christians, received by being in Christ, derived through the Spirit, and teaching them how to walk each day so as to please God and to attract nonbelievers to the gospel. While not all Christians have a special gift of wisdom, we all can display wisdom in how we live.

And in both testaments, the key to becoming wise is fearing the Lord.

9

Thinking About Wisdom

WHAT IS WISDOM? THE previous chapters have suggested several definitions of wisdom: Wisdom is a way of thinking logically or of doing something with excellence. Wisdom is the bridge between the theoretical and the practical sides of life. Wisdom is derived from an understanding of reality—how the world works—and choosing actions in accordance with that reality. According to the wisdom literature, wisdom has to do with the development of good character, leading to better relationships with others—to treating others with respect and kindness. Primarily, wisdom is submission to the God of all wisdom. It was also suggested that wisdom is like a GPS, both because it gives guidance and because it is sometimes wrong.

If those statements define what wisdom is, here are two statements about what wisdom isn't: wisdom isn't a form of genius—geniuses may be evil—nor is wisdom a mystical path to enlightenment—contrary to the stereotype of a hermit meditating in a mountaintop cave. Real wisdom is found in homes, marketplaces, and on the streets where we all live, work, and try to get along with one another in order to survive and thrive. Biblical wisdom, as portrayed in the hundreds of miniature case studies in the book of Proverbs, is neither brainy nor mystical—it is simply practical, and anyone can benefit from applying it.

We can understand wisdom from two perspectives: the thinking side and the being side. The thinking side of wisdom is that it is a way of thinking carefully about life, relying on knowledge, understanding, and moral judgment. It requires insight and foresight—understanding where we are now and where we ought to go next. The other perspective, the being side of wisdom deals with character—with hearts, not smarts. It is an internal compass that guides us in living in relationship with ourselves, with others, and with God. Wisdom teaches us to view ourselves with humility, others with empathy and fairness, and God with fear and obedience. Putting this all together, wisdom is a better way of thinking, leading to better ways of behaving, resulting in better ways of living together.

The advantage of biblical wisdom over generic wisdom is that it is grounded in the monotheistic worldview. Biblical wisdom is grounded on an understanding of reality, truth, and morality derived from the God who made the universe and who administers it according to his own purposes. The disadvantage of biblical wisdom is that God's plans for caring for his world are often unknown. Human wisdom never has access to all of God's ways (Rom 11:33–36). The monotheist's view of wisdom was summarized by the teacher of Ecclesiastes (Solomon):

> [God] has made everything beautiful in its time. Also, he has put eternity into man's heart; yet so that he cannot find out what God has done from the beginning to the end. (Eccl 3:11)

So, it seems humans can appreciate God's wisdom, but not fully understand it.

THE WISDOM BOOKS

While the biblical wisdom writings all share a common worldview and discuss common topics, there are distinct approaches that they each bring to the discussion of wisdom. Understanding the differences in their perspectives is critical to gaining a comprehensive understanding of the Bible's teaching about wisdom.

The book of Proverbs provides a foundation for the whole wisdom genre, applying the monotheistic worldview to choices we make in daily life. But Ecclesiastes questions that simple perspective and the book of Job seemingly denies it—at least at first. The Gospels and Pauline Epistles, after the arrival of the Messiah, reveal a new and very different perspective about wisdom—one which was only hinted at in the Old Testament wisdom literature. And the book of James comes full circle, reconciling the new perspective with that of Proverbs. Thus, the study of the wisdom literature is like a roller-coaster ride—ending back near the beginning.

The Old Testament

In this book, *Wisdom About Wisdom*, parts 3, 4, and 5 will study the three Old Testament books of wisdom: Proverbs, Ecclesiastes, and Job. They each have a very different style of writing, and they differ widely in what they teach about wisdom. These books agree on the promise of wisdom: a successful and long life; and they agree on the problem of wisdom: life doesn't always work out as expected. God is not as predictable as we might like.

Here is a hypothetical case study as to how the three Old Testament books apply wisdom according to their own perspective.

The problem: a student is facing an important exam, the results of which could determine future opportunities. How should that student pass the exam?

- *Proverbs*: Listen to your teacher. Don't try to take short-cuts. Study hard. Learn the material. That is the best way to pass the exam.
- *Ecclesiastes*: Studying hard may not guarantee you will pass. Perhaps your best effort will not achieve a passing grade; even if you pass, you may not be satisfied with the result.
- *Job*: Even if you study and think you understand, you still might fail. This makes no sense until you realize that success in life is not based on passing tests.

In other words, these three books teach the following:

- *Proverbs*: There are normal principles of wise and righteous living, which when applied are most likely to result in success.
- *Ecclesiastes*: Success is overrated. Living a life pursuing success may end in failure, but even achieving success will be disappointing. So then, what is the point of life?
- *Job*: Bad things happen to good people. So why be good? Let God speak to that.

Or, one might contrast the three books in another way:

- *Proverbs*: Life is fair.
- *Ecclesiastes*: Life is not fair, but God is fair.
- *Job*: Maybe God is not fair.

Needless to say, at the end of his book, Job received a stern lecture for suggesting that God might be unfair.

The New Testament

Wisdom itself didn't change in the New Testament but the understanding of it radically changed. And the means of gaining it also changed. The radical change happened when wisdom was born as a man: the Word (*Logos*) became flesh and lived among us. Jesus was not just the Messiah and the Savior, he was Wisdom incarnate, introducing a new and different theology of wisdom. Wisdom could no longer be reduced to a set of verbal instructions in careful thinking or moral judgment. In Christ we meet a person who was not just wise, but actually co-wise with God. Hereafter, gaining God's wisdom became contingent on recognizing that person as Wisdom-in-the-flesh. Apart from Christ, human wisdom was shown to be empty and counterproductive, even deceptive, corrupt, and demonic! The moral of the New Testament wisdom writings is to choose carefully—there are scams out there.

We will begin our studies of the wisdom books with the book of Proverbs, which presents the foundation for all of the biblical wisdom writings. Then we will follow with Ecclesiastes and Job as they delve more deeply into the different understandings of wisdom. Finally, we will look at the new direction the New Testament brings to our understanding of wisdom.

And so, we begin our studies in biblical wisdom.

PART THREE

Studies in the Book of Proverbs

I have heard that Christian missionaries working in parts of East Asia use the book of Proverbs as their entry point for presenting the gospel; not because there are "salvation verses" in Proverbs—there aren't—but the very practical wisdom of Proverbs makes sense in most cultures and can build a bridge to an ethical, monotheistic view of reality. If you can understand Proverbs, you are ready for the gospel.

10

Introducing the Book of Proverbs

MOST OF THE BOOK of Proverbs consists of a collection of brief case studies that offer instruction in living wisely in daily life. The goal of these instructions is to produce better people who will in turn have better marriages, better families, better communities, better government officials, and better nations. This purpose statement applies to both Jews and gentiles, to people living three thousand years ago, and to people today. Proverbs is an important book for us all.

The primary purpose, "to produce better people," raises the question, What does the word "better" mean? What constitutes a better person who will have better relationships and better communities? Proverbs identified two characteristics of a better person: a wiser person and an upright (righteous) person. Proverbs does not define living "better" in religious terms as other books of the Bible might. The book has been called "religion in street clothes": how to live out your faith when you're not in church. The proverbs in Proverbs are practical illustrations of two paths: the way of wisdom and the way of foolishness, which the readers of the book must choose between. The path they choose / we choose will lead to predictable outcomes of success or failure in life. God oversees this. As we shall see, in Proverbs *direction determines destiny*.

The book of Proverbs begins and ends with poems: an introductory poem previewing the themes to be covered in the book and a concluding poem describing an ideal person who is a good example of the wise instructions given in the book.

THE INTRODUCTORY POEM

There is no better introduction to the contents of the book of Proverbs than the poem at the start; it is a six-line poem, which reads like a teacher's lesson plan for the rest of the book:[1]

> To know wisdom and instruction,
> to understand words of insight,
>> To receive instruction in wise dealing,
>> in righteousness, justice, and equity;
>>> To give prudence to the simple,
>>> knowledge and discretion to the youth—
>>> Let the wise hear and increase in learning,
>>> and the one who understands obtain guidance,
>> to understand a proverb and a saying,
>> the words of the wise and their riddles.
> The fear of the Lord is the beginning of knowledge;
> fools despise wisdom and instruction. (Prov 1:2–7)

This poem provides a list of the book's educational objectives, identifies its intended students, details the lessons that they each should learn, and how those lessons will be taught:

- The goal of the curriculum is to gain wisdom and instruction.

- The teaching method will be sayings in various forms: proverbs, sayings, and riddles.

- One group of students targeted for these instructions are the simple (meaning, the naïve and inexperienced youth) who will be taught prudence (meaning, actions based on careful thought and good judgment resulting in positive outcomes).

- The other group of targeted students are older, wiser individuals who need a refresher course in wisdom. They will receive guidance.

- The youth will also learn moral living: righteousness, justice, and equity (fairness). In other words, their wisdom will be seen in how they treat others.

---

1. I have formatted the introductory poem with matched indentations, which show its reverse symmetry (ABCC'B'A'), a common form used in Hebrew poetry. This symmetry is seen in the first and last lines having the repeated phrase "wisdom and instruction," which describes the content of the poem and of the book as a whole.

- And all of us who read Proverbs will learn that the beginning of knowledge is the fear of the Lord. This is the theme of the whole book.
- Sadly, the poem also informs us that fools will despise such instruction.

To summarize the poem—and the entire book of Proverbs—wisdom can be learned through instruction. Wise words from wise teachers and parents impart knowledge, understanding, and insight—the building blocks of wisdom. But acquiring wisdom is a choice, and fools will choose to ignore such instruction.

The book of Proverbs is a wisdom curriculum. This introductory poem is the lesson plan for that curriculum. The remainder of the book contains six-hundred-plus brief case studies, applying the book's wise instructions to daily life. Anyone who heeds those instructions can become wise. And, as we have said, the purpose of the book is for each of us to become better individuals, with better lives and better relationships. That is the kind of wisdom God blesses!

THE CONCLUDING POEM

The final section of the book of Proverbs is a twenty-two-line poem dedicated to a wise woman, sometimes called "the Wife of Noble Character" (31:10–31).[2] She cares for her household by cooking, sewing, and gardening; she runs a small business and makes prudent investments; she gives to the needy; she teaches with words of wisdom; and most important of all, she fears the Lord. Because of her well-run household, her husband is respected in the community, therefore he honors her, and their children praise her. She is the ideal wife and life partner! She is a role model of living wisely.

The poem begins,

> An excellent wife who can find?
> She is far more precious than jewels.
> The heart of her husband trusts in her,
> and he will have no lack of gain.
> She does him good, and not harm,
> all the days of her life. (31:10–12)

---

2. The Hebrew poem is an acrostic. The twenty-two verses each begin with the letters of the Hebrew alphabet in order from א to ת (A to Z).

And the poem concludes,

> Give her of the fruit of her hands,
>   and let her works praise her in the gates. (31:31)

It may surprise us that in the book of Proverbs, a book written by men and for men, that the most detailed description of a wise individual is of a woman. This poem teaches that the success of the home, the family, and the family business are due to the wisdom and hard work of the wife and not just to her husband. Indeed, his reputation among the men of the town is due in part to her. We might say that the wisest choice he ever made was to marry her. Implicit within the Hebrew grammar of the poem is an imperative to him as her husband to praise her for her good works!

But a good wife is recognized not for physical beauty but for her heart:

> Charm is deceitful, and beauty is vain,
>   but a woman who fears the Lord is to be praised. (31:30)

This line not only summarizes the poem about an excellent wife; it summarizes the whole book of Proverbs: one who fears the Lord is to be honored!

Ideals in Proverbs

Let us notice two additional points about this woman: First, she is too perfect. Second, she is Wisdom.

Some writers criticize this poem for creating an impossible standard for women:

> To some women, the figure described in Proverbs 31 is a superwoman, who is more than any human can be expected to emulate. Truly, she is that. She is an ideal and ought not to be seen as a norm for women.[3]

The excellent wife is too perfect. The poem begins by saying that a wife of such excellent character is a rare find. In other words, she is not supposed to be the norm. Her perfection sets an ideal that all wives (and husbands) can strive for. Perhaps we should consider the ideal wife as a personification of a human trait.

---

3. Tucker, *Women*, 75.

Proverbs is a book of ideals. Many of the characters referred to in the book are too perfect to be real. They are either too wise or too foolish. That does not mean that we shouldn't pay attention to them. Teachers often use ideal examples to illustrate a point. The perfect wife is an illustration of an ideal to which we all, women and men, can aspire.

What is the ideal she represents? Look at the description of her in 31:10 (quoted above): she is a rare find; she is more precious than jewels; she brings profit to her husband; she is good for him. Therefore, he can trust her.

Now compare that to the description of wisdom in a brief poem in Proverbs 3:

> Blessed is the one who finds wisdom,
>   and the one who gains understanding,
> For the gain from her is better than gain from silver
>   and her profit better than gold.
> She is more precious than jewels,
>   and nothing you desire can compare with her.
> Long life is in her right hand;
>   in her left hand are riches and honor.
> Her ways are ways of pleasantness,
>   and all her paths are peace.
> She is a tree of life to all who lay hold of her;
>   those who hold her fast are called blessed. (3:13–20)

The Wife of Noble Character (ch. 31) sounds a lot like wisdom (ch. 3). Not only is she a good role model of wisdom in action, but she actually personifies wisdom and its effects. Perhaps she is the same person whom I call Lady Wisdom who gives a lengthy speech in Prov 8. In any case, this wife personifies wisdom in how she acts, how she treats others, and her religious views.

AUTHORSHIP AND ARRANGEMENT

These two poems give a preview of what we shall learn from studying Proverbs. However, before we begin, there are some technical matters to consider.

The opening line of the book of Proverbs attributes its authorship to "Solomon, son of David, king of Israel." It makes sense that Solomon wrote many of the proverbs since we are told that he spoke three thousand proverbs during his life (1 Kgs 4:12). It is unclear if Solomon wrote all of the proverbs attributed to him in Proverbs or if he was a collector who gathered them. One section of Proverbs attributed to Solomon (25:1—29:32) is said to have been collected later by King Hezekiah's men.

Besides Solomon, two other authors are named for brief portions of Proverbs: Agur wrote 30:1–33, and King Lemuel wrote 31:1–9 and maybe 31:10–31. Lemuel gives credit for the content of his writings to his mother who taught him these things. Beyond these brief references, we don't know any more about the identity of these two men.

About half of the sayings in Proverbs are the brief two-line kind we typically mean when we say "proverb" (chs. 10:1—22:16; 25–29). The other half of the book consists of a variety of longer sayings, poems, parables, and speeches. Chapters 1–9 may be a school textbook intended to instruct the sons of court officials in learning wisdom, thus preparing them for future roles as government officials.

One other portion, 22:17—24:34, is attributed to the "sayings of the wise," including both "thirty sayings of the wise" and "further sayings of the wise." We don't know who this group of wise individuals was. The section of thirty sayings resembles collections of Egyptian wisdom writings, such as *The Instruction of Amenemope*, which may have inspired the wise in writing this section of Proverbs.[4]

Exactly how the book of Proverbs was assembled in its present form, and by whom, is not stated. Perhaps it was by Hezekiah's men (Prov 25:1).

Unlike other biblical books, the book of Proverbs cannot be outlined based on its contents. Verses regarding the specific topics covered in the book are scattered throughout the book making outlining difficult.

The following outline of Proverbs is based on authorship, not content:

1. Solomon's Lessons for Young Men (chs. 1–9)
2. The Proverbs of Solomon (10:1—22:16)
3. The Words of the Wise (22:17—24:22)
4. More Words of the Wise (24:23–34)
5. The Collected Proverbs of Solomon (chs. 25–29)
6. The Words of Agur (ch. 30)

---

4. Much of the wisdom in Proverbs is based on general revelation. God's revelation through creation is available to all people, whether or not they are theists. The similarity of the wisdom writings of Israel and Egypt is therefore not surprising. That theists can learn wisdom from nontheists is also not surprising.

7. The Words of King Lemuel (31:1–9)
8. The Wife of Noble Character (31:10–31)

11

Learning from Proverbs (Small *p*)

JOHN IS A RESIDENT in the nursing home where my wife and I work as feeding assistants. During the past few years, John and I have become friends and prayer partners. He is a retired pastor and when I go to his room, he is often reading his Bible, and often he is reading Proverbs. He says that he likes Proverbs because every verse is a complete lesson by itself. John is enjoying one of the appeals of the literary genre of proverbs: they are brief, memorable, and practical.

THE PROVERBS OF PROVERBS

Unless a Christian is a student of the Bible, their acquaintance with Proverbs may have come from a few verses they have seen on posters, coffee mugs, or internet memes. Here are a few popular examples:

> Trust in the Lord with all your heart
>   and lean not on your own understanding,
> In all your ways acknowledge him
>   and he will direct your paths. (Prov 3:5–6)

> Pride goes before destruction,
>   a haughty spirit before a fall. (16:18)

> Iron sharpens iron,
>   and one man sharpens another. (27:17)

> An excellent wife, who can find her?
> For her worth is far above jewels. (31:10 NASB)

> Train up a child in the way he should go;
> even when he is old, he will not depart from it. (22:6)

The theme verse of Proverbs is as follows:

> The fear of the Lord is the beginning of wisdom,
> and the knowledge of the Holy One is understanding. (9:10 NASB)

My favorite and least favorite verses from Proverbs:

> The path of the righteous is like the light of dawn,
> That shines brighter and brighter until the full day. (4:18 NASB)

> Spare the rod and spoil the child. (Actually this verse is not in Proverbs!)[1]

Such proverbs are useful for printing on posters because they deliver a complete thought in a couple of lines that read like poetry and teach a truth. Unlike other scriptural genres, many of the individual proverbs in Proverbs can be understood without considering the context of surrounding verses, but they should be considered within the context of the book as a whole—understanding the worldview of Proverbs is necessary for understanding the meaning of the individual sayings. And all of the proverbs should be interpreted in the context of life in general—we can all recognize that many of the proverbs describe our personal lives and our modern society!

LEARNING FROM PROVERBS (SMALL *P*)

The best way to learn any language or any culture is to be born and raised there, but for a newcomer one of the best ways to learn a new culture is to study the idioms and proverbs that the locals use. Learning proverbs not only helps with learning vocabulary but provides a window into the beliefs and values of the culture—a way to understand its wisdom. Therefore, the proverbs in the book of Proverbs are a window into the worldview of ancient Israel, and particularly the worldview of the wisdom writers.

---

1. See Prov 13:24; for further comments on this proverb, see the section on spankings at the end of ch. 13 of this book.

According to the worldview of Proverbs, life is divided into binary alternatives: wise versus foolish, right versus wrong. The world is black and white with almost no shades of gray. People can choose between the options, ultimately receiving the consequences of their choices. In addition to the two primary pairs of choices, the book presents other pairs of contrasting values including humility versus pride, honesty versus deceitfulness, and faithfulness versus untrustworthiness. Each of the approximately six hundred proverbs in Proverbs are brief case studies illustrating how to live well, based on these contrasting truths.

Reading proverbs is like reading brief poems. They are couplets that present a general truth based on the writer's observations about life. Many proverbs present two options and two consequences, possibly in this form:

> Do this good behavior
>   and receive this happy ending.
> But do this bad behavior
>   and suffer this sad ending.

That generic proverb is a template for the message of the book as a whole.

TYPES OF PROVERBS

Most proverbs use one of these standard forms: contrast, comparison, or complement. Some use humorous comparisons. Some make their point by listing a number of examples—often four, perhaps with the key one at the end.

Contrast Proverbs

The English translation of many proverbs highlights a contrast by using the word "but." For example,

> Whoever is slow to anger has great understanding,
>   *but* he who has a hasty temper exalts folly. (14:29)

> Righteousness exalts a nation,
>   *but* sin is a reproach to any people. (14:34, emphases mine)

These contrasts provide the reader with clear choices with opposite consequences.

Comparison Proverbs

Other proverbs provide a comparison, using the English words "like" or "better than." They teach a truth about one person or thing by showing its similarity to something else:

> Like a thorn that goes up into the hand of a drunkard
> is a proverb in the mouth of fools. (26:9)
>
> Like a gold ring in a pig's snout
> is a beautiful woman without discretion. (11:22)
>
> Better to be lowly and have a servant
> than to play the great man and lack bread. (12:9)
>
> Better is a little with righteousness
> than great revenues with injustice. (16:8)

To understand a comparison proverb the reader has to pause and think about the similarities between the two things.

Complement Proverbs

In some proverbs, the second half of the statement completes the thought of the first half:

> Leave the presence of a fool,
> for there you do not meet words of knowledge. (14:7)
>
> He who is often reproved, yet stiffens his neck,
> will suddenly be broken beyond healing. (29:1)

In some proverbs the second half is a parallel statement to the first:

> Whoever gets sense loves his own soul;
> he who keeps understanding will discover good. (19:8)
>
> Pride goes before destruction,
> and a haughty spirit before a fall. (16:18)
>
> With patience a ruler may be persuaded,
> and a soft tongue will break a bone. (25:15)

This last proverb illustrates the use of absurdity, a form of humor, to create a comparison: just as patience is the best way to persuade a reluctant king, gentle words can overcome resistance.

Numbered Lists

Some proverbs use several illustrations to make a point. Sometimes they focus attention on the final item in the list:

> There are four things that are too mysterious for me to understand:
>
>> an eagle flying in the sky,
>> a snake moving on a rock,
>> a ship finding its way over the sea,
>> and a man and a woman falling in love. (30:18–19 TEV)
>
> There are four things that are impressive to watch as they walk:
>
>> lions, strongest of all animals and afraid of none;
>> goats, strutting roosters,
>> and kings in front of their people. (30:29–31 TEV)

Contradictory Proverbs

Sometimes there are two proverbs that seem to contradict each other. Actually they teach two sides of the same coin. For example, in English we are told that both of these contradictory sayings are true:

- Birds of a feather flock together.
- Opposites attract.

Both of these proverbs together ask us something about friendship: Do we prefer friends like ourselves or do we choose friends (and mates) who differ from us? Both may be true at times—which is part of what makes life interesting. Many other proverbs in English and in other languages have a contrast proverb that teach a balancing truth.

In the book of Proverbs there are two seemingly opposite sayings placed adjacent to each other:

> Answer not a fool according to his folly,

> lest you be like him yourself.
> Answer a fool according to his folly,
> lest he be wise in his own eyes. (26:4–5)

Though these two proverbs appear contradictory, they are actually complementary, revealing two approaches to responding to a fool. Commentators don't agree on how to reconcile the two statements. My explanation is yes, do correct a fool's irrational statements, or he will never learn better. But, no, don't use his style of reasoning or you will also sound foolish. (A similar American proverb says, "Don't argue with a fool, or bystanders won't be able to tell the difference.")

OTHER TEACHING METHODS IN PROVERBS

In addition to its use of proverbs as a teaching method, Proverbs also uses lectures, poems, idioms, and figures of speech. The most prominent figure of speech is personification—the presentation of an abstract idea as though it were a person. In Proverbs two significant topics, wisdom and foolishness, are both personified as women. I call these fictional women Lady Wisdom and Lady Folly. Their role within the book is to invite young men to choose either the right path in life or—hopefully not—the wrong path.

Lady Wisdom is the personification of wisdom. She speaks several times throughout the first nine chapters, including lectures extolling the value of wisdom and warnings about the dangers of foolishness. She also recites her memoir of being present at the time of creation. But her most important role is to invite naïve young men to come to her house and partake of her "feast" of insight.

On the other hand, Lady Folly, the personification of foolishness, only appears once (9:13–18). Like Lady Wisdom, she invites young men to come to her house and eat at her "feast," saying, "Stolen water is sweet; food eaten in secret is delicious!" (v. 17).

These two ladies play a significant role in the teaching methodology of Proverbs. While the proverbs of Proverbs offer numerous choices regarding specific circumstances, the dueling invitations by Lady Wisdom and Lady Folly (in Prov 9) present the ultimate choice in the book: wisdom or foolishness. Every smaller choice we make in daily life contributes to the ultimate choice between the fear of the Lord and going one's own way. This choice is offered not only to impressionable young men of that day but to every reader then and now.

12

Four Kinds of Wisdom in Proverbs

PROVERBS IS A BOOK about wisdom and becoming wise. But is wisdom more about becoming a successful person, becoming a good person, or becoming a godly person? Proverbs gives instruction in four kinds of wisdom: tips for a successful life, character formation, good relationships, and wisdom as the gift of God. If we listed every verse that teaches one of these types, we would have to print the entire book of Proverbs! So, to be brief, this chapter provides summaries of the four types of wisdom.

TYPE ONE: TIPS FOR A SUCCESSFUL LIFE

Basically, wisdom is the art of being successful, of forming the correct plan to gain the desired result.

—HUBBARD[1]

That definition of wisdom fits many of the instructions in the book of Proverbs. Most of those sayings will not sound surprising to modern ears. The keys to success haven't changed much in three thousand years.

---

1. Hubbard, "Wisdom," 1244.

Twenty-Six Tips for Success Found in Proverbs

Success in Business

1. Plan ahead (Prov 16:3, 9; 20:18; 21:5). But remember that God ultimately decides whether or not your plans will succeed. "Man proposes but God disposes" (19:21 TLB; see also 16:3, 9).
2. Get good advice from many advisors (12:15; 13:10; 15:22; 20:18).
3. Negotiate shrewdly—that is, with prudence (1:3-4; 8:5; 14:8).
4. Work hard—avoid laziness (10:4; 12:27; 14:23; 20:4; 28:19; 31:13-19).
5. Invest and save for the future (6:6-8; 13:11; 21:5, 20).
6. Invest in your community (11:24-26; 14:31).
7. Be honest in business dealings (11:1; 20:10, 17, 23; 22:28; 23:10).
8. Avoid going into debt (22:7), and pay your debts promptly (3:27-28).
9. Don't lend or cosign loans (6:1-5; 11:15; 17:18; 22:26-27).
10. Don't give or take bribes (15:27; 17:23).

Appropriate Use of Words

11. Honesty is the best policy (12:17, 19, 22; 23:26; 6:16-19).
12. But sometimes silence is the best policy (10:19; 15:28; 17:27-28).
13. Don't use flattery or insults (10:32; 15:1; 16:24; 26:28).
14. Don't gossip (11:12-13; 20:19).
15. Don't stir up strife or quarrels (20:3).

Good Relationships

16. Respect government officials (22:21-22).
17. Maintain good relationships with family, friends, and neighbors (17:17; 18:24; 27:6, 9, 10)—but don't overdo it (25:17; 27:14).

18. Choose your friends carefully (24:24–25).
19. Honor your spouse (12:4; 18:22; 19:14; 31:28–31).
20. Train your kids (22:6; 6:20–23).
21. Never take revenge (20:22; 24:29).

Personal Guidelines

22. Avoid drunkenness (20:1; 23:20–21, 29–30).
23. Avoid adultery (5:15–23; 6:32–33; 7:24–27; 30:20).
24. Never stop learning (1:5–6; 9:9–10).
25. Heed correction (9:7–8; 3:11–12; 13:1; 15:31).
26. "Those who trust in themselves are fools" (28:26a NIV).

Proverbs is a book of practical wisdom. For example, the first item above—"plan ahead"—is still common advice. Proverbs presumes that everyone plans ahead, whether for righteous goals or for wicked purposes (16:3; 19:21). Strategic planning is made stronger by listening to counsel (20:18), which will lead to profit (21:5). However, wisdom recognizes God's oversight of our lives; he will determine whether our plans succeed or not. The most practical path to success is to commit our ways to him.

> Commit your work to the Lord, and your plans will be established. (16:3)

But the final tip in the list above may surprise us. "Trust yourself" is common advice in most contemporary self-help books, but Solomon placed more confidence in trusting advisors and trusting the Lord than in trusting oneself.

Each of these proverbs suggests a wise course of action and reveals a positive outcome for choosing that action: wealth, abundant harvests, long life, and being respected in one's community. There are, however, costs for not heeding this advice: poverty, being cursed, sin, vomiting, and being hated.

However, Proverbs is more concerned with becoming a better person than with acquiring personal success. That brings us to the role of good character in wisdom.

TYPE TWO: CHARACTER FORMATION

A basic principle underlying the book of Proverbs is that character counts! Proverbs may seem to be a random assortment of rules or rules of thumb to follow as needed, but taken together they are guidelines for developing character traits. The four main character types in Proverbs are wise, foolish, upright, or wicked. Wisdom and uprightness go together, as do foolishness and wickedness. If each person becomes wiser and more righteous, they will become a better person; therefore they be more successful and their families and communities will be better places to live. (See ch. 8 for a discussion of character.)

According to Proverbs, human character matters a great deal because the consequences of character are real. Good character results in good behavior, which will obtain good outcomes such as long life, honor, wealth, and success. Foolish character, however, produces bad behavior, leading to danger, harm to self and others, shame, and possibly a premature death. Therefore, character reveals who can be trusted based on past behaviors. Contrary to the disclaimer at the end of many advertisements, Proverbs suggests that past performance is a predictor of future performance.

This cause-effect relationship between character, behavior, and outcomes has been described as the basic pattern of the book of Proverbs. Bruce Waltke, a leading commentator on Proverbs, expresses this basic pattern as "character—act—consequence."[2] The following is a paraphrase of this pattern:

> Character → Conduct → Consequence

"Character determines conduct which determines consequences."[3] Life is not a series of random behaviors that we choose each time we act. One's character shapes one's conduct and vice versa: one's conduct shapes one's character. Over time character becomes increasingly fixed, resulting in predictable patterns of behavior. But Proverbs adds a fourth element to this model of character formation:

> Choices → Character → Conduct → Consequences

Proverbs is a book about daily choices that shape character. Character is not inborn. No one was born wise or foolish. Each person's character

---

2. Waltke, "Proverbs," 1093.
3. Martin, "Donald Trump." Dr. Martin was my pastor for twenty-five years.

has been formed daily as they walk along the path they have previously chosen by the kinds of choices they have made.

Proverbs lists the character traits that will typify the wise: being humble, teachable, prudent, having integrity, honesty, kindness, generosity, respect for the rights of others, keeping confidences, self-controlled, faithful, moral, associating with the wise, and fear for the Lord. (As we shall see in ch. 14, Proverbs also lists opposite traits to describe the fool.)

These positive traits compose an internal compass that gives guidance for a wise and moral life. This moral compass is located in the heart. In Scripture, the word "heart" is the closest equivalent to the English word "character." According to Proverbs, wisdom and morality both reside in a person's heart.

> My son, pay attention to what I say;
>   turn your ear to my words.
> Do not let them out of your sight,
>   keep them within your heart;
> For they are life to those who find them
>   and health to one's whole body.
> Above all else, guard your heart,
>   for everything you do flows from it. (4:20–23 NIV)

Everything you do flows from your heart, so guard it. Whether for good or for evil, the heart is the center and the source of one's life. Whether we are wise or foolish today depends on whether we have been storing wise or foolish teachings in our heart. This is the core wisdom taught by Proverbs.

Jean and I used to live in northern Minnesota, a place where fishing can be a year-round recreation. When there is no ice on the lake, you can fish in the water. When there is ice on the lake, you drill a hole in the ice and fish through the hole. But fishing, walking, or driving on ice is risky business. The ice must be thick enough to support a person or a vehicle. We were told that during the winter months, the ice thickness is constantly changing. The ice is always getting thicker or thinner. It may take weeks of warmer or colder temperatures for the changes in the thickness to make a difference, but every day the ice becomes safer or less safe.

That is how character forms: slowly, imperceptibly, but surely. And after years of choices in either a wise or a foolish direction, one's character has hardened such that others can recognize one to be wise or a fool. It's all about character. The wise can be trusted to behave correctly. Fools can be trusted to behave selfishly and crookedly.

According to Proverbs, character determines whether or not a person is trustworthy. Character counts!

TYPE THREE: BETTER RELATIONSHIPS

It has been suggested that Proverbs is a commentary on the biblical commands to love.[4]

> You shall love the Lord your God with all your heart and with all your soul and with all your might. (Deut 6:5)

> You shall not take vengeance or bear a grudge against the sons of your own people, but you shall love your neighbor as yourself: I am the Lord. (Lev 19:18)

How do we show love for God and for others? The book of Proverbs is not an advice column such as we might find in a magazine or podcast telling how to have good relationships, but Proverbs does list many practical ways to show love—as well as many practical ways to not show love. For example, how does a friend support a friend? How does a neighbor maintain good relationships with a neighbor?

> Oil and perfume make the heart glad,
>   and the sweetness of a friend comes from his earnest counsel.
> Do not forsake your friend or your father's friend,
>   and do not go to your brother's house in the day of your calamity.
> Better a neighbor who is near
>   than a brother who is far away. (27:9–10)

In other words, friends and neighbors may support one another even better than family. Good friends will be honest with each other, even if the truth hurts. Good neighbors will take care of each other, even in times of trouble. However, if you want to keep a good relationship with your neighbor, don't mow your grass early on a Saturday morning:

> Whoever blesses his neighbor with a loud voice,
>   rising early in the morning,
>   will be counted as cursing. (27:14)

---

4. Hubbard, "Proverbs," 979.

The purpose of the book of Proverbs is to make better people, resulting in better marriages, families, communities, and nations. Proverbs also instructs how to treat one's enemies and even one's animals (Prov 25:21–22; 12:10). Thus, a good test of one's wisdom is how they treat others. Here are six summary statements from Proverbs about better relationships:

1. All people and animals are God's creatures. God cares for all his creatures and he expects us to care for one another as well. This standard is implicit in the worldview of ethical monotheism: God is good and he expects his people to be good—to one another.

2. All people are created by God as equals; therefore equity and justice are the standards for how we treat others. This includes being humble, fair, kind, truthful, respectful, and generous with others.

3. The flip side of the second standard is the behavior we must avoid: do not take advantage of others for your own profit. Specifically, do not deceive, cheat, or steal from your customer, your neighbor, your parents, from widows, or from the poor. And never offer false testimony in order to condemn the innocent.

4. Be faithful to those with whom you are in a covenant relationship. Such faithfulness includes fidelity in marriage, keeping promises made to others, and seeking the good of all in one's community. In each of these relationships the standard is mutual love, honesty, and cooperation.

5. The wise should give instruction, counsel, correction, and, if need-be, discipline to restore any who have wandered from the paths of righteousness. Instruction and discipline are especially important for one's children. But the goal of such correction must always be to help others and must be motivated by love.

6. In all matters be honest, pay what you owe, never cheat, don't gossip, don't be a troublemaker, and don't take revenge.

Hopefully none of these standards for maintaining good relationships surprise us. They are taught in Proverbs, as well as throughout Scripture, and they were also taught by Jesus. They are practical applications of loving your neighbor as yourself. Though these standards are not new, they are easily forgotten, which is why familiarity with Proverbs is so important.

TYPE FOUR: GOD'S WISDOM

The fourth type of wisdom is the most critical for understanding biblical wisdom: wisdom comes from God. This truth is foundational to the worldview of Proverbs. Therefore, fear of the Lord is the necessary first step in learning wisdom (9:10).

God is wise. He administers his world and oversees the lives of his people in such a way that his wisdom "works" for those who possess it. But God is not just the keeper of wisdom, he is the giver of wisdom. He gives wisdom to those who seek it by seeking him.

Proverbs gives three lines of evidence for God's wisdom: he is the Creator of all; he sees, judges, and rewards every human heart and every human deed; and he gives wisdom to those who ask him.

First, God Is the Creator

> The Lord by wisdom founded the earth; by understanding he established the heavens; by his knowledge the deeps broke open, and the clouds drop down the dew. (3:19–20)

The point of this passage is that God made the world and he made it wisely. Wisdom works because God designed the world with natural order and with moral order. The implication is that for us to be wise our lives should fit in with the world as God designed it.

Second, God Supports Wise Choices

God assures us that wisdom "works" by sovereignly administering the world, particularly the lives of people to give success to those who plan and live wisely. In Proverbs, God is not mentioned often—only in ninety-four verses; thus, about 10 percent of the verses explicitly mention God, but he is always there in the background guaranteeing that wisdom works. God not only sees and knows all, he judges all, determining a just consequence for each behavior. Here is a sample of proverbs showing God's role in judging human behaviors:

> The eyes of the Lord are in every place, keeping watch on the evil and the good. (15:3)

> A good man obtains favor from the Lord,
>   but a man of evil devices he condemns. (12:2)
>
> The Lord tears down the house of the proud
>   but maintains the widow's boundaries. (15:25)
>
> The Lord has made everything for its purpose,
>   even the wicked for the day of trouble. (16:4)

Because of God's sovereign rule over life, fear of the Lord is the beginning of wisdom.

> The fear of the Lord prolongs life,
>   but the years of the wicked will be short. (10:27)

Third, God Gives Wisdom

> For the Lord gives wisdom;
>   from his mouth come knowledge and understanding;
> he stores up sound wisdom for the upright;
>   he is a shield to those who walk in integrity,
> guarding the paths of justice
>   and watching over the way of his saints. (2:6–8)

God's revealed words are at the heart of learning wisdom.

REVIEWING THE FOUR KINDS OF WISDOM

Perhaps some readers of the book of Proverbs never go deeper than the first kind of wisdom. They view Proverbs as a collection of useful statements about how to be successful in life. They choose their favorite texts and put them on their coffee mugs or post them as internet memes. Hopefully they also abide by the other teachings as well. This shallow approach to wisdom is not wrong. The teachings of Proverbs will work at that level.

But to understand Proverbs within the context of the wisdom literature, it is necessary to see the book as a whole. Proverbs is a collection of individual verses collected over centuries of time, but together they present a consistent package of values, attitudes, and actions—character traits—that describe a wise person and the contrasting attitudes and actions—character traits—that describe a fool. Taken as a whole, Proverbs describes good character and teaches that character counts! Character is important because it determines how we treat others. Good character leads us to fulfill the law of love in all our relationships.

However, to understand Proverbs the way that Solomon, Agur, and King Lemuel understood it, we need to see it as presenting a worldview, the ethical monotheistic worldview, in which God, the Righteous One, is the key actor in every single verse. That is the reason that within the worldview of Proverbs wisdom must begin with the fear of the Lord.

13

"Get Wisdom"

Get wisdom; get insight;
  do not forget, and do not turn away from the words of my mouth.
Do not forsake her, and she will keep you;
  love her, and she will guard you.
The beginning of wisdom is this: Get wisdom.

—Proverbs 4:5–7

PERHAPS THE MOST SURPRISING idea is that wisdom is possible—some people do become wise! In Proverbs there are about forty references to "the wise." It can be found among both men and women, kings and servants, elders and children, and even animals can be wise! Anybody, it seems, can become wise.

The wise can be recognized by the kind of choices they make, by the way they treat others, and by their fear of the Lord. Another piece of evidence of wisdom is that the wise seek to increase in wisdom: they keep learning from wise teachers, they gladly accept rebuke and correction, and they seek wisdom more than gold or silver. And they avoid behaving foolishly!

Proverbs offers instruction about how to "get wisdom."

SEVEN STEPS TO BECOMING WISE

Step One: Admit We Lack Wisdom

According to Proverbs, we are not born wise; we are born "simple," meaning we are born novices, inexperienced, and naïve. For some, unfortunately, this lack of understanding continues throughout life. For others, being simple degenerates into foolishness and wickedness. But for a few, those who heed the invitation of Lady Wisdom, they acquire insight and prudence.

A key lesson in Proverbs is that no one should be wise in their own eyes (3:7; 26:12). That is step one to becoming foolish!

Wisdom begins with honest humility.

Step Two: Fear the Lord (1:7; 3:7; 9:10)

Because we all lack knowledge and wisdom, the wise choice for all is to trust the One who has perfect knowledge and wisdom. When we rely on him, he will make our paths straight (3:5–6).

The introductory poem (1:2–7; see ch. 10) bases the acquisition of knowledge on the fear of the Lord. Fearing God is the ground for a proper knowledge of him, which is the ground for a proper knowledge of everything else.

Perhaps we would have expected knowledge to precede faith—you have to know about something to believe it—but the epistemology of faith is that knowledge and wisdom are not stepping stones to an ultimate goal of finding God; it is the opposite. A proper education in wisdom begins with fearing God. This is the monotheist approach to wisdom. This is where fools go wrong.

Step Three: Ask God to Give You Wisdom (2:3–19)

> Yes, if you call out for insight
>   and raise your voice for understanding,
> if you seek it like silver
>   and search for it as for hidden treasures,
> then you will understand the fear of the Lord
>   and find the knowledge of God.
> For the Lord gives wisdom;
>   from his mouth come knowledge and understanding. (2:3–6)

Asking God for wisdom is more than a quick prayer when we are in a tight spot; it begins with valuing wisdom more than wealth and searching for it as treasure. The result of this search is wisdom, understanding, and the fear of the Lord.

When prompted in a dream, King Solomon asked God for wisdom to rule effectively. For the rest of us, the prompt to ask for wisdom may begin with knowing God's word (2 Tim 3:14–17). The second prompt is the occasion of a trial or test in one's life, a time of realizing that one lacks wisdom (Jas 1:2–5). God blesses those who seek his wisdom with counsel, protection, and moral understanding—as he did for young King Solomon.

Step Four: Learning Wisdom Through Instruction

The premise of the book of Proverbs is that the way to learn wisdom is by listening to and heeding instruction. The introductory poem focused on acquiring "wisdom and instruction" (1:2, 7). According to the poem, the simple (naïve youth) can learn prudence and moral behavior by following the instructions given in Proverbs. And those who already have wisdom can get continuing education by reviewing the book's teachings. Instruction in wisdom can not only be gained by learning from the sayings in Proverbs, it is available to each of us by heeding the instructions we receive from our parents, teachers, and mentors. The wise become wiser by learning from the wise.

> Hear, my son, your father's instruction,
>   and forsake not your mother's teaching. (Prov 1:8)

> Give instruction to a wise man, and he will be still wiser;
>   teach a righteous man, and he will increase in learning. (9:9)

> The way of a fool is right in his own eyes,
>   but a wise man listens to advice. (12:15)

> Listen to advice and accept instruction,
>   that you may gain wisdom in the future. (19:20)

Step Five: Learning from Experience and Observation

The book of Proverbs does not encourage learning by trial and error. While it acknowledges that errors happen to us all and we should learn from them, it is better to avoid them. One way we can avoid making mistakes is by observing the example of others.

Proverbs presents both good and bad examples for us to follow or avoid. A good role model is the Wife of Noble Character, who epitomizes all the characteristics of wisdom taught in the book (31:10–31). Other good role models are animals, such as ants, which are known for their industriousness and foresight (6:6–8), and birds, which will avoid a snare when they see it (1:17; 6:5).

Bad examples to avoid imitating include the lazy farmer, a drunkard, and an adulterer (24:30–34; 23:29–35; 5:20–25). Proverbs also holds out hope that a simple youth might benefit from observing a mocker being punished by being beaten with a rod (19:25; 21:11).

Step Six: Staying on the Straight Path

The book of Proverbs emphasizes making wise choices on a daily basis. When right choices are repeated, they become habits. Good habits are described as walking on right (or straight) paths. But care is needed to avoid straying off in either direction.

> Ponder the path of your feet;
>   then all your ways will be sure.
> Do not swerve to the right or the left;
>   turn your foot away from evil. (4:26–27)

> [Wisdom will deliver] you from the way of evil,
>   from men of perverted speech,
> who forsake the paths of uprightness
>   to walk in the ways of darkness. (2:12–13)

Making choices to stay on the straight paths will internalize these choices in one's heart, forming good character, which is the basis of wisdom. Good choices today are the beginning of the process of becoming wise for the rest of one's life.

Step Seven: Remedial Education—Discipline and Correction

Proverbs does not assume that any of us will become wise by choosing wisdom only once. When we stray from the straight path, remedial education is required. There are many proverbs relating to correction, rebuke, and discipline. Some remedial education is verbal, restating a lesson learned before. This may include a verbal rebuke or criticism for doing something wrong when you knew better. And, in more extreme cases there may be a punishment, possibly even corporal punishment.

> Whoever loves discipline loves knowledge,
> but he who hates reproof is stupid. (12:1)

> My son, do not despise the Lord's discipline
> or be weary of his reproof,
> for the Lord reproves him whom he loves,
> as a father the son in whom he delights. (3:11–12)

This last proverb teaches that just as loving parents correct a disobedient child so a loving God disciplines those he loves. God's discipline may take the form of painful lessons learned from "the school of hard knocks," through painful experiences, or even by facing persecution. Not all painful experiences are discipline for those who have gone astray, but it may be part of God's overall education curriculum.

In Scripture, there are different degrees of punishment for wrongdoing: shaming, shunning, repayment of stolen property, paying a fine, being beaten with a whip or a rod, and death. I expect that the discussion of punishment is the most controversial topic in Proverbs, and some readers will find this discussion offensive.

CORPORAL PUNISHMENT

In Proverbs, corporal punishment often refers to beatings with a rod:

> A whip for the horse, a bridle for the donkey,
> and a rod for the back of fools. (26:3)

> On the lips of him who has understanding, wisdom is found,
> but a rod is for the back of him who lacks sense. (10:13)

Perhaps these verses refer to discipline with a rod in a metaphorical sense, and not necessarily as a literal beating with a stick. But corporal punishment was considered normal in their culture and in most cultures of that day. In the context of Proverbs, it is clear that discipline can be painful.

In order to deal with this controversial topic, let us consider corporal punishment in the context of Scripture and in the context of biblical culture. The controversy centers around the use of the word "rod," which suggests a painful beating on the back or backside. But there are other uses of the word "rod" in Scripture.

First, a rod is a shepherd's tool for guiding and protecting his sheep. As such it gives the sheep confidence and comfort: "I will fear no evil, for you are with me; your rod and your staff, they comfort me" (Ps 23:4).

The sheep feel no fear because the shepherd's rod and staff assure them that the shepherd is watching over them. The shepherd uses a rod to protect them from wild animals. Of course, Ps 23 is not just about sheep and shepherds; it is about God, the shepherd of his people. We are the sheep. We can be comforted because God's rod assures us of his watchful care over us.

Another meaning of a rod is as a scepter, a symbol of rank and authority. Moses, Aaron, and the heads of the twelve tribes of Israel were each given a rod as a sign of their position. At times these rods of authority became very significant in the history of the new nation of Israel (Exod 17:5). Even King Jesus will rule the nations with a rod of iron (Ps 2:9; Rev 12:5; 19:15), which implies both his authority and power.

These two other senses show that the word "rod" can be a positive word. God's rod is one of comfort and authority. But in Proverbs, the rod is used for remedial education:

> Strike a scoffer, and the simple will learn prudence;
> reprove a man of understanding, and he will gain knowledge.
> (19:25)

> When a scoffer is punished, the simple become wise;
> when a wise man is instructed, he gains knowledge. (21:11)

Beatings with a rod are a way to save a fool from walking a crooked path leading to his own destruction. However, in most Western countries today corporal punishment of prisoners is no longer acceptable. Wrongdoing is punished by fines and imprisonment, not by beatings or death. Whippings or canings are still practiced in some countries (e.g., Singapore) but are not allowed in most Western societies.

The point of Proverbs is that punishment now is better than even worse consequences, possibly even death, later. If a painful beating can reform a fool before he or she suffers the consequences of their foolishness, then they should be grateful. But he or she probably isn't.

In order to understand Proverbs, it is necessary to understand that discipline, whether the Lord's discipline of his people or parents' discipline of their children, is an act of love. Without love, discipline is cruelty. But cruelty is never the purpose of discipline.

What About Spanking Children?

This topic is very controversial. In many countries spankings are illegal in schools—and in some places, they are illegal in homes as well. Here are two well-known proverbs about child rearing:

> Spare the rod and spoil the child.

> Train up a child in the way he should go;
> even when he is old he will not depart from it. (22:6)

The first proverb—"Spare the rod and spoil the child"—is not in Proverbs, but the following verses have a similar meaning:

> Folly is bound up in the heart of a child,
> but the rod of discipline drives it far from him. (22:15)

> Discipline your son, and he will give you rest;
> he will give delight to your heart. (29:17)

Solomon seems to have viewed child rearing as requiring strict measures to transform the innate folly present at birth. Solomon believed that an undisciplined child will become an undisciplined adult. Though Solomon expected parents to strictly discipline their children, this should not mean he expected them to discipline them harshly!

Having said that disciplining a child is necessary, what form should that discipline take? It doesn't have to involve a beating with a rod. The scriptural references to a rod may be a metaphor meaning to punish a child who has not responded to verbal instruction or correction. Punishments can vary according to the child. Every child is different, and some will respond to a look of disappointment on their parents' faces while others will require a stronger intervention.

I am old enough to remember the wooden paddle that hung on the front wall of my grade school classroom, and I remember rare occasions of seeing the teacher use it. I was never paddled in school, but I did endure other punishments, such as standing on my tiptoes for ten minutes trying to keep my nose within a circle my teacher had drawn on the chalkboard (because I had talked back to the teacher), or having to write "I will not do [a bad behavior] in class" five hundred times. I assume these activities were meant to be corrective, but they felt like punishment!

In raising our children my wife and I used a wooden spoon for the *rare* occasions when a "rod" was needed. This worked especially well with Heidi, our youngest daughter. When she disobeyed us, we would send her to her room, making her take the wooden spoon with her. When she was ready to come out, she would spank herself with the spoon; we would hear her cry, and then she would come out and give the spoon back to us. Years later, when Heidi got married, one thing she requested to keep was that wooden spoon to have for her kids.

I know that I am out of sync with much of modern culture because I am not totally opposed to spanking. I *am* totally opposed to child abuse, and I shudder when I read about parents who use these verses in Proverbs to justify beatings of their children. Harsh beatings are wrong! But I believe there is a nonabusive form of spanking.

Correction need not mean spanking. Time out, grounding, or additional chores are preferable punishments. But for a young child who does not respond to lesser interventions, a mild form of spanking may be appropriate. Spanking should be a last resort, never done in anger, never done so strongly as to injure a child, and using a "rod" or "wooden spoon" rather than the hand. Can we call this tough love?

As I write this, I am sure that some readers will disagree strongly with my conclusion and with Solomon's viewpoint, but hopefully we can agree with the idea that children need to be taught to do what is right. In Proverbs, training a child for righteousness is a process of instruction, of remedial education, of correction, of rebuke, and then and only then, of punishment. As Proverbs says,

> Do not withhold discipline from a child;
>   if you strike him with a rod, he will not die.
> If you strike him with the rod,
>   you will save his soul from Sheol. (23:13–14)

> Whoever spares the rod hates his son,
> but he who loves him is diligent to discipline him. (13:24)

The bottom line is that discipline in some form is needed but that any discipline should only be done in love (3:11–12).

14

Don't Be a Fool!

THE TRAGIC END OF A FOOL'S LIFE

IN CHAPTER 1 WISDOM was defined as truth applied to life, therefore wisdom is often best seen in stories about life. The same is true of foolishness. The world's literature is filled with stories about fools. The Bible records many such stories as well.

A prime example from Scripture is the story of a man whose name, Nabal, actually means "fool" (1 Sam 25:1–38). When David was fleeing from King Saul, hiding out in the wilderness, his army provided protection for the local farmers, including Nabal. But when David sent messengers to request food from Nabal, he refused, saying,

> Who is David? Who is the son of Jesse? There are many servants these days who are breaking away from their masters. Shall I take my bread and my water and my meat that I have killed for my shearers and give it to men who come from I do not know where? (vv. 10–11)

Nabal's servants were frightened that David might respond to this insult by attacking and destroying them, so one of them went to Abigail, Nabal's wife, and told her what Nabal had done. He asked her,

> Now therefore know this and consider what you should do, for harm is determined against our master and against all his house,

and he is such a worthless man that one cannot speak to him. (v. 17)

Indeed, David was planning revenge against Nabal, but Abigail went to him, bringing food and begging him to avoid unnecessary bloodshed on account of the foolishness of her husband. David praised Abigail:

> Blessed be your discretion, and blessed be you, who have kept me this day from bloodguilt. (v. 33)

This story illustrates both foolishness and wisdom: Nabal, the fool, and Abigail, the wise. I suspect we have all met their descendants along life's way. Perhaps we are also one of their descendants—but which one?

In his greed, Nabal cared only about himself. He mocked David and refused to show kindness to David's men when they requested food and drink. He ignored his indebtedness to David's men for guarding his flocks and protecting his workers. Perhaps the main way in which he was a fool was that he could not foresee the extreme danger into which he, through his poor choice, was placing himself and his workers. David was about to attack them when Abigail quickly intervened and averted disaster.

According to Proverbs, "The way of the wicked is like deep darkness; they do not know over what they stumble" (4:19). But Abigail could see the danger. She acted to save herself and her servants—and her husband Nabal—from certain death. David praised her wisdom, and when Nabal died a few days later, David married her.

Some people think that men are inherently wiser than women or that husbands are wiser than their wives; but they should remember the story of Nabal and Abigail! And they should realize that the book of Proverbs refers to both men and women as wise. The concluding poem, "The Wife of Noble Character" (Prov 31:10–31), describes a woman whose hard work and wisdom made the family business a success and earned her husband a good reputation in the town. The book of Proverbs concludes that she deserves praise for her works, reminding us that David praised Abigail for her wisdom.

On the other hand, Proverbs also refers to both men and women as fools—this chapter on foolishness applies equally to both genders. Proverbs presents both wisdom and foolishness in a gender-neutral way. We would be wise to apply that standard of gender neutrality today.

AVOIDING FOOLISHNESS

Proverbs has a two-fold strategy for acquiring wisdom. The first, as we discussed in the previous chapter, is to "get wisdom." The second strategy is to avoid foolishness.

Surprisingly, Proverbs, a book about wisdom, spends more time talking about folly than wisdom: there are about forty references to "the wise" and seventy references to "fools." Why feature foolishness so prominently? Perhaps it is because wisdom is a long-term strategy for life, but foolish behaviors often offer immediate gratification and short-term pleasures. And by definition, temptations are tempting, so young men may be easily enticed.

Another difference between being wise and being foolish is that there are just a few ways to be wise—really only one—but Proverbs lists multiple varieties of fools:

- the proud (or arrogant) (16:5, 18)
- gossips (11:13)
- drunkards (20:1; 23:20–21)
- gluttons (23:20–21; 28:7)
- the lazy (or sluggards, slothful) (6:6–11)
- adulterers (2:16–19; 5:1–23; 6:27–29)
- mockers (or scoffers) (9:7–8; 15:12)

Each type of fool will experience negative consequences according to their particular foolishness.

Though there are a variety of fools, they all have some character traits in common. One way to define a fool is to contrast him or her, trait by trait, with the wise. The following chart compares traits of fools with those of the wise.

The Wise	Fools
Humble	Proud, arrogant (Prov 8:13; 18:12; 29:23)
Listen to instruction and correction	Despise instruction, avoid correction (1:7; 5:11–13; 9:7–8; 15:4, 12, 32)
Use few words, speak cautiously	Blabbermouths (12:23; 18:2; 29:20)

The Wise	Fools
Prudent	Careless, reckless (4:19; 10:21; 14:16–17; 27:12)
Integrity, honesty	Lie, deceive, steal, cheat (1:19; 6:16–19; 12:22; 24:28–29; 26:28)
Care for others, show kindness, treat others fairly	Selfish, greedy, rude, don't respect the rights of others (22:22; 29:7; 30:14)
Associate with the wise	Avoid the wise, associate with fools (13:20; 15:12; 22:24–25)
Calm, self-controlled	Emotional, argumentative (14:17; 16:28; 19:19; 29:11)
Faithful to his/her spouse	Immoral (6:28–29; 23:27–28; 30:20)
Does not consider himself/herself to be wise	Are wise in their own eyes (3:7; 26:12; 28:26)
Fear the Lord	Choose not to fear the Lord (1:29; 14:2)
Deserve honor and respect	Deserve disgrace and punishments (3:35; 6:32–33; 26:1)

Perhaps the most telling trait of a fool as found in the right-hand column above is that a fool is wise in his/her own eyes. If "the fear of the Lord is the beginning of wisdom" (9:10), it is also true that being wise in one's own eyes is the beginning of foolishness!

Do we see these kinds of people in our world today? Are there more who are wise or more who are foolish? Perhaps nobody is perfectly wise or perfectly foolish (perhaps there are a few perfect fools). But if we were to take a census, I fear that the number of fools would be greater. It is common to hear people say that the world is getting worse—and in some ways it is—but humankind with its mixture of wise persons and fools has always been this way. This was the world as Solomon saw it. And, to be honest, he was sometimes a fool himself.

But the question raised by reading Proverbs is, Which are we—wise or foolish?

Perhaps we could summarize the whole book of Proverbs by saying, "The wise don't know they are wise, and fools don't know they are fools."

The Downhill Path to Foolishness

Proverbs suggests a three-step process leading to foolishness and wickedness:

The Simple → the Fool → the Wicked

The Simple: We were all born simple, meaning inexperienced and naïve. There is hope for the simple to learn wisdom, but without wise guidance, they easily make foolish choices. Proverbs teaches that youth is a critical time when small choices can make a big difference in the future course of a person's life, either toward prudence or toward wickedness. This is why instructing youth is so important for them and for society in general.

One way to teach the simple is to let them watch the punishment of the scoffer (19:25, 21:11). Watching someone get beaten with a rod might be educational for a young person.

The Fool: The English word "fool" often implies a stupid person, like a court jester. The biblical use of the term "fool" is different. A "fool" might sometimes be slow, stupid, or even a madman (Eccl 7:25)—the kind of person you don't want to send on an errand because they'll mess it up; but such a dimwit is not the primary meaning of "fool" in Proverbs. A "fool" is not necessarily dumb, but he or she has a moral and spiritual deficiency. They not only do wrong, they enjoy doing wrong. They love breaking the rules and ignoring instructions (1:22). Fools are controlled by their emotions. They see themselves through the lens of an exaggerated self-confidence. Due to this they bring harm to themselves and those around them.

Fools are walking on crooked paths leading to disastrous ends, and they don't even realize it. "The way of a fool is right in his own eyes, but a wise man listens to advice" (12:15).

The chief fool is the scoffer (also called a mocker): he or she is motivated by arrogance, insults others, and laughs at others who suffer disaster. The scoffer is a troublemaker who stirs up conflict in the community. When he leaves town, life gets better for all. Though a scoffer insults and mocks others, he avoids being corrected himself (9:7–8, 12). The final word about a scoffer is that God mocks them (3:34).

The Wicked: A danger for fools is they may continue on that path becoming wicked (also called an evildoer or sinner). "Wicked" is the generic term for one guilty of all kinds of wrongdoing:

- lying, deceiving (6:12)

- stealing (1:10–19; 2:12–15)
- violence (24:1–2)
- bribery (17:23)
- defrauding the poor (29:7)
- corrupt officials (18:5; 29:12)

But in the end, the plans of the wicked will fail, and they will suffer injury and shame (6:15).

> A worthless person, a wicked man,
>   goes about with crooked speech,
> winks with his eyes, signals with his feet,
>   points with his finger,
> with perverted heart devises evil,
>   continually sowing discord;
> therefore calamity will come upon him suddenly;
>   in a moment he will be broken beyond healing. (6:12–15)

The wicked may feign righteousness, but it is just a front. He may claim to have faith, but his life contradicts that claim. He or she can be described as

> a practical atheist. There is no room in his thoughts for God (Ps 10:4), nor is there any fear of God in his eyes (36:1). As the enemy of Yahweh (37:20), he hates God (68:12) . . . He has no worries that God might intervene with his perversion (10:13). Since God has forgotten and does not see the wicked man's conduct (10:11), his innocent victims are without defense.[1]

Wickedness "connotes disloyalty to Yahweh, rebellion against the covenant standards, and total disregard for the welfare of fellow citizens."[2]

FOOLS' STORIES IN PROVERBS

Many of the proverbs in Proverbs suggest a story. As we read the words our imaginations fill in the rest of the details, yielding either a positive story with a happy ending or a foolish story with a tragic ending. Sometimes a single proverb suggests a story. For example,

---

1. Carpenter and Grisanti, "רשׁע," 1202.
2. Carpenter and Grisanti, "רשׁע," 1203.

> A false balance is an abomination to the Lord,
>   but a just weight is his delight. (11:1; see also 16:11)

This proverb reminds me of the painting by Leslie Thrasher in which a woman is buying meat at the butcher shop. As he is weighing her purchase, he secretly places his thumb on the scales, adding weight and cost to her purchase. But she knew his trick, and had her finger under the scale pushing up so she wouldn't be cheated. Just as the painting tells a story, the proverb above suggests two stories: one of dishonesty and one of honesty, and it tells us the outcome of those stories. God sees both honest and dishonest vendors and judges them accordingly.

Some of the stories in Proverbs are more detailed. For example,

> I passed by the field of a sluggard,
>   by the vineyard of a man lacking sense,
> and behold, it was all overgrown with thorns;
>   the ground was covered with nettles,
> and its stone wall was broken down.
> Then I saw and considered it;
>   I looked and received instruction.
> A little sleep, a little slumber,
>   a little folding of the hands to rest,
> and poverty will come upon you like a robber,
>   and want like an armed man. (24:30–34)

This story suggests a link between foolishness, laziness, and poverty. The outcome of not tending one's fields is as certain as being robbed! A sluggard is his own worst enemy.

Another foolishness story is of a drunkard:

> Who has woe? Who has sorrow?
>   Who has strife? Who has complaining?
> Who has wounds without cause?
>   Who has redness of eyes?
> Those who tarry long over wine;
>   those who go to try mixed wine.
> Do not look at wine when it is red,
>   when it sparkles in the cup
>   and goes down smoothly.
> In the end it bites like a serpent
>   and stings like an adder.
> Your eyes will see strange things,
>   and your heart utter perverse things.

> You will be like one who lies down in the midst of the sea,
>   like one who lies on the top of a mast.
> "They struck me," you will say, "but I was not hurt;
>   they beat me, but I did not feel it.
> When shall I awake? I must have another drink." (23:29–35)

This story is really a series of three snapshots. The first snapshot shows a person who has been drinking too much; he is morose and has bloodshot eyes and bruises—maybe from falling or from fighting. The second snapshot is of the attraction of wine: red, sparkling, smooth; but the hangover is just the opposite: like a snakebite, like seeing delusions, like stumbling around as if you were seasick. The third snapshot is of a man who was assaulted but, because he was drunk, he couldn't quite remember what happened. It seemed like a bad dream. His remedy was to wake up and find another drink.

That story illustrates the general principle about drunkenness in Proverbs: "Wine is a mocker, strong drink a brawler, whoever is led astray by it is not wise" (20:1).

Sometimes drunkenness is paired with gluttony:

> Be not among drunkards
>   or among gluttonous eaters of meat,
> for the drunkard and the glutton will come to poverty,
>   and slumber will clothe them with rags. (23:20–21)

These proverbs are not teaching that all wine drinking or all meat eating is bad, but rather, doing either to excess will lead one into poverty and pain. Anything done to excess is bad.

Two Main Temptations in Proverbs

Though the sayings in Proverbs refer to many sorts of temptations, they emphasize two which are primary enticements for simple youth: "Easy sex and easy money."[3] Warnings about adultery occur nine times in Proverbs. Warnings about violent crime occur four times.

Adultery. Proverbs tells one lengthy story about the temptation to adultery:

> Once I was looking out the window of my house, and I saw
>   many inexperienced young men, but I noticed one foolish fellow

---

3. Waltke, "Proverbs," 1085.

in particular. He was walking along the street where a certain woman lived. He was passing near her house in the evening after it was dark. And then she met him; she was dressed like a prostitute and was making plans. She was a bold and shameless woman who always walked the streets or stood waiting at a corner, sometimes in the streets, sometimes in the marketplace. She threw her arms around the young man, kissed him, looked him straight in the eye, and said, "I made my offerings today and have the meat from the sacrifices. So I came out looking for you . . . My husband isn't at home. He's on a long trip . . ." He gave in to her smooth talk. Suddenly he was going with her like an ox on the way to be slaughtered. . . . He did not know that his life was in danger.

Now then, sons, listen to me. Pay attention to what I say. Do not let such a woman win your heart. . . . She has been the ruin of many men and caused the death of too many to count. (7:6–15, 19, 22, 24, 26–27 TEV)

Proverbs labels a man who commits adultery as senseless, subject to the husband's revenge, open to public disgrace (6:32–34), and as likely to receive an early death. Lest anyone think adultery is a secret sin, the book reminds us that God always sees it (5:21).

Violent crime. The other major temptation that Proverbs warns about is "easy money"—money that might be gained through deceit or violent crime. Proverbs also tells a story about this temptation:

Son, when sinners tempt you, don't give in. Suppose they say,
"Come on; let's find someone to kill! Let's attack some innocent people for the fun of it! They may be alive and well when we find them, but they'll be dead when we are through with them! We'll find all kinds of riches and fill our houses with loot! Come and join us, and we'll all share what we steal.
"Son, don't go with people like that. Stay away from them. They can't wait to do something bad. They're always ready to kill. It does no good to spread a net when the bird you want to catch is watching, but men like that are setting a trap for themselves, a trap in which they will die. Robbery always claims the life of the robber—this is what happens to anyone who lives by violence." (1:10–19 TEV)

Throughout Proverbs there is a warning we might call the *irony principle*: those who try to hurt others in order to help themselves will suffer the fate they tried to cause. They entrap themselves: "Whoever digs a pit will fall into it, and a stone will come back on him who starts it rolling" (26:27).

Therefore, young men, don't join a criminal gang seeking stolen wealth.

The Unfinished Story

Proverbs 1–9 is a series of lessons addressed to young men. Chapter 9 tells the story of naïve young men walking about town and encountering two houses offering free food to anyone who will come inside.

Lady Wisdom speaks from the highest point in the city, inviting young men and all who lack sense to come to her table for a feast:

> "Whoever is simple, let him turn in here!"
> To him who lacks sense she says,
> "Come, eat of my bread
> and drink of the wine I have mixed.
> Leave your simple ways and live,
> and walk in the way of insight." (9:4–6)

Her invitation concludes with the theme verse of Proverbs:

> The fear of the Lord is the beginning of wisdom,
> and the knowledge of the Holy One is insight. (9:10)

Elsewhere in town, Lady Folly, an unruly and senseless woman, sits outside her house "calling to those who pass by":

> "Whoever is simple, let him turn in here!"
> To him who lacks sense she says,
> "Stolen water is sweet,
> and bread eaten in secret is pleasant." (9:15–17)

These competing invitations are the final lesson in the curriculum addressed to young men. This story is unfinished. We don't know whether those young men will choose Lady Wisdom and her offer of insight, or Lady Folly and her offer of stolen water and secret bread. What we do know is that this choice is in reality a choice between life (9:6) and death (9:18).

What About Us?

Lady Folly still invites the simple to enjoy her feast. I suspect we all have heard many of her invitations. Her temptations may be different for each of us, but her suggestion that forbidden things taste better is always part of the invitation: "Stolen water is sweet; bread eaten in secret is delicious!"

Perhaps we all have also heard Lady Wisdom calling out to us. She offers wisdom for those who accept her invitation. Our story is also unfinished: wisdom or folly, which invitation will we accept? It's our choice.

15

Every Good Path

IN PROVERBS THE WAY of wisdom is called the good path (2:9).

The metaphor of life as a path or a journey is one of the most common metaphors used in world literature. Writers use this metaphor in a variety of ways with different, even opposite, meanings. Some writers use the metaphor to emphasize making your own path instead of following someone else's path. Some emphasize the value of diversity as there are many paths from which to choose. Others emphasize the experiences along the way as being more important than the destination. Some writers view a path as leading to a specific destination, while others deny this. The metaphor of life as a "path" seems to be like an inkblot, meaning whatever the writer wants.

In Proverbs a path has one basic meaning: it connects a person today to a destiny tomorrow—*direction determines destiny*. Every life follows a path that the person has chosen. There are really only two kinds of paths: straight and crooked. "Straight" means morally good, abiding by the standards of right attitudes and behaviors. "Crooked" suggests bent, twisted, perverted. Each path leads to a destiny, either desirable or undesirable. But Proverbs also describes the existential moment in which each person is choosing, and every choice, good or bad, places that person onto a path leading to an ultimate destiny.

As foreign as this concept may sound in our poly-moralistic world, Proverbs assumes that there is in fact one straight path, designed by God and leading to life and blessings. At the core of Proverbs' worldview is the existence of good and evil as real categories by which actions and people can be classified and judged. Without understanding morality as a category of truth, one cannot understand Proverbs or, for that matter, any of the Bible.

The introductory poem (1:2–7) said that the purpose of the book is to teach three virtues: righteousness, justice, and equity (1:3). These same three virtues are repeated in 2:9 where they are called the good path: through wisdom "you will understand righteousness, justice, and equity, every good path."

These three virtues are ethical principles that are foundational for the Old Testament law and for wisdom. Biblical wisdom will always be righteous, just, and fair. Moral uprightness will also be righteous, just, and fair. These three virtues ought to be true for God's chosen people: both Israel and the church ought to live according to these principles.

Following is a closer study of these three virtues.

RIGHTEOUSNESS

In Proverbs, righteousness (right-ness) can be defined both by living in accordance with the moral order God built into the world and by doing those behaviors God approves and blesses. Surprisingly, in Proverbs righteousness is not primarily about doing religious things such as temple worship, sacrifices, prayer, or praising God; Proverbs focuses on religion in street clothes, the way to live out your faith when you're not in church. Righteousness includes horizontal right-ness (person to person), such as honest words and honest business practices, being generous, and respecting the rights of others. Righteousness also includes vertical right-ness (person to God), such as humility, the fear of the Lord, trusting him, and steadfast love.[1]

In Proverbs the way to be righteous is not just by what one does, but by what one doesn't do: the righteous avoid walking in the perverted ways of the wicked. Those ways are an abomination to the Lord.

Proverbs reads, "There are six things that the Lord hates, seven that are an abomination to him:"

- "haughty eyes"

---

1. For a more thorough study of righteousness, see ch. 7.

- "a lying tongue"
- "hands that shed innocent blood"
- "a heart that devises wicked plans"
- "feet that make haste to run to evil"
- "a false witness that breathes out lies"
- "one who sows discord among brothers" (6:16–19)

Not only will the righteous not do those seven things, they hate them (13:5), as does the Lord (8:13). Righteousness is not just about outer behavior but also moral purity in one's heart.

Walking Without Stumbling

The Lord blesses the path, the household, the children, and the nation of the righteous. Solomon gave this assurance to the young men he was teaching:

> I have taught you the way of wisdom;
>   I have led you in the paths of uprightness.
> When you walk, your step will not be hampered,
>   and if you run, you will not stumble. (4:11–12)

Every life is a series of steps taken along one's chosen path, and each step involves a choice to stay on the path without straying to either side. The Lord watches over the steps of the righteous, clearing the path before them so they won't stumble. But for the wicked who have strayed from the good path, their steps are hindered by dangers and darkness. To prevent stumbling one should stay on the good path.

However, Proverbs acknowledges that a righteous person might sometimes stumble: "The righteous falls seven times but rises again" (24:16). It is a great reassurance to those of us who do sometimes stumble, maybe up to seven times; there is hope for the righteous who stumble: Get up and walk again!

So, in Proverbs righteousness means living the life that the Lord approves and blesses. Thus, the wisest thing any person can do is to allow God to choose their path:

> Trust in the Lord with all your heart,
>   and do not lean on your own understanding.
> In all your ways acknowledge him,
>   and he will make straight your paths. (Prov 3:5–6)

JUSTICE

The second virtue that comprises the good path is "justice." Justice is the application of righteousness in how we treat others. We usually think of justice as a legal term, but it applies just as much to how we treat others on a daily basis. Justice is required in every relationship—even in how we treat people who mistreat us, even in how we treat strangers who live in distant places, in other countries, whom we may never meet. Justice applies to how we treat anyone and everyone we may pass on a busy street, to people we encounter online, and to those who have wronged us. Everyone deserves justice, meaning equal treatment according to the standards of right and wrong and according to the standard of kindness.

On the other hand, injustice is motivated by opposite desires: to gain personal wealth and status at someone else's expense. Unjust acts include greed, violence, cheating, bribing, giving false testimony, or seeking to convict the innocent or vindicate the guilty. Injustice may involve lying, bullying, and depriving others of their rights.

Legal justice requires equal treatment for all based on laws and judicial procedures that don't favor one person or one group more than others; and officials must apply the laws without favoritism. People expect justice from those who govern and judge, but unfortunately, injustice is common in many legal systems.

The One Exception to Equal Treatment

While Proverbs advocates for equal justice for all, it also allows for and insists upon one major exception to that standard: social justice for the poor, the destitute, the oppressed, widows, and orphans, who require special protection since their rights are often violated by greedy individuals:

> There are those whose teeth are swords,
>   whose fangs are knives,
> To devour the poor from off the earth,
>   the needy from among mankind. (30:14)

> A righteous man knows the rights of the poor;
>   a wicked man does not understand such knowledge. (29:7)

Proverbs explains the need for special protection for the poor and needy because they are the ones most often mistreated by others. When justice is administered, the poor are often at the end of the line. Life for the poor is hard: their neighbors don't like them (14:20); family members may look away from their suffering (19:7); scoffers and the violent steal what little they have (13:23); thus, injustice targets the poor (30:14). The remedy for this injustice is twofold. On the one hand, the government and neighbors should protect their rights. King Solomon, King Lemuel, and Agur agree, calling on government officials to defend the rights of the poor (29:14; 30:14; 31:8–9).

King Lemuel was taught by his mother that his responsibility as king was to

> Speak up for those who cannot speak for themselves,
>   for the rights of all who are destitute.
> Speak up and judge fairly;
>   defend the rights of the poor and needy. (31:8–9 NIV)

A second remedy for the injustice directed at the poor is a general attitude of generosity toward them (14:21; 21:13; 31:20). When people are generous to the poor, God will repay them (19:17).

God's concern for the vulnerable was summarized by W. R. Domeris in this way:

> The God of the Bible is a God with a passionate concern for those whom society has dehumanized or for those whose lack of power and status has made them especially vulnerable to exploitation—widows, orphans, and the poor (and since the two groups are often linked, e.g., Isa 58:6–7, also the oppressed). In the absence of an earthly kinsman-redeemer, God stands as their protector and guardian.[2]

For government leaders, judges, or for ordinary citizens to fail to protect and provide for the poor and needy is a sin because God is their Maker and their defender (17:5). Proverbs calls on the righteous to be the kinsman-redeemer for the poor and the oppressed. But if God's people will not do this, he will do so himself.

> Whoever despises his neighbor is a sinner,
>   but blessed is he who is generous to the poor. (14:21)
> Whoever oppresses a poor man insults his Maker,
>   but he who is generous to the needy honors him. (14:31)

---

2. Domeris, "רוש," 1085.

Justice requires equal treatment for all, but that can only be achieved by providing special care for those who are often left out. God commands that no one, rich or poor, be excluded from justice, and that no one be left hungry or unprotected.

EQUITY/FAIRNESS

Equity or fairness is the third virtue advocated in Proverbs. Since God made all people as equals, we all have equal rights. Fairness is central to all the teachings of Proverbs: "Rich and poor have this in common: the Lord made them both" (22:2).

The Hebrew root translated as "equity" means straight or balanced. Equity is a basic principle underlying justice. Fairness to all includes respecting the rights of others and excludes taking advantage of others for personal benefit.

The motivation for inequality is a false assumption of personal or group superiority. Such prejudice is grounded in arrogance, pride, selfishness, ambition, envy, and jealousy (Jas 3:14). The antidote for this poison is humility before God and humility before all others.

Jesus gave two operational definitions of equity: first, "love your neighbor as yourself" (Matt 22:39; Lev 19:18); and second, the Golden Rule: "So in everything, do to others what you would have them do to you, for this sums up the Law and the Prophets" (Matt 7:12). Both commands require fairness without favoritism or selfishness. Just as God does not show favoritism (Acts 10:34–35; Eph 6:9), Jesus said we should follow his example, treating all others as our equals.

The apostle Paul took the idea of equity one step further: "In humility count others more significant than yourself. Let each of you look not only to his own interests, but also to the interests of others" (Phil 2:3–4). Jesus' attitude of being our servant (Matt 20:28) is our example to follow. The safest way to protect everyone's rights is to be everyone's servant!

An understanding and application of the threefold path of goodness is linked with God's gift of wisdom (Prov 2:5–9). Wisdom and righteousness are partners. People are most like God when we practice righteousness, justice, and fairness for all. We are least like God when we live selfishly.

16

Four Character Traits of the Righteous

Someone has observed that the world is made up of two types of people: those who divide everything into two types and those who don't.

Solomon was clearly a person of the first type. In his writings, virtues and vices came in matched sets. Therefore, he taught goodness by describing a virtue to be sought and a vice to be avoided: Do be humble, don't be proud. Do be honest, don't deceive. Do be generous, don't be greedy. Do show love, kindness, care, and faithfulness, but don't be hateful, unkind, uncaring, or unfaithful. These four traits are taught in Proverbs as values that typify the righteous—and they are also taught in the rest of Scripture, including in the teachings of Jesus. These same values are the standards for Christian character because they are derived from the character of God.

TRAIT ONE: HUMILITY VS. PRIDE

The first test of a truly great man is his humility.
—John Ruskin[1]

> Before destruction a man's heart is haughty,
> but humility comes before honor. (Prov 18:12)

---

1. John Ruskin, quoted in Peck, *Abounding Grace*, 117.

In Proverbs humility and pride are not random behaviors, they are character traits—they reflect a person's heart. No virtue better expresses the character of a saint than humility. No trait better expresses the character of a sinner than pride. In Proverbs, humility is closely linked with wisdom and honor (11:2; 18:12; 22:4)—the opposite of how we often think. And the hallmark of foolishness is to be wise in one's own eyes (3:7), which is a manifestation of pride.

The Hebrew words for "humility" suggest it is an act of lowering oneself,[2] and "pride" is an act of exalting oneself.[3]

Humility

The worldview of monotheism holds that God is God and I am / we are far less than God. Therefore our relationship with God begins with the fear of the Lord, and that begins with humility. Our status before God is the obvious reason for being humble.

In Proverbs, however, the role humility plays does not stop with being humble before God. Humility is also required in all of our relationships with others, and it should also be my attitude toward myself. I should not harbor secret pride in my heart. Humility is the primary trait of good character. It is a necessary step toward becoming wise and toward receiving honor. Humility is honored by God and should be honored by men.

> Toward the scorners he [the Lord] is scornful,
> but to the humble he gives favor. (3:34)

> The reward for humility and fear of the Lord
> is riches and honor and life. (22:4)

In the New Testament, humility is essential to becoming like Christ. Jesus not only taught his disciples to be humble, but he lived out his humility before them. For Jesus humility meant to be a servant to others. Though he was their teacher and Lord, he washed their feet—and said that this was an example for them to follow (John 13:12–15). Jesus' humility meant giving up his divine rights to become a human, to be a servant, to be obedient, and then to die the shameful death of the cross

---

2. Dumbrell, "ענו," 455.
3. Smith and Hamilton, "גאה," 786.

(Phil 2:6–11); therefore, according to Paul, his attitude of lowliness is an example we all should follow.

For Christians to be Christlike, we must consider others as of greater importance than ourselves, looking out for their interests as well as our own (2:3–4), and honoring others above ourselves (Rom 12:10). When Paul wrote, "Do not be haughty, but associate with the lowly. Never be wise in your own sight" (12:16), he may well have been paraphrasing Proverbs.

Pride/Arrogance

A proud person views himself/herself to be wise and his/her actions to be praiseworthy. This arrogance leads to every other form of foolishness and sin. Pride consists of ranking oneself above one's peers and ultimately above God. C. S. Lewis called pride "the great sin."[4] This attitude toward pride is a key feature of the Christian religion.

> The emphasis placed on pride, and its converse humility, is a distinctive feature of biblical religion, unparalleled in other religious or ethical systems. Rebellious pride, which refuses to depend on God and be subject to him, but attributes to self the honour due to him, figures as the very root and essence of sin.[5]

Pride is different from other vices in one significant way: it is found equally among saints and sinners, and perhaps more among saints! Saints may be proud of their good deeds or their religiosity—but such self-righteousness is actually anti-righteousness. Perhaps as Christians we know better than to boast openly about our personal goodness, but we may boast inwardly to ourselves—in our hearts. Jesus listed pride as one of the sins of the heart that makes a person unclean (Mark 7:22–23). James considered such boasting a form of lying (Jas 3:14). Proverbs says that God will judge the proud and boastful:

> Everyone who is arrogant in heart is an abomination to the Lord;
>   be assured he will not go unpunished. (Prov 16:5)

> Do you see a man who is wise in his own eyes?
>   There is more hope for a fool than for him. (26:12)

---

4. Lewis, *Mere Christianity*, 108–9. I recommend this chapter, "The Great Sin," for an insightful study of pride and humility.

5. Tongue, "Pride," 955.

> One's pride will bring him low,
> but he who is lowly in spirit will obtain honor. (29:23)

All human pride is a denial of the central idea of monotheism that God is supreme. We each must acknowledge that God is not merely "King of kings and Lord of lords" (1 Tim 6:15), but that he is *my* King and *my* Lord. If I withhold giving him his glory and my obedience, it is pride, sin, and rebellion, and Proverbs warns that it will lead to shame and destruction.

Another insight from C. S. Lewis is that "the first step to becoming humble is to admit that one is proud. If you think that you are not conceited, it means you are very conceited indeed."[6]

TRAIT TWO: HONESTY VS. DECEIT

We can think of honesty as either a quality of speech, whether spoken or written, or as a quality of business, being forthright and fair in making deals. As a quality of speech honesty means using words that are factually accurate and not misleading, without exaggeration or lying. In this sense, honesty is a character trait of those who would never lie or stretch the truth to mislead or take advantage of another.

While honesty refers to accurate verbal communication, its usage in Proverbs goes deeper than this. Honesty is about a personal commitment to truth and it results in the character traits of truthfulness and integrity. Honesty is the outer behavior expressing the inner trait of truthfulness. Lying, on the other hand, is the outer expression of the character trait of self-centeredness, seeking personal benefit by concealing or distorting elements of the truth.

But the usage in Proverbs goes even deeper than this. If we had asked a Jewish rabbi during biblical times to define "truth," he might have said, "Truth is God's character. It is why we trust him. It is why we believe his words." In Proverbs, Agur expressed it this way:

> Every word of God proves true;
>   he is a shield to those who take refuge in him.
> Do not add to his words,
>   lest he rebuke you and you be found a liar. (30:5–6)

---

6. Lewis, *Mere Christianity*, 114.

Truthfulness is an essential trait of both God's character and Jesus' character (John 14:6)—so truthfulness should become an attribute of every righteous person's character. To be godly is to be a person who values truth and lives and speaks accordingly. Proverbs says that the righteous "hate falsehood" and "buy truth" (13:5; 23:23).

Truthfulness, Integrity, and Trustworthiness

Honesty is the most common expression of truthfulness in Proverbs. To the extent of our knowledge and our requirement to speak,[7] our words should "tell the truth, the whole truth, and nothing but the truth." As Ted Ward described it:

> As God's people, we are to be people of truth. Truth is a basic value in the Christian community. We should even think twice about the little white lies that make things "nice"—half-truths, exaggerations, and insincere compliments. Our commitment to truth should be as complete as the limitations of being mortal will allow. We regard trustworthiness as one of the marks of God being in us.[8]

Notice the link Ward made between truthfulness and trustworthiness. Telling the truth is the best way to earn and keep trust. Marriages, families, churches, communities, nations, and civilization itself depend on both truth and trust to survive and thrive. We earn trust by being honest.

If honesty refers to truthfulness towards others, integrity requires being honest with ourselves. A person with integrity knows the truth about themselves, and they align their behaviors with their inner values. Integrity refers to consistency between character, beliefs, and behavior. It is the opposite of duplicity and hypocrisy. A person with integrity can be trusted to behave consistently and honestly in all situations.

> The integrity of the upright guides them,
> but the crookedness of the treacherous destroys them. (11:3)

> Better is a poor person who walks in his integrity
> than one who is crooked in speech and is a fool. (19:1)

---

7. It may not be dishonest to tell a falsehood the person actually thought was true. But a person who values truth will correct such falsehoods once they are discovered. And it may not be dishonest to withhold negative information that is unnecessary, illegal, or dangerous to others to share.

8. Ward, *Values*, 44.

We have referred to righteousness as an inner compass that guides a person's choices and the path they choose to walk. Honesty and truthfulness are an essential element of that inner compass. And, as the previous verse stated, crooked speech is the mark of a fool.

Dishonesty and Deceit

If we define truth as factual accuracy and as personal integrity, the opposite of truth is falsehood, which is speech that is either totally false or presents a false picture by editing the truth. Deceitfulness knowingly conceals inaccuracies, uses exaggeration, or a biased slant of the facts to prevent the hearer from knowing the full truth. Proverbs strongly condemns deceitfulness.

More verses in the book of Proverbs refer to the use of words than to any other topic.[9] The misuse of words includes lying, deceit, slander, boasting, gossip, flattery, smooth speech, enticement, mockery, insults, cursing, and false testimony. The seriousness with which God views the sinful use of words is shown in this passage:

> There are six things that the Lord hates,
>   seven that are an abomination to him:
> haughty eyes, a lying tongue,
>   and hands that shed innocent blood,
> a heart that devises wicked plans,
>   feet that make haste to run to evil,
> a false witness who breathes out lies,
>   and one who sows discord among brothers. (Prov 6:16–19)

Three of the sins in this list directly involve the deceitful use of words: lying, false testimony, and stirring up conflict; but probably all seven involve misuse of words at some level. God considers all such sins of the tongue an abomination. This list is not simply seven separate sins; taken together they provide a picture of a wicked person disregarding truth for his/her personal benefit. One characteristic of sin is that doing one usually leads to another. Beginning with his/her pride, a wicked person accumulates other sins, especially deceit, in order to enhance their reputation or to advance their personal ends at the expense of others.

Proverbs is particularly concerned with dishonest testimony in court. Eight times it condemns a false witness as perpetuating injustice.

---

9. Ortlund, *Proverbs*, 132.

"A faithful witness does not lie, but a false witness breathes out lies" (14:5).

We should expect that deceivers will be deceptive. Scammers are good at deceiving! Deceit is often a package of which lying is only one part. This package includes half-truths, flattery, and gifts. It may include insults aimed at others—and insults are one form of dishonesty. It may include bribes. A deceiver may deliver his falsehoods with a smile, a handshake, flattery, and kindness. The one being cheated may not recognize that this is all part of the disguise:

> Whoever hates disguises himself with his lips
>   and harbors deceit in his heart;
> When he speaks graciously, believe him not,
>   for there are seven abominations in his heart. (26:24–25)

> A lying tongue hates its victims,
>   and a flattering mouth works ruin. (26:28)

A harmful characteristic of lying is that it intentionally robs another person of his/her right to understand the truth. Of course, the point of lying is to conceal truth, but in doing this, the liar devalues the personhood of the other, not treating them as equals, denying them the right to know the actual situation.

Lying and deceit are wrong at several levels: they violate the principle of truth; they deny others their right to know the truth; they are an attempt to hurt others; they result in the loss of trustworthiness; and they are an abomination in the eyes of God. These principles ought to guide Christians in how we speak in legal situations, in political discussions, online, in business, and in our personal relationships.

Honesty and Wisdom

What does honesty have to do with wisdom?

In Proverbs, Lady Wisdom declared her consistent honesty and her rejection of dishonesty. Therefore, she invited all mankind to listen to her instructions and to follow her example (8:6–21). Truthfulness is found in the heart before it is heard on the lips. A person cannot be considered wise if they don't value truth, and a person can't value truth without consistently practicing honesty.

Is it too idealistic to imagine a world in which a general attitude of truthfulness leads to a general practice of honesty leading to people being able to trust one another? Can we imagine a world in which businesspeople simply tell the truth about their products or services, good and bad, without exaggeration or slandering their competitors? Is a world without false advertising possible? Or can we imagine a world where politicians simply tell the truth about themselves and about their rivals, without exaggeration or slander? As Christians, we can contribute to creating a world of truthfulness and trustworthiness by committing ourselves to being persons of truth!

TRAIT THREE: GENEROSITY VS. GREED

The category of wealth differs in one way from the other three topics in this chapter. Neither possessing riches nor being poor is necessarily a moral issue. How we gain wealth may be a moral issue, but just being rich is not. What is always a moral concern is how we use our wealth. Proverbs refers to generosity as a mark of righteousness and to greed as a form of wickedness. Proverbs does not suggest that "money is the root of all evil," which is a misquotation of Heb 13:5. That verse actually says, "Keep your life free from love of money, and be content with what you have, because he has said, 'I will never leave you nor forsake you.'" Proverbs agrees with those ideas.

> A faithful man will abound with blessings,
> but whoever hastens to be rich will not go unpunished. (28:20)

> The blessing of the Lord makes rich,
> and he adds no sorrow with it. (10:22)

> [Lady Wisdom says] I walk in the way of righteousness,
> in the paths of justice,
> granting an inheritance to those who love me
> and filling their treasuries. (8:20–21)

Thus, wealth may be God's blessing and the result of hard work and wisdom.

However, though God blesses some with wealth, he reserves his right of ultimate ownership of our possessions (Lev 25:8–10, 23; Deut 18:1–5). By his authority he determines the proper way one's personal wealth is to be used. In a biblical worldview, people are not the owners of their possessions but the stewards who must give an account of their stewardship on a day of God's choosing (Matt 25:14–30; Luke 12:16–21; 16:19–31).

What does it mean to be a steward of God's possessions? It includes the law of firstfruits, the law of generosity, and the law of honesty.

The first obligation of having wealth is to honor God by giving the first part back to him—the law of firstfruits:

> Honor the Lord with your wealth
>   and with the firstfruits of all your produce;
> then your barns will be filled with plenty,
>   and your vats will be bursting with wine. (Prov 3:9–10)

This principle of giving God the firstfruits is continued today in the practice of tithing. Tithing is not a tax imposed on church members by the church hierarchy; rather it is the proper way to honor God who has bestowed his blessings upon us. As we return the first portion to God, we remind ourselves who gave it to us in the first place.

Another obligation of having wealth is to contribute to the economic well-being of one's community, including generosity to those in need. We all understand the principle of sharing with others—we teach it to our children—but it seems that adults still need to be reminded of the importance of sharing. Generosity towards others is an expression of the three virtues of righteousness, justice, and equity.

> One gives freely, yet grows all the richer;
>   another withholds what he should give, and only suffers want.
> Whoever brings blessing will be enriched,
>   and one who waters will himself be watered.
> The people curse him who holds back grain,
>   but a blessing is on the head of him who sells it. (11:24–26)

These verses teach that, ironically, the reward for giving generously is prosperity and refreshment, while those who cling to their wealth will become poor. Those who withhold their harvest, trying to drive up the market price, will be cursed by those who are hurt by this practice. Instead, they should contribute to the economy for everyone's sake, and for their generosity, others will pray for God to bless them. "One who waters will himself be watered" (Prov 11:25).

Almost all of God's blessings[10] are given to us to be shared. In this way, God blesses others through us. Generosity is one of the marks of a caring Israelite (Deut 15:7–11; Prov 22:9; 31:20) and of a follower of Jesus (Matt 19:16–24; 2 Cor 9:6–11; Gal 2:9–10).

> The generous will themselves be blessed,
> for they share their food with the poor. (Prov 22:9 NIV)

Finally, Proverbs forbids obtaining wealth through any sort of dishonesty, deceit, corruption, or violence.

> Unequal weights and unequal measures
> are both alike an abomination to the Lord. (20:10; also 11:1; 16:11)

These references refer to the use of balance scales to weigh product or payment as part of a sale. Ray Ortlund, Jr. wrote of this verse,

> "Unequal weights" are any kind of dishonesty, any kind of cheating or cutting corners or false advertising. That is an "abomination" to the Lord. Strong language. An abomination in the Old Testament included sexual sin, for example (Lev 18:22). But here the Bible says that dishonest business practices are an "abomination." They are moral corruption. You might be sexually pure, but if you cheat people for money, your life is an abomination in the sight of God.[11]

Perhaps we are tempted to pray that God will make us rich (or richer), but the only prayer recorded in the book of Proverbs contains this request: "Give me neither poverty nor riches, feed me with the food that is needful for me" (30:8). Both are dangerous. The danger of poverty is that one might be forced to steal in order to survive. The danger of riches is that one might take credit for one's success and forget the Lord.

The concluding statement from Proverbs on the topic of wealth is not that wealth is evil—it may indeed be God's gift—but "whoever trusts in his riches will fall" (11:28). That lesson was true in Solomon's day and is just as true today. Perhaps the only way to avoid "falling" is to hold onto one's wealth loosely and to share it generously.

---

10. The only blessing that I can think of which we are not to share is our spouse. Marriage is an exclusive relationship sealed by a covenant made before God (Prov 2:17).

11. Ortlund, *Proverbs*, 178.

TRAIT FOUR: LOVE AND FAITHFULNESS VS. BETRAYAL AND UNFAITHFULNESS

In chapter 4 I suggested that what the world needs even more than sweet love is wisdom. Now that our study of Proverbs has brought us to the word "love," I offer another alternative lyric for that classic song: "What the world needs now is faithfulness"—that's the only thing that there's too little of. Love is good—and necessary—but faithfulness in love is even better!

Our modern use of the word "love" often refers to a temporary emotional high that will be here today, gone tomorrow. Such a variable feeling is the opposite of faithfulness. The book of Proverbs speaks disparagingly of such emotion-driven love. In reaction to emotion-driven love, Proverbs introduces a better sort of love: steadfast love, which attaches commitment, kindness, and truth to love. Imagine a world in which "love" means both loyalty and truth. That is indeed what the world needs now!

Like English, the Hebrew language has several words for love with a wide of range of meanings. The most common Hebrew word for love has both positive and negative associations. In Proverbs "love" can refer to emotions, to commitments, to sex, and to a preference for abstract concepts such as loving wisdom. On the other hand, the wicked love sin, wine, and dishonest gain. They love sleep and sleeping around. The lists below illustrate the positive and negative uses of the word "love" in Proverbs.

Positive uses of the word "love":

- "The Lord disciplines those he loves" (3:12 NIV).
- "Whoever loves discipline loves knowledge, but he who hates reproof is stupid" (12:1).
- "The one who loves their children is careful to discipline them" (13:24 NIV).
- "Do not forsake wisdom, and she will protect you; love her, and she will watch over you" (4:6 NIV).
- "[Lady Wisdom says,] I love those who love me" (8:17).
- "He who loves wisdom makes his father glad" (29:3).
- "Whoever loves purity of heart, and whose speech is gracious, will have the king as his friend" (22:11).
- [Speaking of a man's wife] "Be intoxicated always in her love" (5:19).

- "Better a small serving of vegetables with love than a fattened calf with hatred" (15:17 NIV).

Negative uses of the word "love":

- "How long, O simple ones, will you love being simple?" (1:22).
- [An adulteress propositioning a young man] "Come, let us take our fill of love till morning; let us delight ourselves with love" (7:18).
- "He who fails to find me [wisdom] injures himself, all who hate me love death" (8:36).
- "Whoever loves transgression loves strife" (17:19).
- "Love not sleep, lest you come to poverty" (20:13).

What we love and how we love reveals what we value in our hearts. The most important use of love has to do with God's love for his people and his expectation that they in turn will love him and love one another.

Faithful Love

Proverbs uses a second Hebrew word for love: *hesed*, which is sometimes translated as kindness, lovingkindness, loyalty, or mercy.[12] *Hesed* love carries the sense of loyalty within a relationship: loyalty between friends, loyalty within marriage, loyalty between a king and his subjects, and loyalty between God and his people. *Hesed*-like love often refers to covenant relationships in which there is mutual commitment, and therefore *hesed* is sometimes translated as covenant love.

In the Old Testament, especially in Proverbs, *hesed*-like love is often paired with the Hebrew word for truth and together they are translated as "love and faithfulness" (NIV), or "loyalty and faithfulness" (HCSB), or "steadfast love" (ESV). This combination of words reminds us that while the world needs love, it needs faithful love even more!

The following verses show the uses of faithful love in Proverbs:

> Let not steadfast love [*hesed*] and faithfulness [truth] forsake you;
>   bind them around your neck,
>   bind them on the tablet of your heart.
> So you will find favor and good success
>   in the sight of God and man. (3:3–4)

12. Baer and Gordon, "חסד," 211–18.

> Steadfast love and faithfulness preserve the king;
>   and by steadfast love his throne is upheld. (20:28)
>
> Do they not go astray who devise evil?
>   Those who devise good meet steadfast love and faithfulness. (14:22)
>
> By steadfast love and faithfulness iniquity is atoned for,
>   and by the fear of the Lord one turns away from evil. (16:6)
>
> What is desired in a man is steadfast love. (19:22)

These verses show the importance of faithful love. It can assure the safety of a king. It is the result for those who seek good for others. And faithful love can even attain forgiveness of sins!

The opposite of faithfulness is betrayal or treacherousness. The adulterous wife has betrayed her wedding vows and therefore betrayed both God and her husband (2:17). "The treacherous will be rooted out of [the land]" (2:22).

"Love" in Proverbs is neither a passing feeling or an emotional commitment; rather it is a character trait of the wise. It implies both loyalty and kindness to others, seeking their good. This is how God loves his people and how he expects us to love one another.

SUMMARY

Being humble, honest, generous, and faithful are behaviors that reflect good character. The teachings of Proverbs describe both how a wise person acts and the values they have internalized, values that shape their character. This combination of traits transforms morality from just following rules about good behavior into an inner compass that guides how we choose on a daily basis.

Thinking about our lives as a series of critical choices may seem overwhelming. Can we really be righteous all the time? All of these individual choices, however, are contingent on one prior choice: the fear of the Lord. Once we have chosen to follow the Lord, humility, truthfulness, generosity, and faithfulness will flow from that. These values describe God's character and therefore describe godliness. Whenever we make a choice to do what is right, we become more the type of person that others can trust and the kind of person that God honors.

17

The Worldview of Proverbs

THE BOOK OF PROVERBS reveals how the worldview of monotheism is connected with wisdom and righteousness. All the other wisdom writings were built on the foundation laid in Proverbs—including Ecclesiastes, the New Testament writings of Paul and James, and even the teachings of Jesus, all relied on the understanding of God's world from Proverbs. This reliance is seen both in the frequent quotations of Proverbs in the New Testament, and in the underlying theology in which the God of Proverbs is the God of the rest of the Bible. Proverbs applies the truths of monotheism to daily life.

THE FOUNDATION OF WISDOM IN PROVERBS

Proverbs is the foundation for understanding biblical wisdom, but it is not a book of abstract theology. It makes no effort to define monotheism or biblical ethics; instead it spells out the practical implications of the ethical monotheistic worldview. If you want to know how to live in the world designed by God, read the book of Proverbs. It is a practical guidebook for wise living. And any reader can benefit from its instructions.

Some critics of the book of Proverbs, however, have called it a secular book. It is secular, they say, in the sense that it doesn't say much about religious rituals or temple worship. The few mentions of those religious things are incidental to the main teachings of the book. These critics also say that Proverbs is secular in the sense that anyone, religious or nonreligious, can apply its maxims and have a more successful life. In fact, the book is not addressed exclusively to the Jews as we might expect but to all mankind (Prov 8:4). And, truth be told, some of the wisest people I know (in the general sense of wisdom) are nonreligious, and a few of the most foolish people I know are Christians. So, it might seem that monotheism isn't required for applying the teachings of Proverbs—as the critics have said.

However, I strongly disagree with the idea that Proverbs is secular. Proverbs is a religious book in a way similar to the book of Esther. While the book of Esther recognizes the hand of God in determining the circumstances of the people in that story, both good and evil, it never mentions God. He is, however, always there in the background. No reader of the book of Esther would ever call it secular. In the same way, we can say that though 90 percent of the verses in Proverbs don't explicitly mention God, it would be a serious misinterpretation of the book to view God as absent in that 90 percent. In every verse he is active in the background. Throughout the book, God is the chief actor.

In all the proverbs of Proverbs, God works behind the scenes as the judge and administrator in each life. He knows each person's heart, he sees the paths they walk, he determines the rightness of their actions, and determines whether their plans will succeed or fail. The book of Proverbs is a commentary on monotheism. The following passage is one example among many; and it includes an unexpected twist:

> The Lord has made everything for its purpose,
>   even the wicked for the day of trouble.
> Everyone who is arrogant in heart is an abomination to the Lord;
>   be assured, he will not go unpunished.
> By steadfast love and faithfulness iniquity is atoned for,
>   and by the fear of the Lord one turns away from evil.
> When a man's ways please the Lord,
>   he makes even his enemies to be at peace with him. (16:4-7)

This passage describes both God's sovereign oversight of the lives of all people. He determines the outcome of each life, whether positive or negative outcomes, and even trouble for the wicked. He punishes those with proud hearts; therefore it is very important that we not harbor pride in our hearts!

But in the midst of these warnings about God punishing sin, the passage also reveals the possibility of atonement (forgiveness) for sin.

This atonement, however, is not based on temple sacrifices, as we might expect in an Old Testament book; rather, it is based on each person's love and faithfulness. This unexpected reference to faithful love bringing forgiveness for iniquity is a reminder that, even in the Old Testament, forgiveness was based on grace through faith. As the New Testament also reminds us, "Love covers a multitude of sins" (1 Pet 4:8).

While the passage speaks of forgiveness, it also speaks of the fear of the Lord as the way to avoid evil. That verse summarizes the teaching of Proverbs that, for us to remain on God's good side, we must fear him and avoid evil, wickedness, and pride. Just as we cannot understand Proverbs without recognizing God's activity behind the scenes, we also cannot understand Proverbs without recognizing that we are the actors on stage, choosing our paths, our plans, and conducting our relationships. God's sovereignty incorporates our responsibility.

The picture of our lives shown in Proverbs is like an interactive game in which players win or lose based on the choices they make! Perhaps this interaction between God's sovereignty and individual choices is difficult to understand (and theologians disagree about how to define the relationship between sovereignty and free choice), but this interactive relationship is clearly presumed in Proverbs. God designed the game so that we play a genuine part to which God responds. His response is the deciding factor. The wise understand that "man proposes but God disposes" and live accordingly. They make the kind of choices that God will approve.

An Alternate Path to the Covenant Blessings

Proverbs implies another surprising connection between wisdom and righteousness: wisdom is a path to righteousness; therefore, it is an alternative path to receiving God's approval and blessings. In the Sinai covenant God promised to bless Israel for keeping his commandments, and to curse them if they didn't (Lev 26; Deut 6:18–19). Most of the Old Testament books of history and the prophets record Israel's successes or failures—usually failures— in keeping the covenant laws and the consequences they receive. Surprisingly, without ever mentioning the covenant or the law, Proverbs promises those same blessings to those who choose to live wisely day by day.

This similarity between the covenant blessings and the wisdom blessings can be seen by comparing two passages, one by Moses, the second by Solomon:

> I call heaven and earth to witness against you today, that I have set before you life and death, blessing and curse. Therefore choose life, that you and your offspring may live, loving the Lord your God, obeying his voice and holding fast to him, for he is your life and length of days, that you may dwell in the land that the Lord swore to your fathers, to Abraham, to Isaac, and to Jacob, to give them. (Deut 30:19–20)

> So you will walk in the way of the good and keep to the paths of the righteous. For the upright will inhabit the land, and those with integrity will remain in it, but the wicked will be cut off from the land, and the treacherous will be rooted out of it. (Prov 2:20–22)

The promises made to Moses in Deuteronomy were based on love for God and obedience to God's commandments. The blessings Proverbs offered were based on wisdom, the conclusion of a passage that began, "For the Lord gives wisdom . . ." (2:6). The two sets of blessings are very similar to each other. Thus Proverbs offers an alternative path to God's blessings!

Another surprising innovation found in Proverbs is that wisdom is available to all mankind; therefore wisdom-based righteousness is available to all mankind; therefore the blessings of the covenant are available to all mankind (Prov 8:1–4, 31). By seeking biblical wisdom, even gentiles could enjoy the blessings God gives!

WISDOM-BASED THEOLOGY

I used to serve as the academic dean at Oak Hills Christian College in northern Minnesota. Part of my role was to meet with prospective students who came to visit the campus. I recall the time that a mother and son came to check out the school. She explained to me that her son had the spiritual gift of prophecy, and they were seeking a Christian school which would enable him to develop this gift. This request was a first for me, and I wondered what to say. Though our Bible College studied the topic of spiritual gifts in our Bible classes, we were not what might be called a charismatic school. Though individual students might practice the so-called charismatic gifts in their private devotions or in small group times, such gifts were never part of our public worship. Chapel usually consisted of singing and preaching from the Bible—but never spoken prophetic messages. None of our faculty knew how to prophecy in the way that this mother wanted. I suggested to her the names of several other Christian colleges in the region where her son might be taught how to prophecy and be given the opportunity to do so in public worship. And so, they left our campus seeking a school that better fit their theology and practice.

As I reflected on this conversation, I decided that the way I would describe our college was as a wisdom school, not as a prophecy school. We believed and taught the Bible as the revealed word of God, but we were not seeking new revelation based on prophecies. In retrospect, this is how I would describe the book of Proverbs as well.

In Proverbs God does not speak through prophets nor does he give new revelation. Totally missing is the prophetic commentary on the contemporary history of Israel, which is so prominent in the history books of Scripture. The theology of Proverbs is a wisdom theology, not a prophecy theology. God speaks, but he speaks through parents, teachers, and advisors. The prophets of Proverbs are "the wise," those with the knowledge and understanding of God. The wise know the kind of life that God approves, and they are experts at applying that knowledge to the daily lives of believers.

The closest thing to a spokesman for God in Proverbs is Lady Wisdom. She witnessed God's activities in creation, which serve as the basis of wisdom. She knew God's role as the arbiter of morality, which underlies the understanding and practice of wisdom, his role as supervisor of human plans, and his watching over our ways of treating others. Lady Wisdom understood truth to a degree that most people don't, and she invited us all to learn from her. Her secret of living a life that God approves and blesses is simple: embrace wisdom.

There are two places in Proverbs that refer to God's word but not in the sense of prophecy:

> For the Lord gives wisdom;
> from his mouth come knowledge and understanding. (2.6)

God's mouth—his words—is the basis of the wisdom he gives. The knowledge and understanding found in his words are not new but what has always been known by his words in the past. There is consistency, not new revelation.

The second reference to God's words occurs in what may be the strangest passage in Proverbs; this speech by Agur:

> I am weary, O God, and worn out.
> Surely I am too stupid to be a man;
>   I have not the understanding of a man.
> I have not learned wisdom,
>   nor have I knowledge of the Holy One.
> Who has ascended to heaven and come down?
>   Who has gathered the wind in his fists?
> Who has wrapped up the waters in a garment?
>   Who has established all the ends of the earth?
> What is his name, and what is his son's name?
>   Surely you know!
>
> Every word of God proves true;
>   he is a shield to those who take refuge in him.
> Do not add to his words,
>   lest he rebuke you and you be found a liar. (30:1–6)

This soliloquy by Agur begins with sarcasm: a rejection of wisdom for himself and seemingly for everyone else. None of those who claim to speak for God have ever been to heaven or seen how God formed the earth (a speech very similar to God's speech to Job from the whirlwind; see Job 38–41). No human has such understanding and any human effort to add to God's word is a lie.

This speech by Agur reveals an important aspect of wisdom that we often miss: the inadequacy of human wisdom to understand God or his ways. As Scripture states in several places, having wisdom leads one to doubt one's wisdom. Proverbs expresses this idea in other ways as well:

> A man's steps are from the Lord;
>   how then can man understand his way? (20:24)

> Trust in the Lord with all your heart,
>   and do not lean on your own understanding.
> In all your ways acknowledge him,
>   and he will make straight your paths. (3:5–6)

These verses seem to contradict the advice to "get wisdom" that dominates most of Proverbs, but they are identical to the theme of the inscrutability of God's plans as found in Ecclesiastes and Job. The reality that no one can actually understand the path God has chosen for their life explains why the theme verse of Proverbs is that wisdom begins with the fear of the Lord. If God alone understands the world and if he administers our lives, including both judging us for sins and hearing and answering prayers, then the only way to live wisely in God's world is to trust him.

Each proverb in Proverbs is an individual piece of the whole jigsaw puzzle. The truth presented in each of the six hundred plus proverbs is a piece of the bigger picture of Proverbs, of the wisdom literature, of Scripture, and of life experience. My summary of the basic truth of Proverbs is, living morally and trusting God are always the wise choice. And, fearing the Lord is the approach to life that God always blesses.

God is the chief actor in Proverbs, so fear him. He will give you a level path, so fear him. To fear the Lord means to humbly submit to him as the all-wise, Almighty God whose word instructs us to live wisely and who rewards those who do so.

> But the path of the righteous is like the light of dawn,
> which shines brighter and brighter until full day. (4:18)

18

The Wisdom of Proverbs for Today

I HAVE A PERSONAL observation about the importance of the book of Proverbs: the Christian church today needs Proverbs as much as did the people in Solomon's day. Though Christians are saved by grace and indwelt by the Spirit, though we study and memorize our Bibles, we still wander from the straight path onto various crooked paths. Tragically, the amount of sinfulness inside the church may seem as great as that outside the church! We can see this in the recent revelations of immorality, dishonesty, and disrespect in evangelical churches.[1] Instead of turning to God for heavenly wisdom, we fall back into earthly wisdom. In the book of James, the warning about the dangers of worldly wisdom was addressed to Christians, not to pagans. James saw the effect of worldly wisdom in the church as catastrophic! (Jas 3:13—4:17). It still is.

Most people desire the outcomes of success and prosperity that the book of Proverbs offers, but many choose to bypass the path the book prescribes to such blessings: the path of wisdom, of good character, and of seeking God's approval. Proverbs does not suggest that there is any

---

1. While I don't want to exaggerate these problems in churches, they are real. For example, in 2022 the Southern Baptist Convention, of which I am a member, had to acknowledge that sexual abuse among a few leaders in a few churches had been covered up by the association's top leadership for decades. Or another example, in recent years the former pattern of debate using civil speech and courtesy in American politics has degenerated into dishonesty, vicious personal attacks and insults, ridiculous conspiracy theories, and even violence—a degeneration into sin in which evangelicals have not only participated but have themselves accelerated.

shortcut to success. Only fools would seek such a shortcut—fools then and fools now.

One shortcut that seems common among Christians today is bypassing good character. I have even heard Christians explicitly say character doesn't matter, and the only thing that matters is success. And so they ignore Proverbs' instruction on the importance of good character. Lacking the wisdom that Solomon taught, Christians can easily become the fools that Solomon warned about. (And I am writing to myself as much as to anybody else.)

Why should Christians today care about character? Why should we try to get wisdom and avoid foolishness? Why should we be righteous and not wicked? Proverbs gives three reasons:

First, character counts because consequences count—and the consequences of bad character are devastating to the soul and therefore to the church. Lady Folly still sits alongside the road leading to shame, stumbling, and ultimately death (9:13-18). She still invites those who should know better to partake of her feast of secret bread and stolen water. But those who read and follow Proverbs' instructions on character, as evidenced by wise and upright choices, can avoid her enticements (2:6-22). Proverbs instructs us that character, good or bad, has predictable consequences; so choose the good.

The second reason that good character is important is that relationships are important. Good relationships require trust, and trust requires honesty and integrity. Proverbs teaches us how to treat others in order to help them and to encourage them to become better people. Good character is contagious.

The most important reason to value good character is that it is a mark of godliness. Godliness is a condition of the heart. As we shall see in chapter 39, Christ was/is the incarnation of Wisdom, so to become Christlike requires becoming wise. If, as Christians often say, we want to become like Christ, we should not only read the gospels, we should also read Proverbs! Jesus did.

In addition to Jesus, who else read Proverbs? We know that the apostles Paul, Peter, James, and the author of Hebrews all read Proverbs, because they quoted from the book. David Hubbard lists nine quotations from Proverbs and three allusions to the teachings of Proverbs found in the

New Testament.[2] For the New Testament writers, reading Proverbs shaped their worldview, their understanding of wisdom, and their theology of how God interacts with his people.

In chapter 41 seven parallels are listed between Proverbs and the book of James, beginning with "Proverbs and James provide the reader with practical applications of ethical monotheism: if you believe in God, this is how you ought to live." And both James and Peter quote Proverbs 3:34, making one of the primary themes of Proverbs their own:

> He mocks those who mock,
>   but gives grace to the humble. (HCSB)

This verse does two things. It summarizes the two main character types: the mocker and the humble; and it shows how God responds appropriately to people with those types of character: he mocks those who mock others, and he shows favor to the humble. This verse reveals the worldview of Proverbs, and it should matter as much to us now as it did then. Therefore, read Proverbs.

---

2. Hubbard, "Proverbs," 979. The quotations Hubbard lists are Rom 12:16, 20; Heb 12:5–6, 13a; Jas 4:6, 5:20; 1 Pet 4:8, 5:5b; and 2 Pet 2:22.

PART FOUR

Studies in Ecclesiastes

I used my wisdom to test all of this. I was determined to be wise, but it was beyond me. How can anyone discover what life means? It is too deep for us, too hard to understand.[1]

—Qoheleth (a.k.a. Solomon)

And if wisdom itself is vanity, where does that leave our study of wisdom? Welcome to the paradox of Ecclesiastes!

---

1. Eccl 7:23–24 TEV.

19

What Is an Ecclesiastes?

Ecclesiastes is the strangest book in the Bible.
—R. B. Y. Scott[1]

Not many sermons get preached on Ecclesiastes, for it is one of the Bible's most confusing books.
—Philip Yancey[2]

WHY WOULD SCOTT CALL Ecclesiastes strange or Yancey call it confusing? The book is filled with unexpected twists and turns, at times raising questions that the reader may find uncomfortable. And the answers the book provides to those uncomfortable questions raise additional questions needing to be answered. Maybe the most unexpected answer the book gives to its own questions is "I don't know." It never says this quite so bluntly, but as Ecclesiastes explores the challenging inconsistencies of life, it often concludes "only God knows." In my opinion, to say, "I don't know, only God knows," is the mark of an advanced stage of wisdom!

---

1. Scott, *Ecclesiastes*, 191.
2. Yancey, *Bible Jesus Read*, 161.

WHO IS QOHELETH?

The first mystery of the book of Ecclesiastes is its name: What is an Ecclesiastes? The name "Ecclesiastes" is the English version of the Greek word *ekklesiastes*, which in the Greek New Testament is the word used for "church." But this Greek word was, in turn, a translation of an older Hebrew word, *qoheleth* (pronounced ko-hel'-eth), which means "the leader of a group." So the Hebrew title for the book which we call Ecclesiastes is *Qoheleth*, a group leader.

Qoheleth is also the pen name of the author and narrator of the book (see Eccl 1:1). Qoheleth is probably not a personal name but the title of someone in an official position. Because of this, English versions variously translate Qoheleth as "the preacher," "the teacher," or "the philosopher." I will call him the teacher.

This mysterious pen name discloses a second mystery: Who actually was the author of the book? The traditional answer is that Solomon wrote Ecclesiastes—though it never names him directly. The evidence that it was Solomon is found in the author's description of himself as "the son of David, king in Jerusalem" (1:1), a man who had more wealth and wisdom than anyone who was there before him (1:16). This sounds very much like King Solomon, and so I accept the traditional view that Solomon was Qoheleth, the teacher, the author of Ecclesiastes.

But many scholars have doubted that Solomon was the book's author. One reason for this doubt is linguistic. Over long periods of time languages change: grammar changes and vocabulary changes. For an example of such change, compare contemporary American English with King James English—very different. Readers who are not accustomed to King James English find the King James Version (KJV) difficult to understand. Because of those linguistic changes, the KJV has recently been updated to the New King James Version (NKJV) using more contemporary English. In a similar way, linguistic changes happened over time in the Hebrew language, and the Hebrew of the book of Ecclesiastes is from a later period of time than the Hebrew of Proverbs, which was spoken at the time of King Solomon. However, this linguistic difference is easily explained if we assume that Solomon wrote both books but centuries later an editor updated the Hebrew in Ecclesiastes—just as modern editors have updated the language of the KJV to the NKJV. So, the linguistic differences don't disprove Solomon as the author of Ecclesiastes.

The more significant reason to doubt Solomon's authorship is that the style and content of Ecclesiastes are quite different from that of Proverbs. The book of Proverbs presents an optimistic view of life—at least for those who choose wisdom. The wise can expect to be blessed with success, health, wealth, honor, and a long life. And fools can expect the opposite of those good things. In Ecclesiastes, however, life is not so clear cut: bad things happen to good people, and good things happen to bad people. Life can seem unfair. According to Proverbs, injustices can happen because of sin—corrupt people taking advantage of other people. But in Ecclesiastes, "unfair" things happen according to God's plans. Ecclesiastes dares to question the easy optimism of Proverbs while not doubting that God is still in control. The two books look at life from different perspectives. But different viewpoints doesn't mean that Solomon couldn't have written both. Good authors can write about both sides of the same coin, and readers, hopefully, can learn from both perspectives.

The perspective of the book of Ecclesiastes might be summarized with a two-phrase statement: "Life is not fair, but God is fair." The first phrase is easy to understand. We all have experienced times when we felt that life wasn't fair. But can we then think of the God who is sovereign over all of life as fair? Ecclesiastes explores that question, and its answer is perhaps the greatest contribution of the book of Ecclesiastes to our understanding of God and to our understanding of wisdom. But, as Yancey said, it is confusing.

INTERPRETING ECCLESIASTES

This chapter's opening quotations stating that Ecclesiastes is strange and confusing both relate to the challenges of interpreting the book. There are a wide range of interpretations of Ecclesiastes.

One common interpretation is to take the repeated phrase "under the sun" as the interpretive key. This view sees Ecclesiastes as contrasting the secular view of life (life under the sun) with the theistic view (life trusting God). The secular view always ends up as meaningless. While this interpretation is attractive, I find it difficult to separate a secular view and a religious view within the text. The teacher finds both sides of life as "vanity of vanities."

> It is the same for all, since the same event happens to the righteous and the wicked, to the good and the evil, to the clean and

the unclean, to him who sacrifices and him who does not sacrifice. As the good one is, so is the sinner, and he who swears is as he who shuns an oath. (Eccl 9:2)

Reading this verse makes us realize that we are not in Proverbs anymore! This balanced perspective that good and bad people share a common destiny has been labeled as cynical. Or perhaps it is simply realistic: life is tough for everybody.

Some commentators like this pessimistic view of life. They prefer it to the optimism often associated with monotheism. Other critics view Ecclesiastes through a postmodern lens in which life has no inherent meaning or purpose, and, like an inkblot, everyone can make of it whatever they will. Life, they say, is simply unfair to all—and they conclude that therefore God is also unfair; or perhaps they conclude that the inconsistencies of life prove there is no God. But such a negative conclusion is clearly not derived from the book of Ecclesiastes. To only read the book as saying that "everything is vanity"—which it says many times—is to ignore the ending of the book, which is neither postmodern nor nihilistic. In the end, Ecclesiastes is not even pessimistic.

While the teacher raises the possibility that all of life is meaningless, that is not his ultimate conclusion. Though his search for meaning in the aspects of life where people often seek meaning return empty, the teacher finds life's meaning in the last place he looks (which is where you always find what you are looking for). Ecclesiastes provides a strong defense of monotheism as the only reasonable explanation of the multiple inconsistencies in life.

Probably the most common interpretation of Ecclesiastes—and it is my view—is that the teacher makes a deliberate investigation into all of life's experiences, seeking lasting purpose and meaning, and one by one, he finds them empty. Even wisdom, his own preferred source of meaning, turns up empty. Therefore, at the end of his investigation, the only remaining source of meaning is God. But since God's plans and purposes remained beyond the teacher's reach, the only access to his meaning was—and is—through faith!

Thus, Ecclesiastes is a book of pre-evangelism. While it does not tell the gospel story, it shows us that every other idol we may worship—wealth, health, pleasure, success, adventure—provides at best temporary purpose and happiness. Thus, Ecclesiastes eliminates all the most common answers people give for why life is worth living, leaving the reader with no other option but to fear the Lord.

In addition to the teacher's critical investigation of the meaning—or lack of meaning—of life in general, the teacher also wrote about his view of time, about the positives and negatives of work (mainly negatives), and he even offers investment advice while also criticizing estate planning. The book discusses good and bad luck, youth and old age, and the value of friends and family. Maybe most surprising is the book's fixation on death as the great evil at the end of every life, and the teacher recommends that we all attend as many funerals as possible to remind ourselves of our mortality. And along the way he reaches an unexpectedly blunt conclusion about the limitations of human wisdom—which was his own personal strength.

As we shall see, in the midst of his research concluding that almost everything in life is meaningless, the teacher also finds small bits of joy, which are available to us all. His findings regarding these non-vain aspects of every life make reading the book worthwhile.

20

The Investigation Begins

The unexamined life is not worth living.
—SOCRATES (399 BC)

WHAT MAKES A LIFE, any life, worth living? This famous quote by Socrates suggests that for a life to be worth living, critical self-examination is required. But Socrates did not just examine himself, he examined his fellow citizens in his hometown of Athens, Greece. He was searching for a wise man, any wise man, and repeatedly he couldn't find even one. Needless to say, his critical investigation of his fellow citizens did not make him very popular! The citizens of Athens put Socrates on trial, found him guilty, and gave him a choice of leaving town or being executed by drinking poison: exile or death. The implication that he could only live by leaving town was unacceptable to Socrates. He would rather die than stop questioning the value of life. For Socrates, examining life by asking questions was the only way to determine if his life had been worth it. Therefore, he chose death.

MEET THE RESEARCHER

I think that the teacher, a.k.a. Solomon, would have agreed with the quote from Socrates about the importance of an examined life—though

Solomon's circumstances were totally different than those of Socrates. Solomon was in no danger of being executed for his investigations. He was the king and had the freedom and unlimited resources to question anything and everything. He chose to use his freedom to critically examine his own life and that of his fellow citizens. He was seeking anything that provided lasting meaning in life.

The search for meaning is at the heart of the book of Ecclesiastes. The teacher wrote,

> I turned my heart to know and to search out and to seek wisdom and the scheme of things, and to know the wickedness of folly and the foolishness of madness. (7:25)

We should note that at the end of his investigation the teacher admitted that he had failed to understand the scheme of things (7:27–28).

The teacher considered himself a good case study to answer the age-old question of the meaning of life because he was both rich and wise, indeed richer and wiser than anyone else; plus as king during a relatively peaceful era, he had the free time to reflect on life—a pastime for which most people just don't have time (5:20).

It is interesting that the teacher did not encourage everyone to undertake such a life examination for themselves. Perhaps this was because most people lacked the money to try out the many things that the teacher did, but more likely it was because during his research he exposed himself to numerous temptations by which one without his degree of wisdom might be ensnared. Some of the things the teacher tried for himself—wine, women, and song—can be dangerous to a person's soul! Religious people are often labeled as prudish, but that was not true of the teacher. Some of the things he tried would have kept him out of membership in the church where I attend! But even though he was not prudish, he remained prudent. That is a rare combination.

THE RESEARCH METHOD

If you read an article in an academic journal, it begins with a brief paragraph that summarizes the research problem, the research method, and the results. The teacher provides such a summary for his readers (1:12–17). He is examining everything in life looking for something—anything—that cannot be labeled as "vanity"—as meaningless.

The method of his research is to personally experience the aspects of life he is studying. He puts them to the test to see if they actually achieve the positive results that most people believed. He tests pleasures, wealth, possessions, accomplishments, and even his personal favorite, wisdom.

His methodology for testing these things is his personal experiences and observations, using his wisdom (1:13). Here are observations we can make about the teacher's observations:

- He is investigating life "under the sun," "under heaven," and "on earth." His observations are of real people and events. This is a book grounded in reality.

- He made comments about a wide range of topics: wealth, investing, youth, old age, death, and funerals, wisdom, foolishness, and reading books.

- His observations are generally pessimistic. Near the beginning of his search, the teacher wrote, "It is an unhappy business that God has given to the children of man to be busy with" (1:13).

While Ecclesiastes does have its brighter points, overall, this is not a book to read in order to be cheered up—unless it brings you cheer to know that life is hard for everybody, even for the teacher.

THE RESEARCH CONCLUSION

At the end of his investigation the teacher reaches two seemingly conflicting conclusions about the meaning of life: (1) "Everything is meaningless!" (12:8 NIV); and (2) fearing God and obeying his commandments are everyone's duties (12:13–14).

As he investigated the parts of people's lives, the teacher labels almost everything "meaningless" (NIV)—also translated as "vanity" (ESV), "futile" (HCSB), "useless" (TEV), or "soap bubbles."[1] The teacher uses the Hebrew word for "meaningless" thirty-five times to express his conclusion about the meaning of life:

> Vanity of vanities, says the Preacher, vanity of vanities! All is vanity. (1:2; cf. 12:8)

---

1. Dr. Thomas McComiskey, my Old Testament professor at Trinity Evangelical Divinity School, liked this translation of Eccl 1:2. He had heard it from his Old Testament professor before him. It means the beauty of life is as brief as a soap bubble.

Or, "Soap bubbles, soap bubbles, everything is just soap bubbles." The actual Hebrew word the teacher uses is the word for "breath," reflecting the temporary nature of life. "Soap bubbles" is a good paraphrase for that word. Life is like soap bubbles that exist for a few moments and then disappear forever. Soap bubbles are similar to seeing your breath on a chilly morning—you can see it, but it isn't real and doesn't last. The teacher uses "breath" to describe all the things we think give meaning to our lives. Those things last about as long as a soap bubble.

The teacher also uses another metaphor to make the same point: all of our frenetic activity in pursuit of all this vanity is just a "striving after wind" (1:14)—meaning, what a waste of time! As much as we need breath, as much as we need the wind, they are transitory—like our hopes, our dreams, our accomplishments, and even life itself.

Certainly, the teacher was not the only social critic to observe the shallowness of our accomplishments and the brevity of life—many have done so—but he pushed this conclusion as consistently as possible to include everything: all is vanity, a striving after wind.

We will follow the lines of evidence that brought him to this gloomy conclusion in the next chapters.

21

Vanity Fair

THE TEACHER WAS LIKE Michelangelo who, replying to the question as to how he carved the statue of David, reportedly said, "I just chipped away everything that did not look like David."[1] The teacher was a sculptor not of statues but of something much more important: the meaning of life. As he examined each component of life, he found them to be without meaning, so one by one he chipped them away. He even chipped away his own investigation of life! At the end of his search, there was nothing remaining except the actual meaning of life: humble submission to God and keeping his commands.

The teacher investigated all the parts of life people may think will make their life meaningful: success, wealth, pleasure, a good job, and wisdom, and he found them each, even wisdom, to be a vanity of vanities. What is most surprising is that he found life itself to be a vanity! Why? Because we all will die and that wipes away everything we have accomplished in life.

In this chapter we will summarize the teacher's preliminary conclusions about the vanities in life and the vanity of life. (I say preliminary because these were not his final conclusion.)

---

[1]. The origin of this quote is unknown. Similar quotes have been attributed to various sculptors. Whether Michelangelo actually said it is uncertain, but he is often credited with saying it.

VANITY ONE: PLEASURES WITHOUT PLEASURE

The teacher enjoyed life. He had all the proverbial pleasures of "wine, women, and song." He described his life as positive, "I accomplished great things" (2:4 TEV).

But as he reflected on his accomplishments and possessions, he switched to calling it all "meaningless," "vanity."

> I also piled up silver and gold from the royal treasuries of the lands I ruled. Men and women sang to entertain me, and I had all the women a man could want.
>
> Yes, I was great, greater than anyone else who had ruled in Jerusalem. . . . Anything I wanted, I got. . . . Then I thought about all that I had done and how hard I had worked doing it, and I realized that it didn't mean a thing. It was like chasing the wind—of no use at all. (2:8–11 TEV)

Suppose we could be like Solomon and have anything we wanted all the time, would that make our lives full or empty, better or worse, happy or depressed? I remember that as a child Christmas morning was often disappointing. The anticipation exceeded the event. The teacher faced such a Christmas disappointment every day! Philip Yancey calls this "the curse of getting what you want."[2]

Here is what the teacher learned about money:

> He who loves money will not be satisfied with money, nor he who loves wealth with his income; this also is vanity. When goods increase, they increase who eat them and what advantage has their owner but to see them with his eyes? . . .
>
> As he came from his mother's womb, he shall go again, naked as he came, and shall take nothing for his toil that he may carry away in his hand. This also is a grievous evil: just as he came, so shall he go, and what gain is there for him who toils for the wind? (5:10–11, 15–16)

We often think of poverty in terms of lacking money or food, but there is a different kind of poverty: the insatiable hunger for more than one has.[3] Perhaps some of us daydream about being like Solomon, a king

---

2. Yancey, *Bible Jesus Read*, 148–52.

3. I do not mean to downplay the very real hardships and the tragedies of absolute poverty. Around the world billions of people suffer serious shortages every day. As 5:12 says, some people go to bed hungry, providing a moral obligation for those of us who can help them to do so.

or queen served by a large staff with musicians and maybe even a few concubines. Wouldn't that be great? The teacher's answer is that it is more frustration than fulfillment. He found no meaning there.

During my seminary years, I had a part-time job as a personal attendant for a wealthy, elderly man who lived inside a hospital room. He suffered from a debilitating disease that would eventually take his life. He was rich enough to hire graduate students for round-the-clock service. His whole life was reduced to trying to be comfortable in bed, waiting for his next pain pill and getting foot massages. Once he told me that I wasn't very good at most things, but he appreciated that I could give a good foot rub (I thought of it as Jesus washing his disciples' feet). Here was a man who could have afforded almost anything in this world, but he lived for his next foot rub. Vanity of vanities.

VANITY ONE: WORK WITHOUT REWARDS

Immediately after introducing his book with the exclamation, "Vanity of vanities!" the teacher launches his investigation into the meaning of life with a simple question about the value of work:

> What does man gain by all the toil at which he toils under the sun? (1:3)

The teacher repeats that same basic question four times throughout the remainder of the book. He asks such rhetorical questions expecting a negative answer: There is no real benefit to one's work! That seems an unduly blunt conclusion—one that the teacher would walk back later.

Ecclesiastes gives two contradictory answers to the question about the value of work: one answer is that work, like everything else in life, is vanity, chasing the wind. (Perhaps we have all felt that way about our jobs.) The other answer is that one can obtain pleasure from their work—in fact enjoying one's job is part of the reward for doing it—and such pleasure is a gift from God. The teacher gives both answers in the same paragraph:

> My heart found pleasure in all my toil, and this was my reward for all my toil. Then I considered all that my hands had done and the toil I had expended in doing it, and behold, all was vanity and a striving after wind, and there was nothing to be gained under the sun. (2:10b–11)

Which answer better describes your job: pleasure or vanity? Or both? The teacher uses the following words to describe work: toilsome (2:20), hatred (2:18), despair (2:20), and vexation (2:23). Why did the teacher, a king, hate his work? What bothered him the most was that the person who works hard in this life is often not the one who benefits from his labor. Once he dies, his success will be enjoyed by his successor, who didn't work for it. His successor might even be a fool—and that is an injustice!

> I hated all my toil in which I toil under the sun, seeing that I must leave it to the man who will come after me, and who knows whether he will be wise or a fool? Yet he will be master of all for which I toiled and used my wisdom under the sun. This also is vanity. (2:18–19)

The teacher was concerned that his heir might turn out to be a prodigal who would waste it all. His son Rehoboam fulfilled his worst fears in that regard.

VANITY THREE: LIFE AND DEATH

It is not surprising that a perceptive researcher such as the teacher, when investigating the reputed bases for meaning in life—the ones which many people use to prop up their self-esteem—concludes that they are all shallow, unsatisfying, and vain. But it may be surprising that he pays so much attention to one single event that we might have expected him to accept as a simple reality: death.

It is not uncommon for people to dread death. In many cultures it is impolite to even mention death (in English we prefer euphemisms like "pass away" or "go to sleep"), but some cultures have such an extreme taboo that they will never say the word "death" or speak out loud the name of a dead person. To avoid thinking about their own mortality some people won't make a will or buy life insurance. People who are otherwise level headed think of death with fear and resistance. But a fear of dying was not the teacher's hang-up. He knew that death was coming, but one aspect of death troubled him.

The teacher wrote frequently about death. In his poem about the seasons of life (3:1–8), the teacher begins by naming every life's beginning and end: "A time to be born, and a time to die" (3:2).

So, on the one hand, the teacher says that both birth and death are universal and normal. But, in other passages he seems to say that death transforms every other experience of life into vanity. If his use of the word "breath" ("vanity") is a metaphor for the brevity of life, death is what made it so.

In a book about realism, for the teacher to be so upset about dying seems to be unrealistic. Since the teacher acknowledges that "generations come and generations go" (1:4), which is how it has always been, why call it an evil?

Perhaps the teacher was upset that prior generations were soon forgotten, which meant that present and future generations will also be quickly forgotten (1:11; 2:16). Our time on earth is short, and our impact on life is minimal. Throughout life we may seek ways to distinguish ourselves from the crowd, declaring, "I am the greatest of all time" (the GOAT), or, "I am better"—that is, more moral, more religious, more gifted, more successful, or wiser—"than other people," but death is the great equalizer. We often say that life is unfair—and it is—but death is very fair: "The same event happens to all" (2:14).

The teacher was not afraid to die—at least he never said so—but two facts about dying bothered him. First was the fact that everyone receives the same destiny no matter whether they were wise or foolish, good or bad, religious or nonreligious; everybody dies in much the same way, and so would the teacher.

> It is the same for all, since the same event happens to the righteous and the wicked, to the good and the evil, to the clean and the unclean, to him who sacrifices and him who does not sacrifice, As the good one is so is the sinner; and he who swears is as he who shuns an oath. This is an evil in all that is done under the sun, that the same event happens to all. (9:2–3)

> The wise person has his eyes in his head, but the fool walks in darkness. And yet I perceived that the same event happens to all of them. Then I said in my heart, "What happens to the fool will happen to me also. Why then have I been so very wise?" And I said in my heart that this also is vanity. For of the wise as of the fool there is no enduring remembrance, seeing that in the days to come all will have been long forgotten. How the wise dies just like the fool! So I hated life. (2:14–17)

Solomon, the teacher, was also the primary author of Proverbs, a book in which he declared that a long life was the reward for righteousness and an early death was the future for the fool and the wicked. Yet, in Ecclesiastes, that same Solomon observed that everybody faces the same fate, a fact which he called an evil. He protested because the wise and the upright don't live longer than anyone else. Since everyone dies, why be wise? Why be moral? The universality of death seemed to be an injustice—at least according to retribution theology (see the discussion of retribution in ch. 7).

The teacher wrestled with this apparent injustice, but he backtracked a bit by affirming that overall things will go better for those who fear God:

> Though a sinner does evil a hundred times and prolongs his life, yet I know that it will be well with those who fear God, because they fear before him. But it will not be well with the wicked, neither will he prolong his days like a shadow, because he does not fear before God. (8:12–13)

The teacher also struggled with the fact that animals and people both die in a similar way:

> I said in my heart with regard to the children of man that God is testing them that they may see that they themselves are but beasts. For what happens to the children of man and what happens to the beasts is the same; as one dies, so dies the other. They all have the same breath; and man has no advantage over the beasts, for all is vanity. (3:18–19)

People die like animals die: vanity of vanities! Death is the great equalizer—even for animals.

But there was a second fact about death that greatly bothered the teacher: the question of legacy. Who would inherit his wealth when he dies? Since nobody gets to "take it with him," the teacher would have liked to think that his estate, the results of all he worked hard to achieve, would be left to someone who would appreciate its value and continue the work he had started, but he knew that this was often not the case. As we noted in the previous section, one's heir might be a fool (2:18–19), a prodigal who would waste the inheritance for which his or her parents had labored hard.

The teacher believed that it was an injustice that a person's whole life could be ingloriously summarized as "naked to naked" (5:15), meaning we all enter and exit life in the same condition. No matter how much we may accomplish in between, in the end, we all die empty handed. Perhaps the teacher wondered why God allowed such an injustice for every human life. Part of the sorrow for having wisdom (1:18) is the knowledge that sometimes we have no easy answers as to why God does what he does.

As we have seen, for the teacher the pleasures and accomplishments of life are all empty and last no more than a breath, but death turns life itself into vanity; therefore death is an evil. There are three reasons that he believed that death makes life an evil:

- We all leave the world as we entered it. However much wealth a person has gained through hard work, he can't take it with him. And whoever inherits it may be a fool. Vanity!
- Whether a person was wise or foolish, righteous or wicked, doesn't matter, for everybody dies in the same way. Vanity!
- Even being human or animal doesn't matter: all die. Ultimately, humans have no advantage over the beasts. Vanity of vanities!

When any person dies, we can say with the teacher, birth to death, dust to dust, sunlight to darkness, feasting to mourning, remembered to forgotten. The teacher declared that all of this is an injustice. It is evil. It is vanity. It is reality.[4]

The conclusion of the first part of the teacher's investigation of life is that there is no meaning here. There is frustration, sorrow, and nothing that lasts longer than a soap bubble.

---

4. New Testament believers may object to Ecclesiastes's pessimistic view of death. We have been taught that justice will ultimately be found in the next life on judgment day, when God sends us to either heaven or hell—though to be technically correct, being sent to heaven is an injustice, while going to hell is not.

It is unclear how Solomon understood the afterlife. We know that people in his day believed in Sheol, which is often translated in English Bibles as "the grave."

22

"Wisdom Without Wisdom"

My friend John, a resident at the nursing home where I work, has been interested in the fact that I am writing a book about wisdom. Recently he asked me what the title of the book would be, and I replied, "*Wisdom About Wisdom.*" John, who is hard of hearing, wrote down "*Wisdom Without Wisdom.*" At first, I laughed at this funny error, but then, as I thought about it, I realized his title is correct—especially for Ecclesiastes. It may surprise us, but the teacher (Solomon the Wise) lumped wisdom into the "all is vanity" category!

VANITY FOUR: WISDOM WITHOUT WISDOM

Who better to investigate wisdom than one who possesses wisdom? Solomon was such a man.

He wanted to understand "the scheme of things" (7:25), meaning the principles by which life operates. Schemes may refer to plans made by men or, more significantly, those made by God. Understanding the scheme of things takes wisdom. Regarding wisdom, the teacher observed,

> I applied my heart to know wisdom and to know madness and folly. I perceived that this also is striving after wind. For in much wisdom is much vexation, and he who increases knowledge increases sorrow. (1:17–18)

Wisdom and knowledge lead to sorrow and grief. The teacher's investigation led him to frustration, not satisfaction. This was due in part to the vanity of everything, but it was also due to his observations of the crookedness and incompleteness of life—flaws that can't be fixed.

> What is crooked cannot be made straight,
> and what is lacking cannot be counted. (1:15)

What is even more discouraging is his observation of the human condition:

> This alone I found, that God made man upright, but they have sought out many schemes. (7:29)

Ironically, as he set out to understand the scheme of things—God's principles for administering the world—he discovered just the opposite: human schemes by which we devise our own paths. Though God made humankind upright, we use our intelligence to plot contrary ways, ways that the teacher labeled as madness and folly.

In describing what people are like, the teacher does not temper what he saw. His conclusions are pessimistic and depressing. Looking at life with the eyes of wisdom hurts!

The teacher not only saw the gloomy side of life, he also saw it as beautiful and intriguing:

> [God] has made everything beautiful in its time. Also he has put eternity into man's heart; yet so that he cannot find out what God has done from the beginning to the end. (3:11)

So, is life beautiful, gloomy, or both? What is clear was the teacher said that nobody, no matter how wise, has got this all figured out! Even wisdom cannot understand God's ways!

> All this I have tested by wisdom. I said, "I will be wise" but it was far from me. That which has been is far off, and deep, very deep; who can find it out? (7:23–24)

> When I applied my heart to know wisdom, and to see the business that is done on earth, how neither day nor night do one's eyes see sleep, then I saw all the work of God, that man cannot find out the work that is done under the sun. However much

man may toil in seeking he will not find it out. Even though a wise man claims to know, he cannot find it out. (8:16–17)

Maybe one of the most important takeaways from the book of Ecclesiastes is that "the wise," those who claim to know what's going on, don't really know! Therefore they can't solve our global problems. They can't even solve our personal problems. The wise don't know what they claim to know. In fact, not even the teacher could understand all that happens on earth or why God does what he does.

Many people claim to be wise and claim to understand all the "schemes of things" happening in our world, our country, and our individual lives. But, the teacher, who sought such understanding, concludes that it is very deep and far beyond our reach. This is so because God made it so.

Though the teacher doubted the ability of the wise to understand the scheme of things, he remained a believer in the value of wisdom. He gave examples of how wisdom can make a person's life better: it can make his work easier (10:9–10); it can calm the temper of an angry king (10:4); and it can even defeat an attack by a superior military force. But there is one thing wisdom can't do: assure respect.

He told this story: once upon a time the citizens of a small city did not know how to save their city from an attack by a superior army. But in the city was a poor man who had wisdom and knew what they should do, and the city was saved. But afterwards nobody remembered this insignificant man whose wisdom saved them.

> But I say that wisdom is better than might. Though the poor man's wisdom is despised and his words are not heard.
> The words of the wise heard in quiet are better than the shouting of a ruler among fools. Wisdom is better than weapons of war, but one sinner destroys much good. (9:16–18)

By wisdom, the city was delivered but by foolishness much good that had been done was undone. Just as dead flies can make perfume stink, foolishness can overturn wisdom and honor (10:1). Nothing is new under the sun. Foolishness can undo the good accomplished by wisdom.

AVOID EXTREMISM

In the middle of Ecclesiastes, we find a surprising statement:

> Be not overly righteous, and do not make yourself too wise. Why should you destroy yourself? Be not overly wicked, neither be a fool. Why should you die before your time? It is good to grasp the one and not let go of the other. Whoever fears God will avoid all extremes. (7:16–18)

It is not surprising that the teacher warned against extreme forms of righteousness, wisdom, wickedness, or foolishness. He advocated moderation instead of extremism. We can understand the dangers of hyper-religiosity or an overly strict morality. Self-righteousness often ends up as religious hypocrisy.[1] And hyper-wisdom, the putting on of airs, claiming to be wiser than one is, is as foolish as self-righteousness. Boasting about one's wisdom or righteousness is just a form of lying against the truth (Jas 3:14).

The teacher's warning to avoid being excessively wicked or foolish also makes sense. He even warned that by foolishness one could hasten the day scheduled for their death—a shocking thought!

But what did he mean that we should hold onto both? Are we supposed to hold on to righteousness and wickedness? Or to hold onto wisdom and foolishness? However we understand that phrase, the teacher was clearly advocating staying in the middle of the road, away from all extremism.

It is encouraging that the teacher concludes by saying that the fear of the Lord is not a form of extreme religiosity or extreme righteousness. If we fear God he will guide us on a path of moderation in all things.

Perhaps the teacher was wiser than we might have expected: he recognized the limitations on wisdom—it cannot discover the things God has done. He confessed his own ignorance in understanding "the scheme of things." And he advised that wisdom be applied in moderation. Trying to be overwise is foolish!

---

1. Jesus condemned the kind of strict religion that led to hypocrisy and judgmentalism. He condemned any righteousness that emphasized outer cleanliness while condoning inner filthiness (Matt 7:1–5; 15:7–9; 23:1–36). He also showed compassion for people caught in sin (Luke 13:15; John 8:1–11).

23

"Round and Round It Goes..."

I RECENTLY HEARD THAT they are removing wall clocks from school classrooms in Britain. The reason being that children don't know how to tell time on a clock face anymore. They can only read digital clocks, usually on their mobile phones. I have seen this happening among American teenagers as well. The teacher of Ecclesiastes might have said that digital clocks are another evil. (Not that he knew how to tell time either way.)

I am doubly old-fashioned: I still wear a wristwatch rather than tracking time on my cell phone, and I use a watch with a round twelve-hour clockface. When digital watches first came out decades ago, I quickly switched to the new, modern technology. I wore digital watches for years but then decided to go back to the analog watches I grew up with—not because I prefer old-fashioned things, but because I prefer a visual representation of time. A digital clock only shows the time at the moment. An analog clockface enables me to see the current time in relation to the time of the day. A quarter past the hour or twenty minutes till the hour is shown in visual form. That is how I think of time, so I prefer analog clocks.

THE MERRY-GO-ROUND

The old analog clockface teaches another important lesson, one with which the teacher would have agreed: time is not linear, as implied by a digital clock. It is circular. One o'clock today is neither the first nor the last occurrence of that time; it happens every day—or twice each day. The same observation applies to calendars: July 26 this year is neither the first nor the last occurrence of that date—which is why my age increases by one on that date every year.

It is possible to think of time as linear, as a vector that goes in one direction forever. Computers calculate dates in a linear fashion beginning January 1, 1900.[1] Before that date I suppose that for computers time didn't exist. For the teacher, however, time, *as we live in it*, is circular. The keyword is *time repeats*: days, months, years repeat; even generations repeat: great-grandparents to grandparents to parents to children is circular time. Consider this passage, which introduces the teacher's view of time:

> A generation goes, and a generation comes,
>   but the earth remains forever.
> The sun rises, and the sun goes down,
>   and hastens to the place where it rises.
> The wind blows to the south
>   and goes around to the north;
> around and around goes the wind,
>   and on its circuits the wind returns.
> All streams run to the sea,
>   but the sea is not full;
> to the place where the streams flow,
>   there they flow again. (1:4–7)

A modern rendition of the teacher's view of time is the song "Sunrise, Sunset," from *Fiddler on the Roof*. Like the teacher, we all experience time as a repeated sequence of days and nights, of summer and winter, of weather cycles, and even of waters flowing into the sea without ever filling it up. Natural cycles repeat forever; nothing changes; and therefore nothing is accomplished.

> All things are full of weariness,
>   a man cannot utter it;
> the eye is not satisfied with seeing,
>   nor the ear filled with hearing. (1:8)

Just as the sea doesn't ever get full, so our eyes and ears are never satisfied. Just as the cycles of nature never cease, so our human lives seemingly

---

1. Date zero for the Excel program is 1/1/1900. According to this program, there are no dates prior to this date.

change but are never complete. These cycles have always been there and will go on forever. We are riding a merry-go-round that never stops. The teacher found all of this ceaseless repetition to be monotonous and wearisome. He doubted that things ever change for the better. Despite appearances, nothing really changes.

Not only does time recycle nature, it recycles us. Generations come and go. People's lives come and go. The rites of passage by which we mark the significance of our lives, birthdays and death days and all the celebratory days in between—first-hunt days, quinceañera days,[2] graduation days, wedding days, anniversaries, baby showers, retirement parties, funerals, and, in Asian cultures, tomb-sweeping days—none of these rites, which mean so much to us, make any difference to the earth. Does planet earth even know that I am here? When I die will Mother Earth miss me? Of course not. The way we view our lives on earth and the way the earth views us are opposites.

Nothing Is Really New

An implication of the cyclical view of time is that whatever happens has happened before and will someday happen again.

> What has been is what will be,
>   and what has been done is what will be done,
>   and there is nothing new under the sun.
> Is there a thing of which it is said,
>   "See, this is new"?
> It has been already
>   in the ages before us.
> There is no remembrance of former things,
>   nor will there be any remembrance
> of later things yet to be
>   among those who come after. (1:9–11)

Nothing is really new. For the teacher, the world had lost the gleam of newness that youthful eyes often focus on. His comments are either the reflections of a tired old man or of one who has labored hard to make his life better without results, or perhaps of a philosopher who has seen the same events so many times until their repetition makes them meaningless.

---

2. This is the fifteenth birthday celebration for girls in many Spanish-speaking cultures.

If nothing changes, then why keep pushing forward? If nothing changes, we don't even know which direction is forward!

There is an error we should avoid as we read the teacher's pessimistic statements about life: we should not become pessimists ourselves. The teacher is not a nihilist trying to persuade others to become nihilists. Throughout the book he will slip in brief positive statements about life; all of these lead up to his final conclusion, which is *not* a nihilistic negation of life. He is actually building a case for a positive view of life, and we should not jump to a different conclusion before he has completed his case.

A Proper Time for Everything

The repetitive cycles of nature also occur within the events in each of our lives. Our lives are not new; they are recycled. Perhaps the most quoted passage in Ecclesiastes (thanks to a popular folk song of the fifties)[3] is the poem "A Time for Everything":

> For everything there is a season, and a time for every matter under heaven:
>
> a time to be born, and a time to die;
> a time to plant, and a time to pluck up what is planted;
> a time to kill, and a time to heal;
> a time to break down and a time to build up;
> a time to weep, and a time to laugh;
> a time to mourn, and a time to dance;
> a time to cast away stones, and a time to gather stones together;
> a time to embrace, and a time to refrain from embracing;
> a time to seek, and a time to lose;
> a time to keep, and a time to cast away;
> a time to tear, and a time to sew;
> a time to keep silence, and a time to speak;
> a time to love, and a time to hate;
> a time for war, and a time for peace. (3:1–8)

These fourteen pairs of opposites describe the events of every life from beginning (a time to be born) to end (a time to die), with a whole range of normal experiences in between. Each of these normal experiences comes

---

3. Pete Seeger's "Turn! Turn! Turn! (To Everything There Is a Season)." The lyrics of this song were taken directly from Eccl 3:1–8.

paired with an opposite normal experience, which we will all recognize within our lifetimes.[4] Instead of saying that life's events are new—nothing is really new—the poem tells us that life is a series of recycled events, a merry-go-round that never stops.

These pairs of life experiences in this poem are not organized in a logical pattern. We might ask why these fourteen pairs and not others? Why is there a mixture of major life events (birth/death, war/peace) and relatively minor events (tearing/sewing, losing/seeking, embracing/refraining). Sometimes the good item (embracing, loving) comes first, but in the other pairs the good item comes second. The pairs don't come in a chronological order or any other obvious order. Like life itself, they just happen.

We learn three things from this poem: the cycles of life, the randomness of life, and the non-randomness of life.

1. Opposing life events alternate: You can't laugh and cry at the same time. Today I am happy, but tomorrow I may be sad. Today I am content, but tomorrow I may be disappointed. Today I am healthy, but tomorrow I may be sick. Life happens in cycles, and nobody gets to have all happy, all satisfied, or all healthy. We don't get to choose only good things and avoid the other.

2. Randomness: Life happens unexpectedly. Planting and harvesting are predictable—though not always—but the other experiences in the poem come according to the schedule of "time and chance" (9:11). The good and bad events of life happen at one time or another—usually unexpectedly. Randomness is our perspective on life.

3. Non-randomness: The poem begins by telling us that there is a "time for everything." The Hebrew word for "time" can mean a proper time.[5] Though the twenty-eight events in the poem happen unexpectedly, they each happen at the God-appointed time, which is its proper time. So non-randomness is God's perspective on time. (3:1).

---

4. For clarification, some of the experiences listed in the poem had a different meaning in biblical times than they do now. For example, to embrace (make love) and to refrain (abstain) probably refers to the Old Testament laws of cleanliness in which sexual fasting was sometimes required prior to participation in tabernacle worship (Lev 15:19–24). Killing and healing may refer to warfare. Mourning and dancing, while similar to our meaning for these words, had very different expressions in their culture. Mourning included loud wailing and woeful movements, but dance was joyful movement, either in worship or celebration.

5. Tomasino, "עת," 566.

The teacher expands his thought of a proper time for everything a few verses later:

> He has made everything beautiful in its time. Also, he has put eternity into man's heart; yet so that he cannot find out what God has done from the beginning to the end. (3:11)

God has made everything beautiful "in its proper time." It is easy to say that God's timing is best, but that truth may not satisfy our desire to rearrange the timing of events or even to understand them. Some people cry out against the inscrutable nature of God's timing. They want answers: Why? Why now? Why me? The teacher says we cannot know those answers. But this ignorance is not a cause for pessimism. It is a call for trust.

Just as nature repeats itself daily and yearly, just as generations come and go in cycles of lives composed of experiences that always seem new but never are, just as we all look at the horizon of our world and wonder what's beyond, God has given us both limited experiences and unlimited imaginations—but without an understanding of all that God is doing.

The distinctive view of time in Ecclesiastes could be summarized like this:

> Whatever is has already been, and what will be has been before;
> and God will call the past to account. (3:15 NIV)

Time recycles; events repeat; God schedules this; and God judges what we do with the time we have been allotted.

24

Wisdom for an Uncertain World

THE WORLD WAS CREATED with both a natural order and a moral order. Wisdom requires order and predictability. Nobody can give wise advice without some sense of what will happen if one does this or if one does that. Wisdom is blind in a world of uncertainty.

BAD LUCK

While teaching at a Chinese university my wife and I got to know many Chinese students. The Chinese are wonderful people, very kind, and as a rule, very humble. We had many opportunities to be involved in our students' extracurricular activities—at least those few activities that were conducted in English, our only language. Every year we attended a speech contest for the English majors. Each contestant had to give two speeches in English, one prepared in advance and one extemporaneous. For the second speech, each contestant was randomly assigned a topic and given five minutes to mentally prepare before standing in front of the audience to give a speech.

One year an error occurred in this normal procedure. It happened to a student from one of my classes. Unlike most Chinese, he was a braggart. His English proficiency was excellent, and he was not shy to tell others that he had the best English of any student in the department. For weeks he had boasted that he would win the speech contest. I disliked his boasting, but I knew he was probably right. Everyone expected him to win. I had even prayed that he might lose. (I am ashamed of having prayed such a prayer!)

On the night of the contest, one of the officials made a careless error. The student I just described had been given a paper telling him the topic for his extemporaneous speech, and he had five minutes to prepare. When he went to the stage the announcer made a mistake and read a different topic for him to speak about. The student panicked. He asked for the topic to be reread. Once again, the incorrect topic was read. The student didn't know what to say. In front of the audience, he tried to ad-lib a speech on the new topic but, without any preparation, he stumbled badly. Another student won the contest. The braggart did not even place in the top three. I felt this result was both justice and injustice at the same time.

This true story illustrates a common aspect of life which the teacher also observed:

> Again I saw that under the sun the race is not to the swift, nor the battle to the strong, nor bread to the wise, nor riches to the intelligent, nor favor to those with knowledge, but time and chance happen to them all. (Eccl 9:11)

This verse is my favorite one in Ecclesiastes. Its view that the outcomes of life events are uncertain, that the fastest, strongest, smartest person doesn't always win the contest, coincides with life experiences we have all seen. Why doesn't the best-prepared person always win? "Time and chance," loosely translated as bad luck, happen to everyone. Though possessing superior skills and being well prepared normally lead to success, there is no guarantee. Ask any sports fan why their team lost their game this past week.

Life is filled with many uncertainties! Among them is bad luck.

THE ONLY CERTAINTY IS UNCERTAINTY

It annoyed the teacher that throughout his investigation into the meaning of life, at the end of his search to understand the scheme of things, he continuously bumped into things he couldn't figure out. Often this was due to the uncertainty of many things in life.

"The Worldview of Biblical Wisdom" (ch. 6) made the following connection:

Biblical wisdom is grounded on the knowledge that God created the world to be orderly and therefore somewhat predictable. The wise are those who discern the orderly patterns in nature and in human nature and use that understanding to predict what will happen next in life, making possible rational decisions and good advice. Therefore, the logic flows

God → wise design → created order → predictability → wise decision making.

If wise decision making requires predictability, and predictability requires orderliness, then uncertainty contradicts the basic premise of wisdom. No wonder the teacher was frustrated!

Maybe he felt the same way that Einstein did when he argued against Heisenberg's "uncertainty principle," the principle in physics that an observer can't see and know with certainty all sides of a matter-energy sub-atomic interaction. According to this principle, if a scientist knows one variable, he will always be uncertain about the other variables. This uncertainty principle seemingly implies randomness (or chance) in nature, which in Einstein's thought contradicts the basic assumption of all science: that reality is stable and can be accurately observed by scientists and adequately explained by science. Einstein objected to the idea that uncertainty could be inherent within the physical universe. He famously said, "God does not play dice with the universe."[1]

Like Einstein, the teacher objected to the uncertainties he discovered within the normally orderly reality of the world, but his objection was very different. Whereas Einstein appealed to "God" as evidence that ultimate uncertainty can't exist, the teacher concluded that God was in fact the reason for the uncertainties of life. The teacher might have restated Einstein's quote to say, "God *does* play dice with the universe!" And that frustrated him.

To be clear, the teacher would not have said that God practices randomness. God's planning was precise and purposeful, but to humans, it often seems random. For example,

- Nobody knows when bad luck will cause them to lose a race or a battle (9:11).

---

[1]. For Einstein this reference to "God" was only a metaphor for an orderly universe. Reportedly he did not actually believe in God.

- Nobody understands the explanation for things that happen in life (3:11; 7:23–25, 27–28; 8:1, 16–17; 11:5).
- Nobody can predict the weather with certainty (11:3–4).
- Nobody knows if people, be they righteous or wicked, will get the rewards or punishments they deserve (2:12–14; 8:14–15).
- Nobody knows when the disabilities of old age will come in their life (12:1).
- Nobody knows the future (3:22; 6:12; 7:14).
- Nobody knows the day of their own death (9:12).

Such uncertainties seemingly undercut the possibility of wisdom, at least as we usually understand wisdom. The uncertainties of life make prediction nearly impossible resulting in an inability to give good advice. For a wise person, like the teacher, to deal with uncertainty requires moving one step earlier in the diagram above. If there is limited predictability and if one cannot understand "the scheme of things" (the created order), then one must fall back to God who designed it all—but he put his purposes beyond human understanding. God's creation is indeed purposeful, but not even the wise can discern God's purposes. Therefore, wisdom requires us to adjust to this reality. Ultimately, we can only trust God as the sovereign Creator, but in the meantime Ecclesiastes suggests several strategies for living well in a world of uncertainty.

Planning for the Unknown

One strategy for planning ahead in a world of uncertainty is to diversify. The teacher recommends making multiple investments hoping that one or two will yield a return.

> Cast your bread upon the waters,
>   for you will find it after many days.
> Give a portion to seven, or even to eight,
>   for you know not what disaster may happen on earth. (11:1–2)

This strange proverb about casting your bread on the waters means that giving or lending to several people is an investment in different possible outcomes, some of which will give a return later.

I have seen this proverb in practice in other cultures, especially in China where *guanxi* (meaning reciprocity in gift giving) is the basis of building relationships. Giving money or doing favors for others now is viewed as an investment for the future. Those who receive the favor are in debt and are obligated to repay the favor if the giver is ever in need. Such gift giving is a basic element of Chinese culture, a fact that foreigners must quickly learn if they want to do business there. In China as well as in many other cultures, gift giving "to seven or even to eight" is a way to cast your bread upon multiple waters, expecting a return someday.

Another strategic adjustment to the uncertainties of life relates to the weather:

> If the clouds are full of rain,
>   they empty themselves on the earth,
> and if a tree falls to the south or to the north,
>   in the place where the tree falls, there it will lie.
> He who observes the wind will not sow;
>   and he who regards the clouds will not reap. (11:3–4)

Trying to time your planting and harvesting by reading the clouds is a fool's errand. The farmer is better off to do his work without trying to outguess the clouds. (Perhaps modern meteorological science does a better job of predicting the weather—though not always!)

Many things in nature are difficult to understand and hard to predict:

> As you do not know the way the spirit comes to the bones in the womb of a woman with child, so you do not know the work of God who makes everything. (11:5)

God's plans are as incomprehensible as the wind or as life in the womb. If we quibble that modern science has revealed much more about these topics than the teacher could have imagined possible, we miss the point. There is still much we don't know about the wind or the development of the fetus—especially with regard to spirit entering the child. But even if we knew about those occurrences perfectly, there would remain many other mysteries in nature that we still wouldn't understand. God's works are as unknowable as those mysteries. Therefore,

> in the morning sow your seed, and at evening withhold not your hand, for you do not know which will prosper, this or that, or whether both alike will be good. (11:6)

Just as the farmer shouldn't try to outguess the clouds, no one should try to outguess God! Therefore, do your work morning and night. Diversify. Invest in a couple of strategies, in the hope that God will bless one or maybe both of them.

Surprise!

The uncertainties of life may be frustrating, but they can also be beneficial. If every race was won by the fastest runner, if every battle was won by the strongest army, if every chess match was won by the top-ranked chess master, or if every trivia game by the most knowledgeable player, then living life would be pointless! Every outcome could be predicted based on knowing a little background information. There would be no surprises. Life would be predictable—and boring! Thankfully, surprises—and luck—add zest to the routines of life!

Here is another one of my favorite verses in Ecclesiastes:

> He has made everything beautiful in its time. Also, he has put eternity into man's heart; yet so that he cannot find out what God has done from the beginning to the end. (3:11)

God placed "eternity" into human hearts. Within our hearts, we can imagine "eternity," things beyond the limitations of the known world and the vanities of our transitory lives. We can "see" the past, present, and future. We can imagine other, better worlds. We can even "see" the wonders of heaven. Our God-given imagination adds zest to our limited daily experiences.

Imagination, however, is not comprehension. None of us fully understands what God has done, is doing, or will do. Human wisdom is based on human experiences, and God has not enabled us to see very far beyond the limitations of our physical eyesight. Eternity, while fascinating, remains one of life's uncertainties.

25

The Gifts of God

GIFTS OF DAILY JOY

THE IMPRESSION THAT MANY readers take away from Ecclesiastes is that the book is utterly pessimistic, even cynical in its conclusion that "everything is vanity." This impression of pessimism may seem justified by the majority of the content of the book, but it ignores the optimistic verses also found in Ecclesiastes. The references to joy sprinkled throughout the book counter the pessimism.

Daily pleasures, the little things that give us happiness, are a gift from God. Perhaps we want our happiness to come in big chunks, big things like success, wealth, large houses and fast cars, wine, women, and song. We often look for happiness we create through our own plans and efforts, when what we seek has been given to us at home.

The teacher repeatedly mentions eating and drinking as pleasures, especially when done with friends. Our job, our family, our friends are also gifts of God, intended to bring joy into our life. We just need contentment to enjoy these joys.

Your Job

> There is nothing better for a person than that he should eat and drink and find enjoyment in his toil. This also, I saw, is from

> the hand of God, for apart from him who can eat or who can have enjoyment? For to the one who pleases him God has given wisdom and knowledge and joy, but to the sinner he has given the business of gathering and collecting, only to give to one who pleases God. This also is vanity and a striving after wind. (2:24–26)

We have already seen that work, which the teacher called toil, is vanity (2:19). The antidote for the frustration of work is to enjoy it as a gift from God. It seems that God gives the ability to enjoy one's work to those who please him.

This theme of enjoying one's job as one of life's ordinary pleasures also appears in the following verses:

> I perceived that there is nothing better for them than to be joyful and to do good as long as they live; also that everyone should eat and drink and take pleasure in all his toil—this is God's gift to man. (3:12–13)

> So I saw that there is nothing better than that a man should rejoice in his work, for that is his lot. Who can bring him to see what will be after him? (3:22)

In other words, there will always be frustrations in life, so if you can enjoy your job, you are blessed!

Companionship

The teacher identifies another important source of joy in daily life: having a friend.

> Two are better than one, because they have a good reward for their toil. For if they fall, one will lift up his fellow. But woe to him who is alone when he falls and has not another to lift him up! Again, if two lie together, they keep warm, but how can one keep warm alone? And though a man might prevail against one who is alone, two will withstand him—a threefold cord is not quickly broken. (4:9–12)

Friends do more than hang out together, they share the load, pick each other up, keep each other warm, and have each other's back. The reference to a cord of three strands is probably a proverb referring to the added strength of a rope woven from several strands. Its meaning here is that friends give added strength to each other. The value of friendship is cooperation and mutual help.

There is one other companion the teacher recommends that we should each enjoy: our spouse.

> Enjoy life with the wife whom you love, all the days of your vain life that he has given you under the sun, because that is your portion in life and in your toil at which you toil under the sun. (9:9)

Contentment

The life God has allotted to each of us can bring happiness into our vain lives. Contentment brings happiness, but only if we accept the blessings God gives; we don't gain happiness by striving against our appointed lot in life—happiness comes from enjoying the life we have been given.

> Behold, what I have seen to be good and fitting is to eat and drink and find enjoyment in all the toil with which one toils under the sun the few days of his life that God has given him, for this is his lot. Everyone also to whom God has given wealth and possessions and power to enjoy them, and to accept his lot and rejoice in his toil—this is the gift of God. For he will not much remember the days of his life because God keeps him occupied with joy in his heart. (5:18–20)

The Hebrew word for "joy" means happiness, even great happiness, like at a wedding, or the first year of marriage, or a harvest celebration, or after a victory in war. It can include music, dancing, and stomping one's feet.[1] But the joy Ecclesiastes commends is not limited to exuberance, it also includes the quiet, pleasant times of enjoying ordinary things like food, drink, sleep, and friendship. These daily joys transform the vanity of life. Michael Grisanti commented that this is a primary lesson of Ecclesiastes:

> On the one hand, the Teacher (Qohelet) depicts human inability to master one's own destiny.... He seeks to convince humankind that God has arranged all things according to his own purposes. On the other hand, in addition to accepting God's wisdom and sovereignty and his own limitations, a person should enjoy . . .

---

1. Grisanti, "שמח," 1251–54.

> life as God gives it. . . . Enjoying what God provides and allows is integral to a life that is not dominated by vanity.²

In other words, there is much of our lives that we can't control, but whatever good things we have been given are intended to give us joy in the moment. To be content within each moment comes from trusting the God who allotted our times and our tasks. Joy, plus contentment and trusting God, is indeed a great gift!

IS TRAGEDY ALSO A GIFT OF GOD?

Not every story has a happy ending. What about the tragedies that also come in daily life? What about war, disease, famine, storms, floods, crime, corruption, prejudice, injustice, civil unrest, natural disasters, and accidents? What about my wife's cancer? And what about the teacher's pet peeve: death? Do suffering, tragedy, and death rob life of its joy and its meaning?

> In the day of prosperity be joyful, and in the day of adversity consider: God has made the one as well as the other, so that man may not find out anything that will be after him. (7:14)

God has scheduled the good times and the bad times in every life.

The poem "A Time for Everything" (3:1–8) lays out a list of contrasting life events that happen at some time or another to everyone:

> birth/death, planting/harvesting, killing/healing, tearing down / building up, crying/laughing, mourning/dancing, scattering stones / gathering stones, embracing/refraining, searching / ending the search, keeping/tossing, tearing/mending, silence/talking, love/hate, and war/peace.

This poem acknowledges that life is not all happiness. We might summarize the poem in just two words: happy/unhappy—in which "unhappy" includes a range of experiences from feeling sad to being crushed.

Did the teacher not care about tragedy? Why would he conclude his list of contrasting life events, half of which are negative, with a recommendation to "be joyful"? "I perceived that there is nothing better for them than to be joyful and to do good as long as they live" (3:12).

---

2. Grisanti, "שׂמח," 1253.

I don't think the teacher was trivializing the many real tragedies that happen in our lives. Elsewhere he acknowledges the reality of sorrow, trouble, injustice, and corruption, but his advice is to accept good and bad as both from God. He gives both gifts of joy and gifts of sorrow according to his plan; therefore, our only reasonable response is to accept both and to enjoy the moments of happiness along the way. The ability to find joy in the midst of sorrow, perhaps by sharing a meal with family and friends, may be the greatest gift of God.

We cannot escape tragedy. But we can learn to trust God in the midst of good times and bad times—even when we don't understand how the two fit together—because, as the teacher has told us, nobody can comprehend the scheme of things. Nor can we change them:

> I perceived that whatever God does endures forever; nothing can be added to it and nothing taken from it. God has done it so that people fear before him. (3:14)

Does this verse teach that God flexes his muscles so that we will be afraid of him? Here is a better translation of that verse:

> God acts, and men must stand in awe of him (3:14b).[3]

Whether we like our lives or not, whether we like God or not, we must acknowledge, as Job realized at the end of his book, that God alone is God, and therefore when he acts, however he acts, we must stand in awe of him. Our only reasonable choice in life is to let God be God.

Let me conclude with a story that may seem a trivial illustration of the points above: My wife, daughter, and I made a trip to Europe to visit our oldest daughter and her family who were stationed with the US Army in Germany. During that visit we made a short excursion to see the sights of Paris. We knew that we couldn't possibly see everything in three days so we made a rule that we would enjoy what we were able to see and not regret what we didn't have time to see. That acceptance of the limitations on our visit made the time we had very enjoyable.

The teacher said that all of life is like that.

---

3. Scott, *Ecclesiastes*, 221.

26

The Two Conclusions of Ecclesiastes

THERE ARE TWO VERY different endings to the teacher's research report about meaning in life. The two endings are so different that some commentators say they must have been written by different men. According to the two-author theory, the first ending, "all is vanity" (12:8), was written by the teacher—the author of the earlier chapters of Ecclesiastes. But the second ending, "fear and obey God" (12:13–14), was written later by an unknown author who disliked the first ending and wanted to give Ecclesiastes a more orthodox conclusion. The more traditional theory, the one-author theory, is that the teacher wrote both endings. In order to choose between the theories, let's consider the two endings.

THE FIRST CONCLUSION: ALL IS VANITY

The first ending (Eccl 12:8) wraps up the whole investigation and repeats almost word for word the opening statement: "Vanity of vanities, says the Preacher, vanity of vanities! All is vanity" (1:2). The parallel beginning and ending statements are like matching bookends, giving a sense of completeness to the teacher's investigation. The ending statement concludes all of the previous sections of the book, and it specifically concludes the final section of the book dealing with old age and the end of life. The conclusion describes dying:

> The dust returns to the earth as it was, and the spirit returns to God who gave it. Vanity of vanities, says the Preacher; all is vanity! (12:7–8)

In that final section (11:8—12:8) the teacher contrasts the pleasurable days of youth with the days of old age when pleasure is replaced by trouble:

> So if a person lives many years, let him rejoice in them all; but let him remember that the days of darkness will be many. All that comes is vanity. (11:8)

The teacher said that old age is vanity! That statement is addressed to young people and gives a mixed forecast of sunny days now but gloomy days ahead. The teacher encourages youth to enjoy their strength now while keeping in mind that all they do will be judged by God.

He encourages young people to remember two things: First, they should remember their Creator while they are young. "To remember" means "to live accordingly," to live each day in the light of God's presence. It would be a mistake for youth to postpone serving God until some later time after they have their fun.

But they should also remember that old age and death are coming, days of darkness and trouble in which they will not find pleasure. In 12:2–7 the teacher lists numerous infirmities typical of old age, including physical weakness, unsteadiness, loss of teeth, of sight, of hearing, of desire, fear of falling, all ending in death when "the dust returns to the earth" and "the spirit[1] returns to God" (12:2–7). Thus, for humans, each life ends as it started. There is a return to the beginning, just as there is for the sun, the wind, and the waters flowing to the sea (1:4–7). Even the book of Ecclesiastes ends by returning to the words with which it starts! Time is cyclical. Life is cyclical. Ecclesiastes is cyclical. The teacher's writings also fit the theme of begin, conclude, repeat. It all sounds very pessimistic.

That summation of every human life leads the teacher to his first ending: every human life—its dreams, its pleasures, its work, its accomplishments, and all of the big and little events along the way—are all just a breath, just a soap bubble, just vanity. This is the first conclusion of the teacher's investigation of life.

---

1. The Hebrew word translated "spirit" is literally "breath." Life happens when God breathes into a person the breath of life. Death happens when God withdraws his breath.

As we said above, some modern commentators believe that this pessimistic ending was the true ending of the book; the cycle was complete. They believe that the verses that follow this ending were added by a later writer trying to make the conclusion of Ecclesiastes more orthodox.[2] I, however, accept the traditional view that there was only one author and the second ending is the true ending of the book.

THE SECOND CONCLUSION: FEAR GOD AND OBEY HIM

Logically speaking, the second conclusion to the teacher's investigation is derived from the first conclusion: having looked critically at life and seen the many inconsistencies in all that happens; having seen that bad things happen to good people and vice versa; having seen that, however much any individual may have accomplished through wise planning and hard work, it is all wiped away by death; having seen that the future is uncertain and that time and chance can destroy all of our plans; and having seen that even for the wise—and he included himself among the wise—the meaning of life itself was incomprehensible making wisdom itself just another vanity; having established all of this evidence for his first conclusion, the teacher still held on to his faith in God! He believed that God plans each of our lives, though we will never know his plans. From God's perspective, everything is not vanity, but it is all purposeful. Therefore, the wisest course for any of us is to trust and obey him.

> The end of the matter; all has been heard. Fear God and keep his commandments, for this is the whole duty of man. For God will bring every deed into judgment, with every secret thing, whether good or evil. (12:13–14)

This is monotheism in a nutshell. In the study of the phrase "fear of the Lord" (ch. 7), we saw that "fear" means to submit to one who is higher in rank than oneself. But we should not understand "submit" in the negative sense of a soldier defeated in battle bowing in submission to a conqueror; rather, in a positive sense, it is a loyal citizen joyfully yielding to their awesome king. They submit because he is good and he is God. This is the primary implication of monotheism: God is trustworthy—therefore, let

---

2. Scott, *Ecclesiastes*, 256.

God be God. This alone provides lasting meaning for our lives. This alone cannot be labeled as vanity.

Some people scoff at monotheism. They reject the image of an invisible God who is all-seeing, all-knowing, and all-judging. They prefer to think that they are the master of their own lives and their own fate. God lets them make this mistake, but in the end, he will still be their God and their judge. We all will submit to him then. But Ecclesiastes teaches that allowing God to be my God *now* is the wise path.

The teacher's final conclusion is that to "fear God and keep his commandments" is the duty of all mankind ("this applies to every person" v. 13 NASB). This makes the teacher's investigation more than research about one man's life or about one ancient society. The teacher has spoken for God to the whole human race then and now: a meaningful life begins and ends in fearing and obeying God—or trusting and obeying.

It has been a long journey for the teacher to reach this most elementary and most profound of conclusions! And it is not vanity.

27

The Theology of Ecclesiastes

PROVERBS AND ECCLESIASTES BOTH describe God as sovereign over our lives but in very different ways. The theology of the book of Proverbs set forth a basic pattern by which the Lord guides and guards his people, giving wisdom to those who ask and approving or rejecting people's plans—man proposes but God disposes. The God of Proverbs operates from behind the scenes, but his ways are almost predictable.

The God of Ecclesiastes, however, is much further hidden from sight and much less predictable. He is just as involved in administering the world and he schedules the events of our lives, but his ways are deeper, much deeper—to the level of inscrutability. Therefore, the only wise path is to let him be God, and to trust and obey him.

We will consider the theology of Ecclesiastes in four categories: the vanity and unpredictability of life, the waywardness of humanity, the sovereignty of God, and God's judgment of every deed.

THE VANITY OF LIFE

"Everything is vanity!" A lifetime is but a breath. Events come in cycles that repeat. Generations come and go and are soon forgotten. The pleasures and accomplishments of life are shallow and short-lived.

Life is full of uncertainties. Ecclesiastes even allows for a category of bad luck—not meaning randomness but the reality that we often can't predict the outcomes of our efforts due to the many variables involved and due to the inscrutability of why God does what he does! Therefore, no one knows their future (7:14).

An apt description of every life is "naked to naked": we leave this world in the same condition as we arrived—full circle—whether we are righteous or wicked, religious or nonreligious, human or animal, we all will die, and we rarely know in advance when our time is up. Therefore, the teacher recommends that we attend as many funerals as possible (7:1–4) to keep our mortality in mind. It is a heavy burden placed on us by God (1:13).

The conclusion to the teacher's investigation of life is that there is no meaning apart from trusting God. Everything else is vanity.

THE WAYWARDNESS OF HUMANITY

As the teacher investigates everything, he observes that all people are sinners and many are fools! There may be a few upright individuals, a few wise ones, but generally people use the minds God gave them in stupid ways.

> So I turned my mind to understand, to investigate and to search out wisdom and the scheme of things and to understand the stupidity of wickedness and the madness of folly. (7:25 NIV)

> Also, the hearts of the children of man are full of evil, and madness is in their hearts while they live, and after that they go to the dead. (9:3)

We should note that the teacher's pessimistic description of humanity is not based on a theological presupposition of total depravity but on his observations of real people. He learned about human foolishness and wickedness by watching people in action. His words describe the condition of every human heart. A fool's talk starts with foolishness and ends with evil madness (10:12–13). The teacher contrasts folly and wisdom, and it seems to him that wisdom is less effective than folly:

> Wisdom is better than weapons of war, but one sinner destroys much good. (9:18)

> Dead flies make the perfumer's ointment give off a stench,
> so a little folly outweighs wisdom and honor. (10:1)

> Surely there is not a righteous man on earth who does good and never sins. (7:20)

Here is the conclusion to the teacher's investigation of the people he had observed: "See, this alone I found, that God made man upright, but they have sought out many schemes" (7:29).

The teacher's view of humanity is pessimistic. Though our waywardness is our fault based on choices we make, God allows us to do this as part of his plans.

THE SOVEREIGNTY OF GOD

> I perceived that whatever God does endures forever; nothing can be added to it and nothing taken from it. God has done it so that people fear before him. (3:14)

This verse lays the foundation for the book's ultimate conclusion: it is the duty of all mankind to fear and obey God (12:13). The only reasonable response to the vanity of life and the waywardness of people is to trust God. The book builds up to this conclusion in several ways:

The poem "A Time for Everything" (3:1–8) states that there is a proper time for each of life's experiences—birth, death, and all the events in between. God schedules these events for each of us. He has allotted us time and tasks. He has determined our good times and bad times (7:14), both in their proper season.

Is this a theology of fatalism? Is there no hope of avoiding tragedy, of improving one's life, or of achieving success? That is partially true. There are many things in life that can't be changed. In particular, God has fixed each person's day of death, and the only difference anyone can make is to rush this day of death by being foolish, to die before one's time (7:17). It seems we can shorten life but not lengthen it.

While there are limits to how much we can improve upon the life God has set for each of us, there is also freedom in how we each use the time we have been allotted. If we rebel against the limits God has set and pursue pleasures and profits, we may alter—but not improve—our vain lives. The teacher advocates contentment and the avoidance of extremes. And any attempt to outsmart God will fail.

> Consider the work of God:
> who can make straight what he has made crooked?

> In the day of prosperity be joyful, and in the day of adversity consider: God has made the one as well as the other, so that man may not find out anything that will be after him. (7:13–14)

> But all this I laid to heart, examining it all, how the righteous and the wise and their deeds are in the hand of God. Whether it is love or hate, man does not know; both are before him. (9:1)

Everyone lives in times of uncertainty with an unknown future. God alone knows the future.

But there is another side to God's sovereignty: in a world of vanity, God has given gifts of joy to make life worthwhile. There is the joy of ordinary pleasures: food and drink, a good night's sleep, time with friends and your spouse, and finding satisfaction in your job. The teacher concluded that the meaning of life is not found in pushing the limits, or in trying to overturn God's plans, but in contentment within the goodness of his plans.

GOD IS THE JUDGE

There is a second significant role that God plays in Ecclesiastes: he judges every person and every deed. Unlike the New Testament writers, the teacher did not push judgment off to a future judgment day after we die. The teacher was more concerned about justice in the here and now, happening within our daily lives. As we analyze this teaching, let me warn in advance, it is complicated.

First of all, the teacher was certain about one thing: God will judge everybody and their every deed:

> I said in my heart, God will judge the righteous and the wicked, for there is a time for every matter and for every work. (3:17)

> Rejoice, O young man, in your youth, and let your heart cheer you in the days of your youth. Walk in the ways of your heart and the sight of your eyes. But know that for all these things God will bring you into judgment. (11:9)

> For God will bring every deed into judgment, with every secret thing, whether good or evil. (12:14)

Second, God's judgments are a necessary corrective for the numerous injustices in our world. The teacher expected God's judgment to bring about a relative measure of justice. Therefore, things will go better if we fear God.

> Though a sinner does evil a hundred times and prolongs his life, yet I know that it will be well for those who fear God, because they fear before him. But it will not be well with the wicked, neither will he prolong his days like a shadow, because he does not fear before God. (8:12–13)

Things will be well for those who fear God, but for those who don't fear God it won't go well. Though the wicked commit hundreds of crimes, ultimately, they will be judged on whether or not they feared God. And their lives will end as God has determined.

We should fear God because he schedules the times of our lives. We should obey him because he judges the righteousness of our deeds—even our secret deeds. In spite of the injustices that spoil our plans, Ecclesiastes asserts that God's justice will ultimately prevail.

The inequalities of daily life that so bother us—rich vs. poor, health vs. suffering—these are mainly located in the areas of life the teacher identified as vanity (meaning they last no longer than a breath). Death, on the other hand, which he labeled as the greatest evil, comes to us all: it is the great equalizer. But the two areas of meaning the teacher identified, the enjoyment of daily pleasures and fearing God, are equally available to everyone. So, in the final analysis, life is fair.

As Scott said, Ecclesiastes is strange. As Yancey said, it is confusing. But the good news of Ecclesiastes is that nihilism doesn't win—ethical monotheism survives the teacher's rigorous investigation. Life has a purpose after all: one purpose that is the same for everyone.

28

The Wisdom of Ecclesiastes for Today

RECENTLY I TAUGHT A Sunday school class on the Bible's wisdom books. I was surprised that some members of the class, some who had enjoyed studying the other wisdom books, did not like Ecclesiastes. Perhaps they agreed with R. B. Y. Scott and Philip Yancey that the book is just too strange or confusing. Some disliked Ecclesiastes because they don't like Solomon who they thought came across in Ecclesiastes as a wealthy playboy. And they knew that he fell into idolatry in his later years. Perhaps some didn't like the book because its general assessment of life and of humanity seems so pessimistic. And one person objected that the book's conclusion that the whole duty of all mankind is to fear God and obey his commandments falls far short of the gospel's message of salvation by grace through faith.

I told the class that while I agreed with their concerns, I still love Ecclesiastes—sometimes in spite of their concerns, sometimes because of them. I don't see the book as pessimistic but as realistic. Its observations about life ring true to my experience; its tough questions are also my questions; its blunt assessment of the vanity of life is unquestionably true; and its final conclusion makes sense as the only possible response to the vanity of life. As I said earlier, Ecclesiastes is a book of pre-evangelism. While it does not tell the gospel story, it shows us that every other idol we may worship—wealth, health, pleasure, success, adventure, wisdom—provides at best temporary purpose and happiness. Thus, Ecclesiastes eliminates all the most common answers people give for why life is worth living, leaving the reader with no other option but to fear the Lord.

I believe that Christians today need the lessons taught in Ecclesiastes just as much as did the readers in Solomon's day.

Why should Christians who have the gospel of Jesus Christ bother to read Ecclesiastes—especially if they don't like its tough medicine? We should read it because it overthrows our idols, challenges our fixation on dying, deflates our so-called wisdom, and reminds us of our duty.

ECCLESIASTES OVERTHROWS OUR IDOLS

Maybe we don't think of ourselves as idolators. Most of us will never bow to an actual idol, a pagan image—as, unfortunately, Solomon did at the end of his life. But even before he did that, he fell into the playboy lifestyle with wine, women, and song, all of which are popular idols in contemporary society—even among Christians. We also have idols of success, sports, keeping up with the latest technology, and seeking political power. Ecclesiastes overturns all of these idols with a single word: Vanity! How tragic if at the end of one's life one hears this assessment of that life: "Vanity, vanity, all is vanity."

The book offers us an alternative to this vain lifestyle: contentment with the simple joys given by God. Enjoy the fulfilling times at work and the good times at home with family and friends. These are the real gifts God gives!

ECCLESIASTES CHALLENGES OUR OBSESSION WITH DYING—OR RATHER WITH NOT DYING

The emphasis in Ecclesiastes on death as a great evil surprised me. The poem, "A Time for Everything" (3:1–8), includes the time to die as a normal event—as normal as a time to be born. But the teacher seems obsessed with death—he protests against it as an injustice wrought by the hands of a sovereign God!

I wonder how many modern readers share his obsession with death. It seems that we are not so much obsessed with death as with the process of dying. Our goal seems to be to postpone death by prolonging dying. We have become very good at prolonging dying with miracle medicines, high-tech machines, and even robots who do delicate surgeries on and in our bodies—all at great expense.

What would the teacher have thought about our obsession? Obviously, he knew very little about human physiology, epidemiology, and modern medicine. Since he disliked death so strongly, perhaps he would have welcomed the advances in medical science as wisdom. But, more likely, he would have considered our obsession with prolonging dying as just another vanity. In the end, every person still faces the same destiny: "The dust returns to the earth as it was, and the spirit [breath] returns to God who gave it" (12:7). For all of us, there is a proper time to die. Contentment in life implies accepting that I will die.

I am not suggesting that we should stop fighting to live longer and just go gentle into the last good night, but, as we fight to live, we must keep in mind that for each of us there is a day set by God for our death (9:12). For rich and poor, righteous and wicked, wise and foolish, like it or not, death is everyone's destiny.

Danny Dutton, an eight-year-old from California, wrote an essay about God. In a child's simple words he expressed a lot of good theology. His essay ends, "I figure God put me here and he can take me back anytime he pleases."[1] My wife and I have accepted that simple truth as valid for us.

ECCLESIASTES DEFLATES OUR CLAIMS OF WISDOM

Our podcasts and social-media posts offer authoritative opinions on many topics. Perhaps sometimes the writers are experts, and we should pay attention; but often these pundits profess to know things nobody can know. Their so-called wisdom is really just another form of idolatry.

Such intellectual idolatry is also found within the Christian community. Our teachers, preachers and theologians often claim to know about things that neither they nor anyone else can know. (For example, their frequent claims to know when Christ will return.) The teacher says that he had set out to understand the scheme of things but found that it was too deep—it was beyond him. He also says that nobody can comprehend what God does or why he does it, and those who claim to know

---

1. Dutton, quoted by Campolo, "Let Me Tell You a Story," 2–3.

don't (8:17). I am still waiting to hear a sermon on God's reasons for current events in which the preacher concludes, "I really don't know." That would be wisdom!

For all who like to speculate about God's purposes and God's timings, a good motto is, "He has made everything beautiful in its time. Also, he has put eternity into man's heart; yet so that he cannot find out what God has done from the beginning to the end" (3:11). We should remember that imagination is not the same as comprehension.

MANKIND'S DUTY

By calling his conclusion (12:13–14) the whole duty of mankind, the teacher makes clear that to "fear God and keep his commandments" really is his final thought on the whole matter.

Why should we care what a writer three thousand years ago said is our duty? His conclusion lacks the New Testament emphases on God's love, mercy, joy, and a Savior. In Christian theology, the whole duty of mankind is to believe in Jesus as Savior and Lord. Can't we leave Ecclesiastes behind and move on to the New Testament gospel of salvation by grace through faith?

Before we jump to that conclusion, let us acknowledge that all three parts of the conclusion to Ecclesiastes—fear, obedience, and judgment—are reaffirmed in the New Testament. All three are part of the gospel of grace! Consider Phil 2:12, where Paul, the apostle of grace, says to the Philippian believers that they should work out their salvation with fear and trembling. That New Testament verse sounds similar to the teacher's conclusion.

But to view the conclusion to Ecclesiastes as being either old covenant or new covenant is to miss the point! Ecclesiastes takes us back further than either of those historical covenants. The conclusion of "fear God and obey him" is a purpose derived primarily from monotheism: God is God—and I am not God. The emphasis on obedience to God's commands places the book within the worldview of ethical monotheism. There is only one God who is good and expects his people to be good. And "this applies to everyone." This duty is for New Testament believers as well.

I realize that the teacher's idea that the greatest happiness comes from accepting our limitations as a gift from God has never been popular.

It wasn't in Solomon's day either; perhaps that is why he stressed it in writing Ecclesiastes. God's goodness and sovereignty are the basis of our contentment and happiness. But many/most still choose to push against the limitations on their lives, resulting in frustration.

It is still true that the sovereign God holds the times, the deeds, and the outcomes of our lives in his hands. Will we enjoy prosperity or face adversity? Will we face love or hate? We don't know. He knows. If we seek to overturn God's schedules and God's plans, we can only make things worse, not better. That is the vanity of it all. But if we accept the limitations of our allotted time and our allotted tasks, God will bless us with the ability to enjoy our portion of life. And accepting the life God has allotted for us is not vanity.

PART FIVE

Studies in the Book of Job

Saint Teresa of Avila (1515–82), a nun and religious mystic who was later canonized as a Catholic saint, could be very honest with God. On a rainy day she slipped and fell into the mud, whereupon she exclaimed to God, "If this is how you treat your friends, it is no wonder you have so few."[1]

We may laugh at St. Teresa's critique of how God treats his friends. Perhaps Job would have agreed with her! Her predicament of falling in the mud has a parallel in the book of Job. He exclaimed,

> God has cast me into the mire,
>   and I have become like dust and ashes. (30:19)

Job was just being honest and not trying to be humorous.

---

1. Father Horton, "Fauxtations."

29

A Drama in Five Acts

If God is in control, why can't I afford to get insurance for my car?
—A COLLEGE STUDENT[1]

THIS QUESTION MAY SEEM trivial compared to the bigger questions of life, yet it is a microcosm of some of the hardest questions anyone ever asks: If God is in control, why do bad things happen to good people? Or, more to the point, If God is in control, why do bad things happen to me?

This question gets asked in different forms throughout the Bible. Various scriptural answers are given to this question, but in no place is the question asked so directly or with such force as in the book of Job.

Why did I place this study in the book of Job in the third place among the Old Testament wisdom book studies? Job is the first of the three wisdom books in the order of our English Bibles, and it was probably the earliest of the three to be written, so why did I put it last in my Old Testament book studies? In my mind, there is a logical progression among the three books. In chapter 9 I suggested a summary statement for each of the wisdom books:

> Proverbs: Life is fair.
> Ecclesiastes: Life is not fair, but God is fair.
> Job: Maybe God is not fair.

[1]. This was asked by a student at the Christian college where I used to teach.

Proverbs is the foundational wisdom book upon which the others are based. It expresses an ideal picture of how life works, and it assumes that life is generally predictable and fair. Good people can expect good outcomes in life; bad people can expect bad outcomes. Wise people understand this and choose to live accordingly.

Ecclesiastes, however, questions the predictability of life. Bad things happen to good people and vice versa. Because God's ways are unknowable, not even the wise can comprehend them. Therefore wisdom has to adjust to the many uncertainties of life. But Ecclesiastes never questions whether God is in control or whether his ways are just. The book concludes that, for those who live in an uncertain world, the only wise response is to trust and obey God who is in control.

But the book of Job takes this uncertainty one step further. Job's life was indeed unfair—even God said so. So, Job had to wrestle with the conflict between the reality of his unfair life—which is a common reality for many people—and his faith that God was just and would always be fair to everyone. Throughout most of the book of Job, God's fairness is in question. In the first two chapters of the book, the reader learns that Job's faith is being tested. But throughout the book we learn that God is also on trial: Can he be trusted? And, strangely enough, wisdom is on trial as well: How does wisdom work when life doesn't make sense? The book of Job is complicated!

THE BIG QUESTIONS OF LIFE

The book of Job is about suffering. The man Job suffered in the extreme: physically, emotionally, and spiritually. The first question the book raises is, Why? Why does Job (or anyone else) suffer so much?

But that is not the hardest question in the book. The book is also about justice. Since human suffering is clearly not distributed equally among individuals, is it distributed at random or according to some plan? Why do some people suffer more than others? The book asks, Is suffering distributed fairly? Is it an injustice when good people experience the same (or worse) afflictions as bad people? And if there is no advantage for being good, then why be good?

There is an even harder follow-up question to those first two questions: What is God's role in determining who suffers and who doesn't? When a tornado destroys one house and skips over the neighbor's house, the neighbor thanks God for sparing him; so does that mean that the resident of the first house can blame God for not sparing him? If God is responsible when Job suffers more than his friends—and all the characters in the story of Job believed that God was responsible for Job's suffering—then the troubling question is, Why does God decide in favor of one and not the other? As St. Teresa asked, Why would God cause his friends to fall into the mud?

In the book of Job, there is another important question raised by Satan: What motivates human righteousness? Are "good" people motivated to do good just to gain God's blessings or to avoid sorrow? If this is the case, is righteousness just a quid pro quo arrangement between humans and God? Doesn't this prove that God is not good enough for people to love him just for who he is? Does God have to buy followers using health and wealth as bribes? Satan seemed to think so.

And the most important question, the one that greatly troubled Job is, Can God be trusted? Couldn't—shouldn't—God prevent needless suffering? Job reluctantly challenged God's competence to run the world and to administer people's lives.

Perhaps we have all heard those who deny God's existence using these difficult questions as proof that God is either too weak to prevent suffering or too uncaring to do so. Or these critics may conclude based on the suffering in the world that there is no God at all! Though Job wondered about these things, he never denied God's existence or his trustworthiness.

But there is one more unspoken question raised by the book's unknown writer: What does wisdom mean in the midst of a life crisis such as the one that confronted Job? What is wisdom when we ask why and get no answer? The book of Job does not answer the why question, but it does answer the question about the role of wisdom—it may be the most important answer given in the book. And, as we have seen in the other wisdom books, wisdom is not what we expect.

Our study of the book of Job will cause us to rethink our understanding of righteousness, of justice, of faith, of wisdom, and even our understanding of God. It is safe to say that Job's understanding of these five topics was very different at the end of his story than at the beginning.

In summary, the book of Job is about suffering, justice, guilt and innocence, and faith. But, more importantly, the book is about a man named Job and his relationship with his God.

THE MAN JOB

Centuries later, a man named Paul would suffer with an infirmity he called a "thorn in his flesh," and he would pray that God would remove it (2 Cor 12:7–9). God didn't. If Paul had a thorn, Job had a briar patch!

The book of Job reports the life experiences of Job. It also records the lengthy disagreements he had with his friends about the reasons for his suffering. The reality is that none of the human actors in this drama knew the truth about why Job was suffering. As far as we know, not even Job ever learned the real reason he suffered so much, but he did learn a much more important lesson about his faith: he learned what faith is, what wisdom is, when we don't know the answer to the question Why?

All we know about the man Job is found in the book that bears his name as well as in three brief references in Ezek 14 and Jas 5. He lived in the country of Uz, which is otherwise unknown. Uz was evidently located in the east (Job 1:3), perhaps to the southeast of Israel, but this is all speculation.

We know that Job had a wife; ten children, including seven sons; and that he was very wealthy, with many servants and large herds of livestock. He was one of the greatest men in his region. Job was also respected as a wise man, and when his life fell apart, the circle of his wise friends gathered to console and counsel him.

We know that Job left a legacy of personal righteousness and patience. In Ezek 14:14 and 20 he is listed as one of three righteous men: Noah, Daniel, and Job. In Jas 5:11 he is cited as an example of patience during times of suffering.

Job was indeed righteous to a scrupulous degree. He even offered sacrifices for sins his children might have committed that he didn't know about. God declared him to have integrity (1:1). While Job's friends thought that his suffering was due to an unknown flaw in his character or behavior, in reality his suffering was due to his perfect character and unshakable faith.

Ironically, it was Job's total faith in God that led him to challenge God when God seemed to behave out of character. One lesson we learn from the story of Job is that not only skeptics question, but those with unshakable faith may question God as well!

THE BOOK OF JOB

Unlike the other wisdom books, the book of Job is a story, a dramatized retelling of Job's story from beginning to end. The written version was probably based on oral traditions that eventually brought the story to the ears of an unknown writer who composed it as a drama. Perhaps not every speech in the drama is word for word, but the oral traditions preserved the main points of the story. The drama was written in the style of Hebrew poetry.

We don't know who wrote the book or when it was written. Perhaps it is better that we don't know the bibliographic details of the book because, if we knew them, they would cause us to focus on one individual and one incident and perhaps miss the universal significance of his story. The universality of the story of Job is reflected in its having been retold in numerous novels and plays, some of which are based explicitly on the book of Job and others which tell tragic stories that parallel Job's story. The frequent retelling of Job's story in art and in literature assures that his memory will last for generations.

I understand the book of Job as a drama in five acts. Many Bible books are a challenge to outline, but not Job. The plot line is obvious, and the main points are usually marked by the beginning and ending of speeches. Here is a brief outline:

1. Act 1: The Heavenly Perspective (chs. 1–2)

    Scenes 1–2: God and Satan discuss Job's righteousness

2. Act 2: The Earthly Perspective (chs. 3–27)

    Scene 1: Job's lament
    Scenes 2–4: Three cycles of speeches by Job's friends, along with Job's responses

3. Act 3: Closing Arguments from the Defense and the Prosecution (chs. 28–37)

    Scene 1: Interlude: a poem about wisdom
    Scene 2: Job's defense
    Scene 3: Elihu's accusations

4. Act 4: God Speaks to Job from a Windstorm (chs. 38—42:6)

    Scenes 1–2: God's two speeches and Job's responses

5. Act 5: God's Verdict and Consequences for Job and His Friends (42:7–17)

30

"Have You Considered My Servant Job?"

THE BOOK OF JOB is what literature teachers call a "dramatic irony," a story in which the reader knows what is going on but none of the characters do. The backstory that we learn in Job 1 and 2 is very important for readers because it enables us to understand how all the human characters in the drama consistently erred in their attempts to explain Job's sufferings. We know what they didn't know.

The book opens with a brief introduction to the man Job, his wealth, and the righteous way he has conducted his life. Then, without further explanation, readers are taken to heaven to witness two meetings between God and the sons of God (angels).

TWO MEETINGS IN HEAVEN

The First Meeting

The sons of God regularly report to God. Satan[1] also does this. In two of these heavenly meetings God brought up Job as a topic for discussion:

---

1. The Hebrew text calls Satan "the Satan," which indicates it is an official title, not a personal name. The Hebrew word means accuser, indicating the position this angel held. In Rev 12:10 he was called the one who accuses our brothers—meaning believers—before God. The NET Bible Job 1 n35 gives a more detailed explanation of the Hebrew word "adversary" translated as Satan, or the Satan.

> Have you considered my servant Job, that there is none like him on earth, a blameless and upright man, who fears God and turns away from evil? (Job 1:8)

In the first two chapters of the book of Job, we have God, the judge of all the earth (Gen 18:25), and Satan, the accuser of mankind (Rev 12:10), discussing one individual and actually being in agreement that this person was blameless and upright![2] Wouldn't God, who knows every heart, know better than to call Job (or anyone) perfect? And couldn't Satan, the accuser, have objected that Job was guilty of some sin, major or minor? But he didn't. Instead, he charged Job with a hypothetical offense (to curse God), which Job might commit under different circumstances. A person must have amazing integrity if the best that Satan can do is to charge him with a hypothetical sin!

At the beginning of this story, God was impressed with Job's integrity, and Satan wasn't. Satan charged that Job's consistent faith was based on self-interest. Job was good only because he had it so good, but if God would stop blessing him, Job would quickly turn against God. Job's heart was good only so long as God propped it up with goodies. Satan scoffed, If God would remove those props, Job's faith would crumble, and he would curse God to his face. So, God agreed to allow Satan to test Job's integrity, but he placed boundaries around this test: Satan could not use illness to test Job.

So, Satan arranged a series of catastrophic events: bandit raids and severe storms, which destroyed all of Job's livestock and took the lives of his servants and his children. He lost everything but his wife and his health. Job mourned this series of tragedies by tearing his clothes, shaving his head, and worshiping God—an amazing response!

> Naked I came from my mother's womb, and naked shall I return.
> The Lord gave, and the Lord has taken away; blessed be the name of the Lord. (1:21)

Job's viewpoint was that he had been born with nothing, he would die with nothing, and everything he possessed in between was a gift of the sovereign God. So the appropriate response when God blesses us or when God removes a blessing is to praise him.

> In all this, Job did not sin or charge God with wrong. (1:22)

---

2. The HCSB translates this phrase as "perfect integrity," a phrase we will often come back to as we proceed with Job's story.

The Second Meeting

God and Satan meet in heaven again, and, as before, God raises Job's righteousness for their discussion:

> Have you considered my servant Job, that there is none like him on earth, a blameless and upright man, who fears God and turns away from evil? He still holds fast his integrity, although you incited me against him to destroy him without reason. (2:3)[3]

This statement by God is crucial for our understanding of the remaining sections of Job's story: God acknowledges that what he had allowed to happen to Job was unjust! Job's friends will condemn him for saying that God had dealt unjustly with him—but that is what God had also said. In spite of this injustice, Job's faith had held firm.

Satan was ready with a quick retort:

> Skin for skin! All that a man has he will give for his life. But stretch out your hand and touch his bone and flesh, and he will curse you to your face. (2:4–5)

Once again, God consented for Satan to test Job, this time with a painful disease, but without taking his life. Satan afflicted Job with painful boils over his entire body. Job sat woefully in an ash heap, a place of mourning and moaning.

Job's wife said to him, "Do you still hold fast your integrity? Curse God and die!" (2:9). But Job replied, "Shall we receive good from God, and shall we not receive evil?" (2:10). Thus, he still did not sin.

Satan's goal was not simply to entice Job to sin. We can assume he had tempted Job before without success. His goal was to attack Job's integrity, to unmask the shallowness of his faith by getting him to curse God. As we proceed through the rest of Job's story, keep watch to see if he gives in and curses God.

TAKEAWAYS

Having seen the heavenly backstory, we now move on to the human drama consisting of a lengthy debate between Job and his friends as to why he suffered so greatly. But first, let's note the following takeaways from the meetings in heaven:

3. The HCSB translates "without reason" as "without just cause."

1. Job was innocent of wrongdoing.
2. Job's suffering was a test of his faith, not a punishment.
3. Satan believed he could destroy Job's faith by afflicting him with extreme loss and suffering. This included physical pain, social rejection, emotional distress, and spiritual disorientation—as God's actions no longer made sense.[4]
4. Satan's goal was to prove that Job's righteousness was motivated by self-interest—not by a heartfelt love for the Lord. Satan believed that Job would turn against God if his sheltered life was removed. As Job and his friends debate the causes for Job's suffering, the real question becomes whether Job's trust in God will survive Satan's assault. Will Job turn against God?
5. We are also being tested along with Job. He is our champion in this challenge. If his faith can be destroyed by suffering, then the faith of the rest of us, who lack his perfect integrity, can also be defeated.
6. God himself is being tested in this challenge. If Job only loves God for the blessings he receives, then God is not worthy to be loved for his good character. If Job fails his test by cursing God, then Satan proves God has to buy followers.

The deeper question in the book of Job is not about the reason for human suffering; it is not even about how an innocent man can be so falsely accused. Ultimately, the real question in the book of Job is, Will Job continue to trust God even when God appears to be untrustworthy? For thirty-six long chapters, God is silent. As far as Job is concerned, God's silence just adds to his misery.

---

4. Hartley, "Job," 782–83.

31

With Friends Like These...

IS IT POSSIBLE TO fact-check orthodoxy?

What happens when defenders of orthodoxy encounter a situation that doesn't fit their beliefs? Such confrontations occur frequently within religious circles—and to be fair, they also occur within any form of orthodoxy: scientific orthodoxy, academic orthodoxy, political orthodoxy, cultural orthodoxy, and in any social group in which one perspective has been accepted as truth and is therefore not subject to question. The typical result of an encounter between belief and experience is conflict and division. The defenders of orthodoxy don't like to be challenged with inconvenient facts! We currently see such ugly divisiveness happening all around us.

Such a conflict leads to the lengthy debate between Job and his "friends." At the beginning of their debate all five characters—Job, Eliphaz, Bildad, Zophar, and Elihu—agree on two orthodox doctrines: divine sovereignty and retribution justice. While God's sovereignty is never in question during their debate, Job's reality doesn't fit with the doctrine of retribution. Job declares that his personal experience is unjust—as God himself had said (2:3). Job struggles with understanding this injustice, but his "orthodox" friends insist on denying the facts rather than questioning their belief. So, the conflict between Job with his experience and the friends with their orthodoxy quickly turns ugly.

NINETEEN SPEECHES

As Job suffers, he sits alone in an ash heap. Three friends—Eliphaz, Bildad, and Zophar—come from their hometowns to comfort him. (A fourth friend, Elihu, also comes though he doesn't speak at first.). When they first see Job, the three friends are overwhelmed by the sight of him in such sickness and sorrow. They weep, tear their clothes, and throw dust on their heads. They sit silently on the ground alongside of Job for seven days. That silence is the best thing they say in the whole drama.

Job breaks the silence by lamenting the tragedy that his life has become. He wishes he had never been born. He just wants to die, but death won't come (Job 3).

The three friends initially express sympathy for Job, but then quickly switch to making harsh accusations against him. In a series of three cycles of speeches, they take turns stating that Job is to blame for his own suffering. He has sinned and needs to repent of his sin so that his good fortunes can be restored. In their minds, their accusations against Job are the "tough love" he needs to hear.

After each friend speaks, Job responds with a declaration of his innocence. He has not sinned—so he is clueless as to why God has sent such extreme sufferings upon him. It is unfair. Job raises examples of other apparent injustices in the world: the wicked often enjoy easy lives; his three friends are not suffering for their sins; and wild animals know that life is often unfair—thus, animals understand justice better than his friends do! Needless to say, Job's friends do not like him fact-checking them!

As the debate regarding Job's guilt or innocence continued, both sides become increasingly angry and begin casting personal insults against the other. Both sides claim that wisdom supports their viewpoint and that the other view lacks wisdom. After the three friends fail to convince Job to confess his alleged sin, Elihu, a relative youngster, attacks Job for the blasphemy of blaming God rather than himself.

Through nineteen speeches, neither Job nor his friends are able to discern the real reason why God allowed an innocent man to suffer so much. Rather than detailing the lengthy back-and-forth arguments between these supposedly wise men, here is a summary of the key points made by Job's friends. They said that Job was guilty of three sins: he had done something bad, he had concealed the first sin, and he blamed God for treating him unjustly.

First, they assert that Job's suffering is his own fault! His tragic losses and sickness are punishment he deserves for some sin or sins. Though they have no clue what his sin might be, their imaginations go wild in speculating what he must have done to deserve such suffering! As Eliphaz falsely accused Job,

> Is not your evil abundant?
>   There is no end to your iniquities.
> For you have exacted pledges of your brothers for nothing
>   and stripped the naked of their clothing.
> You have given no water to the weary to drink,
>   and you have withheld bread from the hungry.
> The man with power possessed the land,
>   and the favored man lived in it.
> You have sent widows away empty,
>   and the arms of the fatherless were crushed.
> Therefore snares are all around you,
>   and sudden terror overwhelms you,
> or darkness, so that you cannot see,
>   and a flood of water covers you. (22:5–11)

Eliphaz has no evidence that Job has done any of these awful things, but he "knows" that Job must have done something really bad.

Job's second sin is to conceal his first sin. In order to have his health and wealth restored he needs to acknowledge and repent of his sin. Confession is the hope of the sinner. As Zophar says,

> If you prepare your heart,
>   you will stretch out your hands toward him.
> If iniquity is in your hand, put it far away,
>   and let not injustice dwell in your tents.
> Surely then you will lift up your face without blemish;
>   you will be secure and will not fear. (11:13–15)

Zophar is offering hope to Job. If he would only repent, it is not too late; God will forgive and restore his reputation and his prosperity.

But Job will not repent; instead he accuses God of treating him unjustly. This was his third sin: blaming God for his suffering, the sin of blasphemy.

Elihu, the latecomer to the debate, accused Job of justifying himself rather than justifying God. God is sovereign and his reasons for bringing affliction into a person's life cannot be questioned. Like the other three friends, Elihu falsely accuses Job of sin. This quote by Elihu serves as a summary of all the accusations the friends made against Job:

> Far be it from God that he should do wickedness, and from the Almighty that he should do wrong. For according to the work of a man he will repay him, and according to his ways he will make it befall him. Of a truth, God will not do wickedly, and the Almighty will not pervert justice. (34:10–12)

Thus, Elihu upheld the doctrine of retribution as God's standard for justice. The fact that Job was suffering meant that God knew he had committed a sin. God would never punish the innocent!

Job's friends thought that there were only two possible options: either they could defend God's righteousness or they could defend Job's righteousness, but they couldn't do both. It never occurred to them that both God and Job could be righteous at the same time. But at the end of the book that was God's assessment. (We will deal with this paradoxical conclusion in ch. 35.)

HOW THE FOUR FRIENDS WENT WRONG

Shallow Orthodoxy

The friends' accusations sound orthodox. Many of their speeches contain good theology: praising God for his wisdom, knowledge, justice, almighty power, and compassion. Those statements are true—except that, in the case of Job, their orthodoxy led them to false conclusions.

Sulia Mason, a Liberian pastor and a wise friend, once described it this way: the friends had "Christmas card theology," pious words that sounded orthodox but lacked depth of understanding. They had put God into a rather small box labeled predictable and reasonable. But as chapters 1–2 and chapters 38–41 show, God is not small, nor is he defined by human expectations. I suspect that even the best theology will sometimes lead believers to false conclusions. This ought to teach all of us to be cautious in judging others.

But the friends did not view their theology as shallow. They saw themselves as righteous and wise, protectors of the faith, and counselors to a backslidden friend. Their theology was beyond question because it was grounded on the traditions taught by their ancestors. And Eliphaz based his views on words he had heard in a dream. In their view, Job was wrong to challenge their orthodoxy!

I expect that the unknown author of the book of Job wanted readers to squirm as they read the lengthy debate between Job and his friends. On the one hand, Job was supposed to be the good guy, but he talked like a bad guy, blaming God. On the other hand, though Job's friends were wrong to assert that Job had sinned and must repent, they defended their accusations with pious words and correct-sounding theology. So, to the reader, it is unclear who was right and who was wrong.

When I used to teach at a Bible College, I occasionally taught the Old Testament survey course. When we got to the book of Job, I wanted my students to squirm. I gave them a "spirituality quiz" using contrasting quotes in two columns and asked them to choose which column had quotes that were more spiritual.

The following chart contains the matched choices I gave to my students:

Column A	Column B
(1) "With God are wisdom and might; he has counsel and understanding" (12:13).	(1) "Behold, I go forward, but he [God] is not there; and backward, but I do not perceive him" (23:8).
(2) "Behold, God will not reject a blameless man, nor take the hand of evildoers" (8:20).	(2) "But when I hoped for good, evil came, and when I waited for light, darkness came" (30:26).
(3) "Agree with God, and be at peace; thereby good will come to you." (22:21)	(3) "It is all one; therefore I say, 'He [God] destroys both the blameless and the wicked'" (9:22).
(4) Repentant sinners will say, "I sinned and perverted what was right, and it was not repaid to me. He has redeemed my soul from going down into the pit, and my life shall look upon the light" (33:27–28).	(4) "As God lives, who has taken away my right, and the Almighty, who has made my soul bitter..." (27:2).

The quotes in the chart above seemingly represent piety vs. impiety, orthodoxy vs. heresy, and truth vs. error. But my students guessed that this quiz was a setup. As children of the postmodern era, they were accustomed to arguments challenging orthodox views, so they weren't surprised when I told them that column A contained quotes from Job's friends and column B contained quotes from Job. And in the end, God sided with Job and against the friends. God says to Eliphaz,

> My anger burns against you and against your two friends, for you have not spoken of me what is right, as my servant Job has. (42:7)

God said that the pious words and theologically correct arguments of the three friends were *not right*! God was not just referring to their false accusations against Job, but he said that they had spoken untruths about "me"—that is, about God himself. How can we understand that pious words in defense of God may be untrue? Where did Job's friends go wrong?

Faulty Logic

Assuming the friends' theology was correct (though it wasn't), that God's justice is solely based on retribution, then people should always get exactly what they deserve. Good people get health and wealth, and bad people suffer pain and poverty. Sin results in suffering. Righteousness earns blessings. This view of retribution theology is common in many of the world's religions.

But in the reasoning of the friends, the logic of retribution theology has been turned upside down. Instead of sin resulting in suffering, the friends argued that suffering was evidence of sin. It was backwards. The problem with this backwards logic is that it ignores other possible causes for suffering—as was the case for Job. But Job's friends did not consider the possibility Job's suffering might be due to any cause other than personal sin, so they wrongly accused him of sin.

Judgmentalism

All four of Job's friends judged Job as guilty of some secret sin. Of course, the readers of the book know that they are wrong, and God later confirms that their words are untrue. The friends' arguments illustrate how religious people often go wrong:

> Ignorance of the facts + bad theology + self-righteousness + a lack of sympathy = false judgment of others

Their judgment of Job was wrong. Job was innocent, and, ironically, they were not. Therefore, Job challenged their accusations by asking them why God wasn't punishing them for their sins. If retribution justice is God's sole standard for judgment, then all of us are guilty and we all should be suffering!

I will defend Job's friends in one way: I don't believe that they were malicious in their false accusations. They were sincerely trying to help Job, not hurt him. But their judgments made them feel superior—they made them feel "right" as they declared Job to be "wrong." Judging others, whether the judgment be true or false, often results in a feeling of self-righteousness and moral superiority.

The following section may help those of us who sometimes judge others to quit doing so.

JOB'S FRIENDS "R" US

I confess that self-righteous judgmentalism is sometimes present within me. Feeling superior to others based on judging them is a common human flaw. We may see it more easily in others, but if we are honest, many of us may also see it in ourselves. Perhaps this false sense of superiority is the primary motivation for people, including Christians, to judge others. But as James told the Christians of his day,

> There is only one lawgiver and judge, he who is able to save and to destroy. But who are you to judge your neighbor? (Jas 4:12)

The wisdom literature makes clear that God will judge every deed (Prov 15:3, 9; Eccl 12:14). As humanity's judge, God is able to balance love and justice—a balance we humans find difficult. God can see each person's heart, whereas we can only see outward behaviors. The narrative of Scripture is that God's mercy will ultimately triumph over justice, offering hope for us all.[1] God is the fair and merciful judge for each of us, but people are instructed not to judge.[2] As Jesus taught,

> Judge not, that you be not judged. For with the judgment you pronounce you will be judged, and with the measure you use it will be measured to you. (Matt 7:1–2)

In other words, if we judge others without mercy, as Job's friends did, we should not expect mercy when we are judged. This warning applies even if our judgment of others is true! Therefore, Jesus said, don't judge at all.

---

1. Chan et al., "רפא," 1171.

2. This is not to discount the need for a formal procedure for judging sin in the church (Matt 18:15–20), but the goal of such judgment is restoration, not condemnation.

Proverbs teaches justice balanced with fairness for all (Prov 2:9). Perhaps this is what Jesus intended when he gave the Golden Rule and the second great commandment (Matt 7:11; 22:37–40). Those who would cast the first stone against an adulterous sinner—or any sinner—should beware that they too are sinners.

Christians may make another error that Job's friends made. We can assume that our prosperity or good health are proof of God's blessing; or, like Job's friends, we might assume that someone's disease or financial reversal is proof of some unrepented sin in their life. Lynn Eib, the leader of a cancer support group, tells this true story about one member of her group:

> My friend Kristie expected to get some words of healing and blessing when she went to talk to her priest shortly after a diagnosis of breast cancer sent her reeling just before her fortieth birthday. She didn't get either. Her priest said, "You deserved this. You've done something wrong, something bad, and this is God's way of showing you that." He was adamant about it.[3]

Hopefully Kristie found a better counselor to give her encouragement based on good theology!

Like Kristie's priest, we might assume that poor people are poor because they deserve to be poor—something the Bible does not teach. I have heard Americans claim that our country is more prosperous because we are more righteous or that some other country is less prosperous due to its sinfulness—a serious misapplication of retribution theology.

I have even heard this kind of faulty logic being used to prove that Jesus could not have died on the cross! Muslims believe that God would not allow a righteous prophet to be humiliated and suffer, so they teach that God selected a look-alike to die on the cross instead of Jesus. Thus, they deny the reality of God's mercy in sending Jesus as the atoning sacrifice for humanity's sins. Tragically, their "orthodox" theology will lead them away from their only hope of salvation.

So, whether by making wrong judgments through shallow theology or by misinterpreting the ups and downs of the daily news, Christians can fall into the same kinds of judgmentalism as did Job's friends. And the outcome of such errors may be someday to hear God's verdict that we are speaking untruths about him.

---

3. Eib, *50 Days*, 131–32.

32

Job's Defense

JOB'S FINAL WORDS TO his friends showed how far apart they had become:

> As surely as God lives, who has denied me justice,
>   the Almighty, who has made my life bitter,
> as long as I have life within me,
>   the breath of God in my nostrils,
> my lips will not say anything wicked,
>   and my tongue will not utter lies.
> I will never admit you are in the right;
>   till I die, I will not deny my integrity.
> I will maintain my innocence and never let go of it;
>   my conscience will not reproach me as long as I live. (27:2–6 NIV)

Job asserted that if he did what his friends wanted and confessed to a nonexistent sin, that false confession would itself be a sin. Job never wavered in claiming his innocence and defending his integrity.

JOB'S FINAL DEFENSE

In Job 29–31 he gives his closing argument, asserting that he has lived as good a life as any person could. His conscience is clear.

Job recalls his former days (29:2–25) when God had been his friend, his children had gathered around him, he had enjoyed the comforts of wealth and the respect of all the townspeople, he had supported the poor and disabled, and rescued the innocent from the attacks of the wicked. He had lived like a king, surrounded by loyal subjects; and he had expected to enjoy this blessed life until he died. His present reality, however, is just the opposite (30:1–15). He is no longer revered as one of the best members of society; now he is ridiculed by everyone and mocked by social outcasts.

But what is worse than the attacks by his former friends is that God himself seems to have turned against him. Job cries out to God for help and hears silence in response. If Job had ignored others in their times of need, he might have deserved this, but this isn't the case. He had always helped others, but now he receives no help for himself.

> But when I hoped for good, evil came,
> and when I waited for light, darkness came. (30:26)

Evil and darkness are his present reality—the opposite of what he is accustomed to and what he deserves.

In his final defense of his righteousness (ch. 31), Job lists the sins he has *not* committed, an impressive degree of moral behavior that few if any can match! Job's acts of righteousness include:

- He did not look lustfully at other women (31:1).
- He did not cheat in his business practices (31:5).
- He did not wander off the good path, allow his thoughts to wander astray, or do anything impure (31:7).
- He did not commit adultery and betray his marriage vows (31:9–10).
- He did not ignore the complaints of his servants (31:13).
- He did not hold back from meeting the needs of the poor, the widow, or the orphan (31:16–21).
- He did not put confidence in gold or in wealth (31:24–25).
- He did not secretly worship idols, thus betraying his faith in God (31:26–27).
- He did not rejoice at misfortunes for his enemy or curse him (31:29–30).
- He did not allow his family or servants to go hungry (31:31).
- He did not withhold hospitality from the traveler (31:32).
- He did not cover up sins with lies or with silence (31:33–34).

- He did not fear the opinions of people (31:34).
- He did not allow the workers in his fields to go unpaid (31:38–39).

Now we know why Satan had not accused Job of any actual sin (ch. 1). Job is indeed a righteous man! This list of sins which he has *not* committed is matched with an equally impressive list of motivations for his righteousness. The reasons he always had done what is right are as follows:

- His integrity in the eyes of men and of God was important to him.
- He feared God and his judgment.
- In order to keep his heart pure, he disciplined himself to control his eyes, his hands, his steps, and his thoughts.
- He considered his servants, the poor and needy, and his enemies as equals, having been made by God, and therefore deserving of treatment equal to his own.
- He did not covet women or wealth.

Thus, Job's righteousness was inward as well as outward. This chapter has been called the highest statement of morality prior to the Sermon on the Mount.[1] A study of Job's righteousness in this chapter would be worthwhile for anyone wanting to live righteously.

Job's speeches have ended. He will give brief responses to God's speeches, but his self-defense is complete. Before we move on to God's response to Job, let us acknowledge that Job is caught in a trap. Like his friends, he has a narrow view of God's justice based on retribution; therefore his circumstances make no sense. In the next chapter we will explore how precarious his position is.

---

1. Hartley, "Job," 784.

33

Job's Paradox

"Do you think I care if Aslan dooms me to death?" said the King. "That would be nothing, nothing at all. Would it not be better to be dead than to have this horrible fear that Aslan has come and is not like the Aslan we have believed in and longed for? It is as if the sun rose and were a black sun."

"I know," said Jewel. "Or as if you drank water and it were dry water."

—C. S. Lewis, *The Last Battle*

This quote is from *The Last Battle*, the final book in C. S. Lewis's Narnia series. Tirian, the king of Narnia, faced a real paradox: Aslan (the lion who symbolically represents Christ), whom he had always believed to be good, was rumored to have reappeared and was reported to be evil. To King Tirian and his friend Jewel this was like finding the sun to be black or water to be dry.

For twenty-seven chapters of the book bearing his name, Job has been confronted by a black sun and dry water. The God he had always feared and faithfully served had seemingly turned against him. The divine justice he had taken for granted had failed him. And his plea for relief had been met with total silence. He had concluded, as did King Tirian in the quote above, that it would be better to die than to live in a reality that contradicted every good thing he had ever believed to be true.

Yes, Job suffered horribly and wanted the pain to end. Yes, he resented the false accusations leveled against him by his so-called friends. Yes, he protested his innocence in the face of circumstantial evidence of his guilt. But none of those things hurt him as much as waking to a black sun or drinking dry water. The good God in whom Job had always believed and longed for now seemed to be not good! Job's circumstances were evidence that God was the opposite of what Job had always believed. This was incomprehensible. What could Job do in the face of such a contradiction?

What can any of us do with such a contradiction? I am sure many people have faced similar paradoxes. What if we discover that a trusted friend has stabbed us in the back—"et tu, Brute?"[1] What if we discover that an organization for which we had long sacrificed, or a movement or religion or country to which we had given total allegiance, or, worst of all, if the view of reality in which we had lived our entire life was actually false—this would be shattering! This would create extreme cognitive dissonance, emotional collapse, PTSD, and loss of identity. It would be a form of death. But such contradictions do happen. Some may respond with denial—retreating into an irrational state of affirming their former so-called truth. Others may erupt in anger—renouncing the person or thing that had betrayed their trust. For a religious person, this may lead them into confirmed atheism. A few people may react to such dissonance by withdrawing into an emotional shell or by contemplating suicide. After all, as King Tirian said, after your identity has been lost, death may seem better than life.

Job was on the edge of such an abyss. He stared down into this darkness, but one thing restrained him from falling in: if only by a thread, he held onto his trust in God—though he wasn't sure why. Job faced a real paradox: God was both good and not good at the same time! To be more precise, the God who promises justice for everyone was being unjust to Job.

That is like saying the water is wet and dry at the same time. How would Job handle such a contradiction?

JOB'S DOWNWARD JOURNEY

Job's integrity was being tested. This required an extended period of continuous anguish. His physical suffering and emotional despair, combined

---

1. Shakespeare, *Julius Caesar*, 3.1.

with social rejection and the judgmental accusations of his friends and compounded by the unexpected silence of God, had all led Job to want to die. He went from wondering why to crying out, "Et tu, Yahweh?"

As we track Job's inner journey, which vacillated between anger and hope, we should remember that the single critical question on which Job was being tested was whether or not he would curse God.

Stage one: Job felt despair: he wanted to die (ch. 3). Who could blame him?

Stage two: Short of death, Job desired God to just leave him alone, let him die in peace. What is implicit in this request is that Job knew that his suffering was God's doing (9:24), and therefore God could and should undo it (7:17–21).

Stage three: Increasingly, Job became less concerned with ending his pain and more concerned with proving his innocence. Job had concluded that God must have judged him guilty of some sin, yet he knew he was innocent. Job vacillated between his conviction that God was just and would therefore acquit him (23:6–7) and his fear that God was unjust and would never acquit him (10:14).

Stage four: So, a new idea rose in Job's mind: he wanted to talk directly to God. Job became convinced that if he could meet God in court, he could present the case for his innocence, and God, because he is just, would acquit him. Even if God did not relieve his pain or deliver him from death, the one thing Job wanted most was vindication—for God to affirm his innocence and his integrity (23:2–7).

But Job faced three difficulties in carrying out his idea of a direct meeting with God. First, God was silent. He never responded to Job's pleas. This frustrated Job because he really wanted an answer. Second, he didn't know where to meet God. He couldn't find him. God didn't post a schedule of court dates that someone like Job could use to meet him (23:8–9; 24:1). Third, and this is crucial, Job would need a mediator to speak for him (9:33–35), and he didn't have one. Job would be on his own facing Almighty God!

Stage five: Eventually Job realized that there was only one possible mediator: God himself! Of course, it seems like a bad idea to go to court when your defender is also your prosecutor,[2] but that was Job's reality. It was the logical outcome of the paradox in which he found himself. Job was counting on the justice of God to affirm his innocence in his trial.

---

2. Job never said this, and numerous writers reject this possibility (see Chisholm, "רפא," 1220), but it seems that this was indeed his reality.

In fact, Job was already doing this: every time he had cried out for God to recognize his innocence and commute his sentence, Job had already appealed to God, his adversary, to be his defender.

There is *no stage six* at this point in Job's story. There is no resolution to Job's legal case and no answer to his questions. Eventually Job will get his wish of a response from God and he will be acquitted, but none of this would happen in the way Job anticipated. And things would get worse before that will happen.

JOB'S HOPE

As Job tried unsuccessfully to understand why he was suffering, he held on to one last shred of his faith: his hope in God to do what was right. But due to the severity of his pain and his losses, having hope was not easy.

> My days are swifter than a weaver's shuttle
> and come to their end without hope. (7:6)

Job's friends said that his only hope was repentance, but Job would not accept that path. As Job had vacillated on almost every aspect of his circumstances, he went back and forth on the possibility of hope. The most likely outcome of his sickness seemed to be death, which he saw as the end of hope. He did, however, still have the hope that at least he would die with his integrity intact (6:10).

Eventually, Job concluded his hope could only be realized if he had an advocate in heaven (16:19), a kinsman-redeemer who would take responsibility for his vindication. In one of the greatest expressions of faith in the Old Testament, Job declares,

> "For I know that my Redeemer lives,
>   and at the last he will stand upon the earth.
> And after my skin has been thus destroyed,
>   yet in my flesh[3] I shall see God,
> whom I shall see for myself,
>   and my eyes shall behold, and not another.
> My heart faints within me!" (19:25–27)

Job was confident that he did have a Redeemer, one who would defend him while he was still on earth. His heart yearned within him at the

---

3. The Hebrew in this verse is very difficult, and it is unclear if Job expected to meet his Redeemer before or after his death (see Chisholm, "בשר," 778).

prospect of meeting his Redeemer, whom he expected to be God! He would see God with his own eyes![4] He was excited at this prospect!

Though his hope of having a Redeemer did not resolve the paradox as to why a just God would treat him unjustly, the hope of meeting his Redeemer was sufficient for him to hold onto his integrity. He did not curse God.

---

4. I will let theologians explain how Job in his hope expected to see God with his own eyes—the God whom no one can see.

34

God Breaks His Silence

THERE IS A SIGNIFICANT contrast between Job's words right before God spoke to him and his words right afterwards. Before God spoke, Job proclaimed:

> Oh, that I had one to hear me!
>   (Here is my signature! Let the Almighty answer me!)
>   Oh, that I had the indictment written by my adversary.
> Surely I would carry it on my shoulder,
>   I would bind it on me as a crown;
> I would give him an account of all my steps;
>   like a prince, I would approach him." (31:35-37)

Job was rather cocky, approaching God "like a prince"! But after God had spoken, Job's self-confidence had completely disappeared:

> "I have uttered what I did not understand,
>   things too wonderful for me, which I did not know." (42:3)

> "I despise myself,
>   and repent in dust and ashes." (42:6)

Before and after—what a change! What happened to Job's cockiness? He had "seen" God.

In the previous chapter, we looked at Job's wonderful statement of hope (19:25-27) in which he longed for the day when he would see his Redeemer—that is, God. In chapters 38 through 41 his wish was fulfilled, but it was not the positive experience he had anticipated! It was eye-opening and transformative! Job became a changed man. Previously, Job had heard rumors of God, but now he had experienced God for himself (42:5), and this encounter transformed both his view of God and his view of himself. God was greater, far greater, than he had imagined.

If you or I wanted to see God, where would we go? Since God is an invisible spirit, theophanies (appearances of God) are rare. But the invisible God sometimes "appears" as fire, an earthquake, a burning bush, a dove, a loud voice, a still small voice, a dream, a vision of heaven, an angel, a human, and, as in Job's case, a voice from inside a whirlwind. It was life changing—even for one who was already a believer, like Job.

Job's transformation was not only due to what he saw but what he heard: God gave two speeches in response to Job's overconfident complaints. God broke his silence.

GOD'S SILENCE

For most of the book of Job (chs. 3–37), God was silent. It was up to Job and his friends to figure out on their own why he suffered. Of all the afflictions that Job endured, it was the silence of God that pained him the most. When his life was good, he took God's silent management of the events of his life for granted. This is the reality in which we all usually live. Most believers, I suspect, are like Job: when things are good, we accept God's silent administration of the universe and of our lives as a good thing. It is only when life falls apart that we question him.

Job's life fell apart, and he demanded that God explain himself. Most of all, Job wanted God to vindicate him. His suffering was not his own fault. Even if his circumstances didn't improve, Job insisted that God's declaration of his innocence would be enough.

But God had remained silent. Job misinterpreted this silence as further evidence of his injustice. The reader, as an outside observer, knows the real reason for God's silence: Job's sorrows, pain, and sickness were a test of his integrity. And, just as God did not give Abraham reassuring words as he led Isaac up the mountain to be sacrificed, so God could not prematurely reassure Job that everything was fine. Nor could he let Job's friends in on the reasons for his secrecy. The hardest test of one's faith has to be hard.

Another reason for God's silence is that his ways are inscrutable. Though we all might wish that God would be more transparent regarding his purposes and plans, the unanimous conclusion of the wisdom literature is that he is not. God is not obligated to tell us his motives or his purposes. And it is unlikely we would comprehend his reasons even if he did reveal them. Therefore, wisdom is not based on understanding but on trusting. Job eventually reached that point, but it wasn't an easy lesson to learn!

Job's final words—"I have uttered what I did not understand, things too wonderful for me, which I did not know"—speak for all of us when we are honest enough to admit that we don't know why God does what he does.

GOD'S FIRST SPEECH

God spoke, and Job's story immediately changed. The voice from the whirlwind did not reveal the reason for Job's suffering. It was not God's intent to explain himself—it rarely is. And God did not vindicate Job—at least not yet. In his first speech, God addressed Job's challenge regarding God's competence to administer the world. This speech was not the answer Job had expected, but it was the answer he needed to hear.

Contrary to Job's expectation that he would get to question God during this encounter, God did all the asking, and Job was going to have to answer (38:3). Perhaps Job was already regretting his request to meet God!

God spoke to Job as the "Lord" (*Yahweh*), using his covenant name. In the preceding chapters of the book when humans spoke about God, they called him by his formal name, "God" (*Elohim*). Now that God was speaking to Job "face-to-face," he used his personal name. He spoke to Job as a voice from a whirlwind, a "talking tornado." That experience would be terrifying and humbling enough, but God's questions took Job to task for his ignorant words:

Question #1: "Who is this that darkens counsel by words without knowledge?" (38:2)

Question #2: God asks, "Where were you when I laid the foundation of the earth? Tell me, if you have understanding." (38:4)

Question #3: "Who determined its measurements—surely you know!" (38:5a)

God sarcastically says, "You know, for you were born then; and the number of your days is great!" (38:21).

There was not a single question God asked that Job could answer. Even if Job had possessed advanced degrees in the study of cosmology, astronomy, meteorology, physics, and biology, he would still have had to acknowledge his ignorance. Did Job know where the snow, and hail, and wind, and rain, and lightning come from? Did Job know the path of the constellations across the sky? Did Job understand the behaviors of the many species of wild animals? Job did not.

Humans are prone to hubris. Like Job before God spoke, we express self-confidence that we can debate God and win. We think we know a lot about the universe and "the scheme of things," enough to challenge God. We boast of learning about distant galaxies, nebulae, black holes, and dying stars, but how much do we really understand of God's immense universe? I like to watch science programs. I learn a lot from the scientists who discuss their latest discoveries, but I am impressed how frequently these scientists honestly say, "We don't know the reason for that yet." This common admission confirms how much we still don't know about how the universe works. All of us, if we are honest, are aware there is much we don't know about what we know. And sometimes, like Job, we must be reminded of our ignorance.

In the middle of God's first lecture was a brief statement about innate wisdom:

> Who has put wisdom in the inward parts
> or given understanding to the mind? (38:36)[1]

In this lecture we learn that God gave wisdom to each species of animals—providing them with the species-specific knowledge they need to survive in their harsh environments. God asked Job, Who provides food for the lions or the ravens? Does Job understand the birthing times of mountain goats or deer? Who set the wild donkeys free or watches over the wild ox? Who made the ostrich to behave foolishly? Who made the

---

1. The Hebrew of Job 38:36 is difficult. Some versions (including the NIV) translate the verse as God giving wisdom to the *ibis* or rooster. Most translations say that God gave wisdom to the human mind. While either translation is possible in the context, I find the idea that God gives wisdom to humans as making God's point stronger.

horse so strong? Who made the hawks to soar and to nest on rocky crags? (See 38:37—39:30.) God gave every animal the wisdom to live in its own environment. He also gave this innate wisdom to his human creatures.

It is a great irony that we use this God-given wisdom to exalt ourselves and to criticize and challenge God! Job had done this, but his contentious words were words of ignorance.

> Shall a faultfinder contend with the Almighty?
> He who argues with God, let him answer it. (40:1–2)

To which Job replied:

> Behold, I am of small account; what shall I answer you?
> I lay my hand on my mouth.
> I have spoken once, and I will not answer;
> twice, but I will proceed no further. (40:3–5)

Job was embarrassed that he had tried to correct God's administration of the world.

Understanding How the World Works

One definition of wisdom is understanding how the world works so that one can choose the best course of action. Job was being given a crash course in how the world works. He was learning wisdom!

By this definition, no human is ever truly wise; only God knows how the world works. But Job had a different sort of wisdom, not based on his own knowledge but based on knowing the One who had that knowledge. To be wise, Job did not have to know how to administer a whole universe, but he did need to trust the One who does. Biblical wisdom is based on trust.

But there was a more important lesson for Job to learn: God has a plan for all he does. In God's wisdom, these natural events fit together: sunrise, sunset, darkness and light, rain, snow, wind, drought, hunting seasons and mating seasons, birth and death—there is a plan for nature, for animals, and for people. Human lives, including Job's sufferings, are all part of a greater plan of which Job had no clue. His suggestion that God had made a mistake in his case were words of ignorance.[2]

---

2. Theologians call God's plan "providence." He rules his world wisely. Qoheleth often referred to this plan in Ecclesiastes, and he also acknowledged that the details of that plan are unknown and unknowable (Eccl 8:17). The apostle Paul's writings mention

So, Job, having been humbled, acknowledged that his criticisms of God were based on ignorance. But God was not yet done questioning Job.

GOD'S SECOND SPEECH

God introduced his second speech as he had the first: "Get ready to answer me when I question you" (40:7). But this time God directly addressed Job's accusation that God was guilty of injustice:

> Would you really challenge my justice?
> Would you declare me guilty to justify yourself? (40:8 NIV)

We might wonder about what God was getting at in this lecture about justice. He spends half of his time talking about two powerful beasts, Behemoth and Leviathan, but what do wild animals have to do with justice?

In this second speech, God made two points regarding justice: First, to administer justice requires more than moral judgment. It takes strength! While "might" does not make "right," "right" requires "might" to support it. To humble the proud and to punish the wicked requires power. The battle for justice includes a battle to defeat the forces of evil. This requires more strength than any human can muster. Job complained about God's administration of justice, but Job's understanding of justice was superficial! He can't even save himself (41:10).

Behemoth (40:15–24) and Leviathan (41:1–10)—perhaps the hippopotamus and the crocodile, though this is uncertain—could not be captured or tamed by men. But God can and does control them. In the culture of that day people feared Behemoth and Leviathan as manifestations of evil (similar to the dragon in Western mythology). But the Almighty God can control the forces of evil. Here we have a declaration of God's victory in spiritual warfare. God is more powerful than anything that Satan, his adversary, might send to fight him. God is also much more powerful than any human-led rebellion against him or his moral rule. To bring justice requires moral judgment *and* might. God has both.

Second, God is always watching over all the creatures he has made. This, however, does not mean that life is easy for any of them. Life is rough for all. It seems that the entire creation has been subjected to futility (Rom 8:22–25) and is awaiting the day of redemption. But God watches and cares

---

a parallel plan to restore the kingdom of God and bring salvation and reconciliation to humankind through his Son (see ch. 40).

for all his creatures, great and small. As Jesus said, he knows about the sparrow that falls from the tree (Matt 10:29-31)—but he doesn't prevent it from falling! Life is rough for all his creatures, including humans, including Job. God knows and cares when his righteous servants, like Job, suffer.

We see in God's speeches that he is not an aloof God who has withdrawn from the world. The worldview of deism, which in its extreme forms viewed God as the clockmaker who made the clock, started it running, and then took his hands off, is wrong. The fact that God allows suffering for humans and animals, for the righteous and the unrighteous (Eccl 7:14-18), is not due to weakness or apathy. Job was reassured of God's competent rule, and of God's constant care, but he is still not told the reason for his suffering. Hard times, times of testing, are times for faith. Job could trust God without having to understand why he does whatever he does.

As Robin Wakely observes,

> It is clear from 42:1-6 that while the philosophical problem of innocent suffering has not been solved, it has been rendered superfluous and transfigured by the theological reality of the communion between God and humankind.[3]

The philosophical question as to why there is suffering hasn't been answered—not for Job then, not for us now. The question that Job and his friends argued about for so long was never resolved, but it was superseded by a deeper understanding of monotheism: God is both competent and good; therefore, let God be God. This is not fatalism but trust in our Redeemer.

So, as we noted at the start of this chapter, Job's concluding words show that he has learned his lesson:

> I have uttered what I did not understand,
>   things too wonderful for me, which I did not know. . . .
> Therefore I despise myself,
>   and repent in dust and ashes. (Job 42:3,6)

The test is over. Job repented, not because he understood why God allowed his suffering but because he understood that God is watching over all of creation in a caring way. God is not only competent to administer the whole universe, but he is intimately involved with each part of that universe: clouds, storms, lions, ostriches, sparrows, humans, and even Job. Therefore, Job can trust God.

---

3. Wakely, "הרר," 292.

35

Vindication!

GOOD NEWS: JOB PASSED the test!

There was only one question on this test: whether Job would curse God, and he never did. Even though he challenged God's wisdom and God's justice, he never stopped hoping that somehow the God he had always trusted would come through and vindicate his innocence. He continued to believe that God was good and just, even if it defied his immediate experience to say so.

But Job's innocence of sin and the integrity of his faith did not excuse the ignorant words he had spoken. His lack of understanding as to why God had allowed his pain and the calamities that had ruined his life had led him to question God's character. As he had vacillated in his efforts to understand God's reasons, Job used brash words that he came to know were based on his lack of understanding. So, he admitted his ignorance and repented.

GOD'S VERDICT

Job's vindication and repentance might have been a satisfactory end of his story, but God's justice was not yet satisfied. In an ironic twist, God also spoke to Eliphaz, defending Job and accusing the three friends:

> My anger burns against you and against your two friends, because you have not spoken of me what is right, as my servant Job has. (42:7)

According to God, Job, who had just repented for his ignorant words, had spoken what was right, while Eliphaz, Bildad, and Zophar, who gave pious speeches in defense of God's righteousness, had not spoken what was right! How can we understand this paradoxical verdict?

The easy explanation might be that Job never stopped trusting God, and the three friends repeatedly defended God's character with falsehoods. It was bad theology that led them to make false accusations against Job. But God did not accuse the three friends of telling falsehoods about Job but of telling falsehoods about himself! God was saying that their orthodox sounding words and hymns of praise were untrue. Evidently God preferred honest doubt to shallow piety—the kind of "Christmas card" piety illustrated by Job's friends.

In the case of Job's "honest doubt," I believe that God understood the paradox in which Job was trapped. Job believed that God shows justice to everyone, so he couldn't understand why God seemed to be unjust toward him. This "dry water" paradox required Job to believe two contradictory things at once: God is good; God isn't good. Job vacillated between those two opposing beliefs.

As Job wrestled with this paradox, he said some blasphemous things about the not-good god. But the not-good god did not actually exist. And, despite his difficult circumstances, Job still believed in the good God. His "words of ignorance" were never aimed at the true God but at the false god he had created in his mind. Fortunately, Job never moved from being troubled by this paradox to a loss of faith. Because of his integrity, Job held onto his faith in the good God in whom he had always believed. His questioning of his faith was not the same as denying it. He did not and would not curse God.

Like Job, we can also believe in the good God, even when we don't understand him. Therefore we can honestly question him. But we should never succumb to the error of turning him into a bad god. Job did not do that. We learn from Job that questioning faith does not mean denying faith. Therefore, God accepted his repentance and vindicated him for his unfailing faith.

The three friends, on the other hand, were caught on the flip side of the same paradox. They defended God as being just and therefore condemned

Job as sinful based on their incorrect theology. Ironically, as they defended God's justice with their pious words, they were actually blaspheming him, saying that God could not have committed an unjust act—though God himself had declared the treatment of Job to be unjust (2:3). True faith does not defend injustice in the name of piety! True faith asks Why? in the face of apparent injustice. Job's honest questions were a better expression of faith than the friends' simplistic "praise the Lord" theology.

Both Job and his friends needed to come to a bigger view of God. They had each placed God into a small box of their own design, and God doesn't fit into our man-made boxes! As Job said, he had heard rumors about God, but now that he saw the reality of God's true greatness, he repented of his ignorant words (42:5). Probably we could all benefit from a conversation with the God of the tornado!

RESTORATION

The remainder of the story involves the restoration of Job and his friends.

God instructed Eliphaz, Bildad, and Zophar to offer a burnt offering to atone for their sin. Then, in a case of total irony, Job would pray for their forgiveness. When they had done as instructed, the Lord accepted Job's prayer on their behalf.

God also restored Job's previous wealth, doubling his possessions. His relatives and friends returned to supporting him. God blessed Job with seven sons and three daughters, the same number as before, and his daughters were as beautiful as any women of the land. Job lived an additional 140 years, living to see his great-great-grandchildren before he died.

Some commentators have objected to this "happily ever after" ending to Job's story. They view it as unrealistic and as a betrayal of the values taught earlier in the book. I disagree. Job is a book about justice. At the beginning of the story, God said that Satan had incited God to destroy Job without just cause (2:3). In the end, the God of justice had to conclude this contest by restoring Job to his previous circumstances, which he himself had unjustly allowed to be taken away. Only then did the story have a satisfactory ending.

36

Wisdom in the Book of Job

Job is considered one of the wisdom books because it teaches about themes often associated with the wisdom literature: righteousness, justice, blessings, punishments, and God's role in administering the world. But one of the most common themes of the wisdom literature is almost missing from the book: teaching about wisdom itself. The book of Proverbs talks about wisdom in almost every chapter, extolling its excellence. Ecclesiastes also focuses on wisdom and identifies its strengths and weaknesses. But the book of Job does not teach about the topic of wisdom; it just assumes it—except for the poem in chapter 28.

THE CENTER OF THE BOOK

Job is a well-written book. The Hebrew poetry is beautiful. The storyline is perfectly balanced. It begins with Job as a successful, wealthy, respected, and righteous man. It ends with Job restored to his prior good fortune times two. In between those happy times is a prolonged tragedy of loss, pain, despair, and hopelessness.

The organization of the book is basically chronological, telling a story in the order it happened, except for an interlude, a poem about wisdom inserted in the middle.

The storyline might be diagrammed as follows:

(a) Job's prosperity / he intercedes for his children
  (b) God and Satan meet twice / they decide to test Job's integrity
    (c) Job's lament: he wishes to die
      (d) Job's friends accuse him of sin / Job defends himself
        (e) Interlude: An Ode to Wisdom
      (d') Job defends himself / Elihu accuses Job of blasphemy
    (c') God speaks twice / Job repents
  (b') God vindicates Job
(a') Job's prosperity is restored twofold / he intercedes for his friends

This literary structure is called reverse symmetry, or *chiasmus* (from the name for the Greek letter *chi*, written as X, the symmetrical letter). The reverse symmetry of the book of Job might not be worth noting except for the middle of the *X*: a poem about wisdom (ch. 28). Its location seems out of place. The poem is not part of the plot. It interrupts the flow of speeches, coming in between two lengthy speeches by Job. But its location at the crux of the *X* draws attention to its teaching.

An Ode to Wisdom

What does this poem teach us about wisdom? The poem is divided into three parts, which are separated by the refrain:

> But where shall wisdom be found?
>   And where is the place of understanding? (28:12; also in 28:20)

Part 1 of the poem (28:1–11) states that unlike precious metals miners can uncover by digging deep, nobody knows where to find wisdom. Part 2 states that wisdom is far more valuable than precious metals like gold, or coral, or pearls. Part 3 begins by summarizing that no living creature and even Sheol have no clue where to find wisdom. At that point v. 23 tells the reader that God—and only God—knows where to find wisdom:

> God understands the way to it,
>   and he knows its place.
> For he looks to the ends of the earth
>   and sees everything under the heavens.
> When he gave to the wind its weight
>   and apportioned the waters by measure,
> when he made a decree for the rain
>   and a way for the lightning of the thunder,

> then he saw it [that is, wisdom] and declared it;
> he established it and searched it out. (28:23–27)

God not only knows where to find wisdom, he carefully tested it to be sure it was worthy. Unlike humans for whom wisdom is the standard by which we are tested, God is the one who tests wisdom! But God still did not reveal the place where we could go to find wisdom. Wisdom is his domain, and we can only "find" it by seeking him:

> And he said to man,
> "Behold, the fear of the Lord, that is wisdom,
> and to turn away from evil is understanding." (28:28)

God revealed this much to mankind: the fear of the Lord is wisdom; turning from evil is understanding. We might claim to be smarter than this poem suggests; but in the end, the only path to wisdom is to fear the Lord and to shun evil. That is the truth about wisdom that the book of Job reveals.

Job had always had more wisdom than his four friends—not because he was smarter or his arguments were better, and not because he understood why he was suffering or why God allows suffering, but because he actually practiced wisdom in how he lived. God had described him as "a man who fears God and turns away from evil" to Satan (1:8). In his debate with his friends and in his dialogue with God, Job was ignorant and borderline blasphemous, but throughout his story, he is the only person to practice true wisdom. His integrity, which Satan had attacked, was actually evidence of his wisdom.

"THE ODE TO WISDOM" WITHIN THE WISDOM LITERATURE

The main point of this poem can be summarized as follows: God—and only God—knows where to find wisdom. Wisdom is his domain, and we can only "find" it by seeking him. This idea is entirely in line with statements about the inscrutability of God's plans we have seen in the other wisdom books:

> Trust in the Lord with all your heart,
> and do not lean on your own understanding.
> In all your ways acknowledge him,
> and he will make straight your paths.
> Be not wise in your own eyes;
> fear the Lord, and turn away from evil. (Prov 3:5–7)

> A man's steps are from the Lord;
> how then can man understand his way? (Prov 20:24)

> I have seen the business that God has given to the children of man to be busy with. He has made everything beautiful in its time. Also, he has put eternity into man's heart, yet so that he cannot find out what God has done from the beginning to the end. (Eccl 3:10–11)

> When I applied my heart to know wisdom, and to see the business that is done on earth, how neither day nor night do one's eyes see sleep, then I saw all the work of God, that man cannot find out the work that is done under the sun. However much man may toil in seeking, he will not find it out. Even though a wise man claims to know, he cannot find it out. (Eccl 8:16–17)

> "I have uttered what I did not understand,
> things too wonderful for me, which I did not know." (Job's repentance, Job 42:3)

> And he said to man,
> "Behold, the fear of the Lord, that is wisdom,
> and to turn away from evil is understanding." (Job 28:28)

The Old Testament wisdom books all assert that God alone is wise and that no person can understand his plans. Therefore, the only path to being wise is to "fear the Lord, and turn from evil" (Prov 3:7; see also 9:10; Ps 111:10; Eccl 12:13).

While humanity marvels at the brilliance of our scholars and officials—even Christians do this—these are often people who are wise in their own eyes (a.k.a. fools). Meanwhile the ones that God and the angels take note of are men and women like Job, people of integrity who don't rely on their own understanding but rely on the Lord.

37

The Wisdom of Job for Today

Job was not unique in suffering serious loss and pain. Many people suffer as much or more than Job did. The causes may be different—every suffering is unique—but all suffering is hard. As fellow sufferers, we can learn three lessons from Job's story.

LESSON ONE: HOW TO ENDURE SUFFERING

Job is an example of how to endure suffering. He may be remembered for his perseverance (Jas 5:11) and that is true if we look at the overall picture of his life. But in the immediate situation of his pain and loss, his emotions were all over the map! At times he was angry. At times he complained. At times he wanted to die. At times he cried out, "Why me?" and, "This isn't fair!" At times he wanted his friends to stop giving advice and become more sympathetic. At all times he prayed for a miracle. In other words, Job experienced the normal range of emotions for someone who is hurting. His experience shows us that it is okay for people to wrestle with those same feelings. Everyone will respond to pain or loss differently, but it is okay not to be patient all the time. God did not condemn Job for complaining or for asking honest questions.

LESSON TWO: HOW NOT TO COUNSEL SOMEONE EXPERIENCING PAIN OR LOSS

Job's friends are an example of how not to console someone in the midst of suffering. Job's friends needed to show more sympathy and to stop claiming to know why he was suffering. As it turned out, their theories about his suffering were totally wrong. And their "tough love" actually made his suffering worse.

I have heard stories of Christians who are dealing with a crisis or illness being counseled that they just need to have more faith. That theory states that God withholds his blessings until we have enough faith. Such advice is as harmful today as it was for Job in his day. Perhaps we all need to realize that the God who administers the whole universe, including watching over sparrows and Leviathan, knows what he is doing. We can trust him even if we don't understand his plans for our lives. But trusting him is not a magic key to deliverance from sorrow and sickness.

LESSON THREE: IT IS NORMAL NOT TO KNOW WHY WE SUFFER

One way in which Job's story was not unique was that he didn't know why he suffered. As far as we know, Job never learned the real reason for his suffering. This is normal. Many times, perhaps most times, people have no clue why they suffer. Their friends may make suggestions, but the truth is their friends don't know either.

The readers of the book of Job may have expected there to be an answer at the end as to why bad things happen to good people, but none was given. Even the wager between God and Satan was never explained to Job or his friends. As readers we do know about that wager, but it doesn't help us to understand why troubles happen to us. I think that the wager was a rare event and not very useful for the rest of us to understand our own suffering. The purpose of the book of Job is not to solve the problem of human suffering but to answer a more profound question: Can we trust God even when we don't know why bad things happen?

The answer to this profound question is yes, we can. The assurance God gave to Job in the lecture from the whirlwind was that he has a plan by which he governs this world. Job didn't need to know the details of God's plan in order to know that God can be trusted to rule the world with wisdom and with care—even when it didn't feel like care to him.

So, in conclusion, the book of Job shows us that bad things can and do happen to good people, and we rarely know the reasons why. But we can rest assured that God has a plan by which he governs his world. Though we don't know God's plan, we can trust him to watch over us and care for us.

In summary, the book of Job is about suffering, justice, innocence, motivation, and faith. But, more importantly, the book is about a man named Job and his relationship with God. Satan could shake Job's faith in God, but he could not destroy it. That is the happy ending to Job's sad story.

PART SIX

The New Testament: Redefining Wisdom

By turning one page in our Bibles, we go from one testament to the other. While much changed between the Old and New Testaments, the basic understanding of wisdom didn't change. As the apostle Paul wrote to the Christians in Rome,

> Oh, the depth of the riches and wisdom and knowledge of God!
> How unsearchable are his judgments and inscrutable his ways!
>
> "For who has known the mind of the Lord,
>   or who has been his counselor?"
> "Or who has given a gift to him
>   that he might be repaid?"
>
> For from him and through him and to him are all things. To him be glory forever! Amen. (Rom 11:33–36)

This quote of two Old Testament passages (Isa 40:13 and Job 41:11) is a summary of what we have learned about wisdom from the Old Testament, now applied in the New. God is still the all-wise God, and the wise still do not comprehend his ways. No one is wise enough to give him counsel. Paul, writing to the new Christians in Rome, wanted them to understand this basic truth about biblical wisdom.

However, though the basic understanding of biblical wisdom didn't change, the form it took was radically transformed in the New Testament, and the method of acquiring and using wisdom was updated.

38

The Turning Point in Biblical Wisdom

THE NEW TESTAMENT IS not totally new; it builds on the foundations laid in the Old Testament. The two testaments are part of one continuous story. Having said that, it is also true that the New Testament introduces drastic changes to the older understanding of history, theology, salvation, and wisdom. Almost every important part of Old Testament theology has been transformed in the New Testament. At the heart of this continuity and this discontinuity was the expectation and arrival of the Messiah.

The concept of a messiah developed from the ancient custom of anointing a man as a king or a priest. From this original usage the concept developed of God choosing and anointing selected persons to represent him and to serve his people. Such a chosen one could even be a gentile such as Cyrus, the king of Persia, whom God used to restore his people from exile back into the land of Israel (Isa 45:1). The concept of a God-chosen messiah eventually developed into an eschatological expectation of a coming messiah who would bring national greatness to Israel. In between those two messianic concepts—a historical leader and a future king—was an expectation of another King David.

The Jews believed that God repeats himself. They foresaw the great things he had done in the past being repeated in a bigger and better way. There would be a new exodus, a new covenant, a new law, a new prophet, a new king, a new kingdom, and even a new creation. This expectation included a future messiah, a new appointed leader who would be another

Adam, another Moses, and another David, rolled into one—but better this time. The messiah would rule with righteousness and justice and would bring salvation for God's people. Thus, the expected messiah illustrated both the continuity and discontinuity between the testaments. The messiah would connect the promise and the fulfillment.

This pattern of God repeating himself shaped the early Christians understanding of Jesus, their Messiah. He personally fulfilled the most important Old Testament themes: the embodiment of the Old Testament law, prophets, and wisdom. The man Jesus was incomparably the Messiah—except that he was not the upgraded King David in the way that many Jews of that day expected.

Regarding wisdom, the coming messiah was expected to be exceptionally wise. As Isaiah had prophesied,

> There shall come forth a shoot from the stump of Jesse,
>   and a branch from his roots shall bear fruit.
> And the Spirit of the Lord shall rest upon him,
>   the Spirit of wisdom and understanding,
>   the Spirit of counsel and might,
>   the Spirit of knowledge and the fear of the Lord.
> And his delight shall be in the fear of the Lord. (Isa 11:1–3a)

The promised messiah was described using seven phrases, each of which contained a wisdom word found within the wisdom literature: wisdom, understanding, knowledge, counsel, and the fear of the Lord. In other words, the prophesied messiah would be the fulfillment of the Old Testament wisdom writings.

Isaiah continued his description of the messiah's wisdom in the verses which follow the prophecy above:

> He shall not judge by what his eyes see,
>   or decide disputes by what his ears hear,
> but with righteousness he shall judge the poor,
>   and decide with equity for the meek of the earth;
> and he shall strike the earth with the rod of his mouth,
>   and with the breath of his lips he shall kill the wicked.
> Righteousness shall be the belt of his waist,
>   and faithfulness the belt of his loins. (11:3b–5)

Unlike most rulers, the messiah would not judge based on outer appearances, but in righteousness he would uphold the rights of the poor and overthrow the tyrants and the wicked of the earth. By governing with righteousness, the messiah would fulfill the understanding of wisdom found in the wisdom books.

We see these messianic expectations fulfilled in the life of Jesus. Quoting Isa 61:1–2, Jesus claimed his role as God's messianic servant, bringing God's peace and justice to mankind:

> The Spirit of the Lord is upon me,
>   because he has anointed me
>   to proclaim good news to the poor.
> He has sent me to proclaim liberty to the captives
>   and recovering of sight to the blind,
>   to set at liberty those who are oppressed,
>   to proclaim the year of the Lord's favor. (Luke 4:18–19)

To which Jesus added, "Today this Scripture has been fulfilled in your hearing" (4:21). The Messiah had come.

In the New Testament a new perspective on wisdom was revealed, a deeper understanding of wisdom than anything seen in the Old Testament. Wisdom was no longer just a better way of thinking leading to better character and better relationships—though that is still true—but New Testament wisdom is God's path to salvation and liberty for all. This new understanding of wisdom only became possible when the promised Messiah arrived.

First, the Messiah is the capstone of the Old Testament wisdom tradition. No one had lived or taught as wisely as Jesus did. And by his words and the example of his life he taught his followers how to live wisely.

Second, he is wisdom incarnate. In Jesus, wisdom is more than instructions in an intellectual skill—it is him, flesh and blood. He is God's *Logos* living among us. If we want to see wisdom, we look at Jesus.

And third, as the Messiah, Jesus is central to the fulfillment of the mystery of God—wisdom which had been hidden from earlier generations.

So, the messiah was expected to be wise, not in the ordinary sense of better-than-average human thinking but in the extraordinary sense of possessing the very wisdom of God! The arrival of the Messiah marked a significant turning point in biblical theology in general and in biblical wisdom in particular.

39

Wisdom Incarnate

IF WISDOM COULD TALK, what would she say?

> I, wisdom, dwell with prudence,
>   and I find knowledge and discretion.
> The fear of the Lord is hatred of evil.
> Pride and arrogance and the way of evil
>   and perverted speech I hate. (Prov 8:12–13)

This quote is taken from a speech by Lady Wisdom. This speech also includes a lengthy description of her role in God's creation of the world and concludes with an invitation to her readers to gain the Lord's blessing by seeking wisdom (8:35–36).

Lady Wisdom, of course, wasn't a real person. She was a personification—a literary device used by Solomon to teach young men the importance of seeking wisdom. In the New Testament this idea of wisdom personified is transformed into a reality: the Messiah is God's wisdom incarnated as a person with a name, Jesus. If we want to know what wisdom would say if wisdom could talk, we should read the gospels!

Jesus is wise, but we should see him as more than a precocious child, more than an apt teacher, and more than a smarter-than-anyone-else rabbi; he *is* wisdom. And his role as a wisdom-teacher was all according to God's previously undisclosed plan.

WISDOM INCARNATE

In this chapter we will examine the role of Messiah Jesus as the greatest wisdom teacher, as co-wise with the Father, as the embodiment of wisdom, and as the eternal *Logos*.

GREATER THAN SOLOMON

> The queen of the South will rise up at the judgment with this generation and condemn it, for she came from the ends of the earth to hear the wisdom of Solomon, and behold, something greater than Solomon is here. (Matt 12:42)

Jesus' claim to have wisdom greater than Solomon's is remarkable in view of the high regard in which Solomon's wisdom was held. Jesus did not question the wisdom of Solomon. He wasn't suggesting that the Queen of Sheba had been foolish to travel to hear Solomon teach. She was wise to seek out Solomon. Rather, Jesus said that by contrast with this gentile queen, the Jews of his generation were foolish because they rejected a teacher wiser than Solomon.

In the same passage (12:40–41) Jesus also claimed that his preaching is greater than that of Jonah, which had led the people of Nineveh to repent. Both of these comparisons exalt Jesus and his teaching. In both sayings, Jesus used foreigners as examples of people who were more responsive to God's message than were the Jewish leaders of his day.

Jesus as Wisdom Teacher

Jesus' wisdom was recognized early in his life. As the boy Jesus grew physically, he also grew in wisdom (Luke 2:40, 52). At age twelve, he was recognized by the temple scholars for his insight into the Scripture (2:47). When he grew up, he assumed the role of a traveling rabbi, and his teaching astonished—and offended—the people of his hometown:

> On the Sabbath he began to teach in the synagogue, and many who heard him were astonished, saying "Where did this man get these things? What is the wisdom given to him? How are such mighty works done by his hands? Is not this the carpenter, the son of Mary and brother of James and Joses and Judas and Simon? And are not his sisters here with us?" And they took offense at him. (Mark 6:2–3)

Even today, two thousand years later, the teachings of Jesus are still astonishing—and still offensive—to many readers. One mark of real wisdom is that it ages well.

Examples of Jesus' wisdom are found in the answers he gave to the questions posed by the Pharisees and other Jewish leaders: the request for a sign (Matt 16:1–4), the question of following traditions (Matt 15:1–9), the question regarding grounds for divorce (Matt 19:3–9), the question of gaining eternal life (Matt 19:21–22; Luke 10:25–37), the question of the resurrection (Matt 22:23–33), the question of the chief commandment (22:34–40), and the question of the lineage of the messiah (Matt 22:41–46). After Jesus answered their test questions well, they stopped testing him.

Many of the topics that Jesus taught about were the topics discussed in the wisdom literature: righteousness and justice, honesty and humility, generosity and love; but he also introduced new topics: the kingdom of God, his second coming, and the end of the age.

In the first chapter of this book, wisdom was defined as "truth applied to life," the link between theory and practice. Jesus' teaching exemplified this definition. He taught the "things of God," truths which no one else knew, and he made them practical. His teaching was another example of "religion in street clothes." And his teachings were not just practical, they were moral, applying the three key virtues from Proverbs: righteousness, justice, and fairness (Prov 1:3) to daily life. Jesus explained morality with such clarity and insight that teachers and preachers still turn to his words to understand what God values and what he expects of us.

Jesus' example as a wisdom teacher was not just what he taught but how he taught. He used the instructional methods mentioned in the book of Proverbs: proverbs, parables, and poetic sayings.[1] The common people loved to listen to him teach.

In a world filled with good teachers, to be a wisdom teacher requires more than insight and good methodology. What Proverbs identified as most important in wisdom is character. The following character traits of the wise were listed in chapter 13: humble, teachable, prudent, a person of integrity, honest, kind, generous (especially to the poor), respectful of the rights of others as equals, keeps confidences, self-controlled, faithful, moral, associates with the wise, and fears the Lord.

---

1. Examples of Jesus' teaching methods can be found in Luke 4:23; 6:20–26, 43–45; 7:32; 10:30–37.

Jesus displayed these character traits. He was the role model for wisdom. One way in which Jesus surpassed Solomon as a wisdom teacher was that he walked the talk. His life was consistent with his teachings.

As we shall see in our study of the book of James (ch. 42), James divided wisdom into two opposing camps: heavenly wisdom and earthly wisdom. He summarized the character of those who possess heavenly wisdom as displaying a "good life"—that is, "deeds done in the humility that comes from wisdom" (Jas 3:13). It has been suggested that James gained this perspective on wisdom by watching his brother Jesus. If this suggestion is correct, then James was telling prospective Christian teachers that, to be wise, they should be wise in the ways that Jesus was wise: through good deeds done with humility.

Isaiah had described the coming messiah as having the spirit of the Lord, including the spirit of wisdom and knowledge (Isa 11:2). At the end of his ministry Jesus acknowledged his role as Messiah (Mark 14:61–62), but his earlier self-identification as a wisdom teacher "greater than Solomon" already implied that he was the expected Messiah.

CO-WISE WITH GOD

Inherent in the worldview of monotheism is the belief that wisdom is God's domain. The consensus of the Old Testament wisdom writers is that God's wisdom was unknown and seemingly unknowable to humanity. The book of Proverbs portrays anyone who considers themself wise to be a fool. The "Ode to Wisdom" (Job 28) describes wisdom as being so inaccessible that no human, animal, or even the grave knows where to find it—only God knows and he isn't revealing it. And the assessment of Ecclesiastes is that even the wisest of men, even Solomon himself, couldn't comprehend what God is doing in his world. The only way for anyone to become wise is to trust in the all-wise God.

Now contrast that pessimistic view of human wisdom with this prayer by Jesus:

> I thank you, Father, Lord of heaven and earth, that you have hidden these things from the wise and understanding and revealed them to little children; yes, Father, for such was your gracious will. All things have been handed over to me by my Father, and no one knows the Son except the Father, and no one knows the Father except the Son and anyone to whom the Son chooses to reveal him. (Matt 11:25–27)

In this prayer Jesus made two amazing claims about his knowledge and wisdom.

First, Jesus claimed that he knew his Father in a unique way. His personal knowledge of God and of the things of God—meaning the truths of the kingdom—was greater than that of the educated theologians of his day. He claimed that he alone knew (understood) the Father, just as only the Father knew (understood) who he was. Jesus was saying that his knowledge and the Father's knowledge were intertwined. They were co-wise! So, the pessimistic view that God's wisdom was inaccessible did not apply to Jesus. He knew God and the things of God.

Jesus' second claim was his role in revealing God's wisdom to humanity. God's wisdom could only be received by revelation, either from the Father or the Son. Jesus claimed to have the key role in fulfilling God's plan to reveal the things of God to mankind. According to this plan, the truth of God's kingdom was intentionally hidden from the so-called wise men and instead revealed to "little children." What does this mean?

The reference to "little children" (or "infants") has two possible senses: either humility or faith. First, it could mean that Jesus' teaching was meant for those with the humility of a child. Without such humility, no one can enter God's kingdom (Matt 19:13–15; Luke 18:15–17). But the other possible sense is that wisdom cannot be gained through schooling or the intellect, but only by revelation, which is received by faith. And even a child can have faith. A child may be wiser than a scholar! It is no wonder that the theologians of Jesus' day took offense at such a claim.

In another passage Jesus described how God's plan to reveal wisdom had included sending prophets and apostles as his messengers to the people:

> Therefore also, the Wisdom of God said, "I will send them prophets and apostles, some of whom they will kill and persecute," so that the blood of all the prophets, shed from the foundation of the world, may be charged against this generation. (Luke 11:49–50)

According to God's wisdom, his plan from the very beginning was that his truth would be revealed first by prophets and then by his Son, and that this plan included this message and the messengers being rejected by the Jewish officials (John 1:11). Sadly, those who were the most steeped in the wisdom teachings of Solomon and the other wisdom writers were least responsive to the wisdom of the One who was greater than Solomon. So,

Jesus gave this message to those who, like young children, would receive it with humility and faith.

As the Old Testament wisdom writers had suggested, real wisdom is about hearts, not smarts. Not that smarts are bad, but intellect often leads people to become wise in their own eyes, which leads them to reject the wisdom that Jesus brought.

Jesus' Gracious Invitation

How would we react if we met King Solomon or the apostle Peter or Paul? Would we be so intimidated by these great men that we would be speechless. What if we were to meet the One who is greater than Solomon, Peter, or Paul, who is in fact co-wise with God? That would be even more intimidating! Would Jesus lay down the law about our wayward lives? That is not how he himself described such a meeting: it begins with an invitation, a gentle invitation, to follow him and to find rest:

> Come to me, all who labor and are heavy laden, and I will give you rest. Take my yoke upon you and learn from me, for I am gentle and lowly in heart, and you will find rest for your souls. For my yoke is easy, and my burden is light. (Matt 11:28–30)

A yoke is a crosspiece placed over the necks of two animals so that they work together as a team. Or, a yoke can be a beam placed over the shoulders of a person enabling them to carry two heavy pails. Jesus' reference to a yoke was a metaphor about the heavy burden placed on people who try to fulfill the Jewish law. Living as a good Jew was difficult! But Jesus described himself as gentle and lowly, and the burden of following him was easy. Jesus offered rest not labor. A Sabbath rest had always been a key part of God's plan for his people. Once a generation the law required a year-long Jubilee rest. Now, the Messiah offered God's continual rest to all who would follow him.

The Messiah was not a harsh teacher; he offered rest based on truth, humility, and childlike faith.

WISDOM INCARNATE

The New Testament understanding of the role of Jesus is much more than a wisdom teacher or the revealer of the hidden things of God, Jesus was wisdom personified. He saw himself as the personal embodiment of the Old Testament law, prophets, and wisdom. As R. T. France wrote,

> [Jesus] saw his ministry as fulfilling not only the explicit predictions of the OT, but the whole pattern of God's working in the history of Israel which it records....
>
> The coming of Jesus thus introduces, according to his own teaching, a new era. The many centuries of expectation now give way to fulfilment.... Not simply a *repetition* of the previous patterns of God's working, but as their *climax*.[2]

The New Testament writers saw Jesus as the second Adam, the new exodus, the predicted prophet, the lawgiver like Moses but greater, the new King David but greater, a new Sabbath rest, a new priesthood, and the new Israel. Jesus did not just obey the law, he fulfilled it and introduced a new law. And he did not just cite wisdom teachings from the Old Testament; his wisdom was not just proverbs or principles learned from others; rather, it was an expression of his own knowledge and divine character: he was God's Wisdom incarnate!

In the Old Testament God's wisdom was revealed in verbal form. In the New Testament God's Wisdom is present in flesh and blood: alive, acting, and teaching. Jesus was Wisdom alive. Jesus knew God's wisdom and his teaching ministry—including its rejection by Jewish leaders and teachers—was according to God's plan. Clearly, someone greater than Solomon was present in Jesus!

Earlier in this book (chs. 8 and 13) are instructions about how to become wise. Knowing that Jesus was/is Wisdom incarnate expands those preliminary lessons to include a relationship with Jesus as a significant part of gaining wisdom. Those lessons spoke of the fear of the Lord as the beginning of wisdom and the Holy Spirit's role in gifting wisdom, and now we must add receiving Jesus' teachings with childlike humility to complete the picture of becoming wise.

This gives us a trinitarian view of acquiring wisdom: the Father, the Spirit, and the Son all give wisdom in their own way. But Jesus, by being Wisdom visible in the flesh, gives us the clearest picture of how to live wisely on a daily basis. To be wise, live like Jesus!

---

2. France, "Jesus Christ," 572.

THE LOGOS

The four Gospels primarily focus on Jesus' biography: his words and his works; they present the historical record of his life and ministry as the core of the gospel message. But the opening words of the Fourth Gospel are metaphysical, not biographical. They reveal a profound theological introduction to the gospel by telling the reader who Jesus was before he was Jesus:

> In the beginning was the Word, and the Word was with God, and the Word was God. He was in the beginning with God. All things were made through him, and without him was not anything made that was made. In him was life, and the life was the light of men. The light shines in the darkness, and the darkness has not overcome it. (John 1:1–5)

To Jewish readers these words would remind them of Gen 1 and God's act of creation. Just by speaking, God brought form to formlessness, matter to emptiness, and called light out of darkness. But Jewish readers would have been uncertain about the meaning of "the *Logos*." Who was this Word who was there in the beginning with God and who was the Creator of everything? John revealed the answer to that question at the end of this passage:

> And the Word became flesh and dwelt among us, and we have seen his glory, glory as of the only Son from the Father, full of grace and truth. (1:14)

This mysterious "Word," this Creator of all and giver of life and light, was the Son of the Father, and he had actually been born as a human and lived among us. And, John tells us, the first person to recognize him in his human appearance was John the Baptist who declared,

> Behold the Lamb of God who takes away the sin of the world! (1:29)

So, the Word was not only the Creator, and the divine Son, but he was the Lamb, God's provision of an atoning sacrifice for the whole world.

This opening passage links the beginning to the present, providing the reader with a glimpse of eternal truth and of hope. And though this passage never names this person, it tells us his name in his preexistent life: the *Logos*.

John's use of *Logos* for Jesus has both Greek and Hebrew roots.[3] Greek philosophers had used *logos* to refer to a preexisting rational principle that created the world. Before creation when everything was in an unstable flux, the logos-principle brought about order and drew the world into existence. This rational principle continues to bring order to the world by moral instruction. And the human mind, our rationality, reflects the *logos* within us. The Greek *logos* is impersonal—a view that makes sense within their worldview in which truth exists as abstract ideas.

The Hebrew use of "word" was very different. The "word of God" is God speaking. It is an act of communication, but unlike our words which have no inherent power, God's words are powerful and effective in making things happen. In Gen 1 creation happens because God speaks. He continues to speak through prophets, angels, audible voices, and even through a donkey. The Hebrew "word" is not an abstract principle; it is communication from God, "Thus saith the Lord," and an act of God (Heb 4:12).

For John to call Jesus the Word draws upon both of these roots. Greeks might think of Jesus as the preexisting one who brought order out of chaos. Jews might think of Jesus as the primary means of God's communication to mankind. Both usages connect Jesus to a previous idea of wisdom, but neither fully express all that John meant by Word.

The Gospel of John begins, "In the beginning was the Word" (John 1:1). This Word was both "with God" and "was God" (1:1). This enigmatic description of the Word is suggestive of the trinitarian view of God that would develop as Christians tried to make sense of who Jesus is. Jesus is God; he is everything that God is, and paradoxically he is simultaneously alongside of God, the Son alongside the Father. This Word is neither an abstract principle nor a verbal utterance, it is a divine person who took on human form and flesh in order to live among us (John 1:14; Phil 2:6–8).

"All things were made through him" (John 1:3). Jesus, a baby born to a peasant girl in Bethlehem, is the incarnate Creator of the heavens and the earth (Col 1:15–16). These *Logos* verses link the man Jesus with the act of creation, which was an act of God's wisdom (Prov 3:19–20; 8:22–31). Jesus knew God's wisdom because he had been with him in the beginning.

---

3. Ladd, *Theology*, 237–43.

If wisdom is the capstone of the divine attributes (ch. 6), then the title *Logos* is the capstone of Jesus' identity as well. It speaks of his divine wisdom. We have not fully understood who Jesus was/is until we understand him as the eternal *Logos*.

As we shall see in the next chapter, in his letters to the churches, the apostle Paul took these ideas about Jesus the Messiah and ran with them.

40

God's Mysteries Revealed

WISDOM AND MYSTERY

When I hear the word "mystery," I usually think of a story about crimes to be solved by a detective like Sherlock Holmes or Monk or one of the dozens of other smarter-than-average sleuths in novels or TV shows. When I hear mystery, I don't think of Jesus Christ, but that is who the apostle Paul thought of: "God's mystery, which is Christ" (Col 2:2). When Paul used the word "mystery," he was talking about God's hidden wisdom now revealed in Christ.

The biblical use of the word "mystery" is quite different from both its ancient use and its modern use. The common meaning of "mystery" today is a riddle to be solved. In New Testament times, however, a common use of the word "mystery" referred to mystical secrets about the Egyptian, Greek, or Roman gods. The only way to learn these secrets was to be initiated into one of the "mystery religions," which were popular at that time.[1] But the Bible does not use the word "mystery" in either of these ways. The Bible is not a code to be deciphered, and Christianity is not a cult that sells access to secret knowledge.

The biblical meaning of "mystery" is knowledge that was previously unknown but has now been revealed. Such knowledge was unforeseen

---

1. Finkenrath, "Secret, Mystery," 501. See also Brown, "Mystery Religions," 64.

and unforeseeable and can only be known through revelation. Here are four examples of the biblical use of the word "mystery":

1. When King Nebuchadnezzar had a troubling dream, which he couldn't recall when he awoke, he threatened to execute all his advisors unless they told him the content and interpretation of the dream. Needless to say, none of his advisors could do this and so their lives were on the line. But the prophet Daniel told the king that his God could reveal mysteries (Dan 2:27–28). After praying for God's help, Daniel was able to tell the king his dream and its meaning, thus proving the superiority of Israel's God over the Babylonian gods. The use of the word "mystery" in this story concerned knowledge that could only be known through revelation from God.

2. Jesus used the word "mystery" to describe his teaching about the kingdom of God. In this case, Jesus himself was both the revealer and the revelation. He revealed the truth that he was the expected King only to his disciples (Matt 13:11; Mark 4:11; Luke 8:10), but he concealed the secret of the kingdom from others by using parables. Thus, a mystery was a new teaching that could only be understood by revelation.

3. A different use of the word "mystery" is found in Revelation, the last book of the Bible. The Greek title of the book is *apocalypsis*—meaning the disclosure of something secret or unknown.[2] The "mysteries" mentioned in Revelation refer to the esoteric symbols that compose the majority of the book, symbols such as the seven stars that Christ held in his right hand (Rev 1:20) or the woman Babylon riding on a scarlet beast (17:7–8). In both of those cases Revelation gives clues to help the reader interpret the mysteries—though, to be honest, for me the clues are just as mysterious as the symbols they are supposed to reveal. Revelation is a challenge to understand! The word "mystery" in Revelation relates to the "mystery of God" that would be fulfilled (10:7), a reference to the coming kingdom of God.

4. As we said before, the apostle Paul used the word "mystery" to describe the gospel of Jesus Christ. He called it "God's mystery," "the mystery kept secret for long ages but has now been disclosed . . . according to the command of the eternal God" (Col 2:2; Rom

---

2. Packer, "Revelation," 1014. See also *apokalupsis* in Arndt and Gingrich, *Greek-English Lexicon of the New Testament*, 91.

16:25–26). "God's mystery" refers to the message Paul preached: God's plan for salvation that had been concealed from humanity prior to the coming of the Messiah. Not even the smartest and best educated of mankind, Jew or gentile, had discerned this mystery. As we look into these newly revealed mysteries, we are actually accessing the very wisdom of God, which had been previously inaccessible.

So, the biblical meaning of "mystery" is knowledge that is unknown until it is revealed. We will look at "God's mystery" in three parts: Christ, Christians, and the church.

MYSTERY ONE: CHRIST

The Folly of God's Wisdom

In the New Testament God's wisdom is often contrasted with human wisdom. For example, the apostle Paul wrote to the Corinthians:

> For the word of the cross is folly to those who are perishing, but to us who are being saved it is the power of God. For it is written:
>
> "I will destroy the wisdom of the wise
> and the discernment of the discerning I will thwart."
>
> Where is the one who is wise? Where is the scribe? Where is the debater of this age? Has not God made foolish the wisdom of the world? For since, in the wisdom of God, the world did not know God through wisdom, it pleased God through the folly of what we preach to save those who believe. For Jews demand signs and Greeks seek wisdom, but we preach Christ crucified, a stumbling block to Jews and folly to Gentiles, but to those who are called, both Jews and Greeks, Christ the power of God and the wisdom of God. For the foolishness of God is wiser than men, and the weakness of God is stronger than men. (1 Cor 1:18–25)

This is a shocking passage! Not that it is surprising that God can outsmart the philosophers—that is not at all surprising. What is shocking is that God chose a strategy based on a "foolish" message to offer salvation to the world. Couldn't God have used a scholarly thesis written by someone like Confucius or Plato or Solomon to overwhelm the world's philosophers and theologians and force them to acknowledge his wisdom? But God chose the opposite approach. The key to gaining God's wisdom is not intellect but belief—faith! Faith seems so weak compared to human reason. Even a child can have faith—and, of course, that's the point. God, in his wisdom, bypassed—and surpassed—human wisdom by offering a "foolish" message that even a child could grasp and believe. None of the world's sages had figured this out—but millions of "foolish people" from every nation on earth have found this truth by believing a foolish-sounding message.

Biblical wisdom requires revelation to replace our own limited understanding with God's unlimited understanding. Without relying on revelation, we will become wise in our own eyes, which is another way to say we become fools. That is why the incarnation of divine Wisdom in the person of Jesus was essential. In Christ, we learn a deeper wisdom than anything we had previously considered.

The reason we didn't find this wisdom in our earlier studies is that it remained a mystery until the Messiah came. On the one hand, the link of wisdom to a mystery fits with the Old Testament idea of the inscrutability of God's wisdom: not even the wise could comprehend it. The wisdom-mystery connection (1 Cor 2:7; Col 1:25–28) is a new revelation of the true meaning of wisdom; it is not just more difficult to figure out but a totally different kind of wisdom.

The mystery of God in Christ is not some secret knowledge that Jesus possesses, it is Jesus himself: "Christ, the power of God and the wisdom of God" (1 Cor 1:24). God's power and wisdom were concealed in the humble life of the man Jesus. Who would have expected God to humble himself?

> Christianity is the only major religion to have as its central event the humiliation of its God.[3]

The Unrecognizable Messiah

Some other ancient religions have stories of their gods walking among men, but those so-called divine appearances were never truly human. Being human would mean weakness or ignorance. And that is why the story of Christ's incarnation seems foolish: Jesus was a homeless pauper from the backwater province of a third-world country; lead a ragtag, poorly educated group of followers; hung out with tax collectors, prostitutes, and

---

3. Shelley, *Church History*, 3.

foreigners; was rejected by most of the religious leaders of his day; and was arrested, tried, and executed. All of this was far from what the Jews were expecting for their Messiah, and none of this would be considered the signs the gentiles would have expected for a son of a god. Jesus didn't measure up to their expectations. He seemed foolish by comparison.

To the Romans, the Greeks, and the Jews, "Christ, the power of God and the wisdom of God," was a mystery—a truth they could not have foreseen and they did not recognize when it appeared. But the commonness of Jesus was the very heart of the gospel. "Humbly" describes how Jesus was born, how he lived, and how he died, and it was how the apostles preached about him. And it was how Isaiah had prophesied about him:

> He [God's servant] had no beauty or majesty to attract us to him, nothing in his appearance that we should desire him. He was despised and rejected by mankind, a man of suffering, and familiar with pain. Like one from whom people hide their faces, he was despised and we held him in low esteem. (Isa 53:2b–3 NIV)

God's servant wouldn't glow like an angel or look as handsome as a celebrity. He wouldn't look attractive as our portraits of Jesus usually portray him. Isaiah described the coming messiah as actually unappealing and disfigured, the kind of person we would see and look away. But the humiliation of God's servant went much deeper than his appearance. In order to become a guilt offering for our sins, it was necessary for God to turn against him!

> We all, like sheep, have gone astray, each of us has turned to our own way, and the Lord has laid on him the iniquity of us all. (53:6)

> Although he had done no violence, and there was no deceit in his mouth. Yet it was the will of the Lord to crush him; he has put him to grief. (53:9b–10)

God's servant carried all our iniquities. It was God's will to crush him. This turn of fortunes was totally unexpected because the Messiah was actually God incarnate. This certainly was a "foolish" way to save the world!

The Pattern of Wisdom

The truth that Jesus was God incarnate, while foolishness to nonbelievers, was not a problem for the Christians. The following passage (Phil 2:6–11) is believed to be an early Christian hymn about Jesus. It shows how the early Christians understood Jesus' person and his role in salvation. The first half of that hymn is as follows:

> Who, though he was in the form[4] of God, did not count equality with God a thing to be grasped, but emptied himself, by taking the form of a servant, being born in the likeness of men. And being found in human form, he humbled himself by becoming obedient to death, even death on a cross. (Phil 2:6–8)

The beginning part of this hymn describes how Christ humbled himself by descending from heaven to earth to the grave. His first step downward was to "empty" himself of his divine powers and privileges in order to become fully human, a servant, and obedient unto death, even the shameful death of the cross.

The Messiah died! If we grew up in Sunday school, we may have heard this so many times that it hardly moves us. But to those who lived at that time, it was an incomprehensible mystery. To the Greeks, this thought was utter foolishness. They knew that good men may die, but good people would not be killed as part of God's plan! To the Romans crucifixion was a shameful way to die. They killed the worst of the worst on a cross. Would God subject his own Son to such shame? And to the Jews, the messiah they were anticipating would be an upgraded King David, restoring their national greatness and God's glory. The idea that the messiah would come to suffer and die *according to God's plan* was unthinkable. They did not see it coming. Yet, as foolish as the crucifixion seemed (and still seems), this was and is the very wisdom of God. The execution of the Son of God is the mystery, the truth which no one (except maybe Isaiah) foresaw.

Years ago, I was discussing the gospel with a Muslim *imam* (teacher). He said, "Christianity makes no sense. Kings send their soldiers to die for them. Kings don't die for their soldiers. Strong leaders have employees to serve them. They don't serve their employees." I replied that I disagreed. Even at a human level, I was aware of good leaders who viewed themselves as servants to their workers. Servant leadership might be more

---

4. The word "form" suggests his nature: "who being in very nature God" (NIV).

common than this imam thought. But in this case, the "foolishness" of God sending his Son to die was actually this imam's only hope of salvation. This apparent foolishness was God's mercy at work to save anyone who would accept it by faith.

Before we move on from the mystery of Christ, let us complete the hymn we started above:

> Therefore God has highly exalted him and bestowed on him the name that is above every name, so that at the name of Jesus every knee should bow, in heaven and on earth and under the earth, and every tongue confess that Jesus Christ is Lord, to the glory of God the Father. (Phil 2:9–11)

The humiliation of Jesus was not a failure of God's plan, it was the necessary first step in his exaltation to the position of Lord over heaven, earth, and the nether regions. The seeming foolishness of a submissive, suffering, and crucified Messiah was God's wisdom, a mystery revealed in Christ. Humility is also the pattern for how God would make saints of his people. There is an equally "foolish" revelation of God's wisdom in another unexpected place: Christians.

MYSTERY TWO: CHRISTIANS

If Christ seemed foolish by the world's standards, how much more so Christians! But they/we are also evidence of the hidden wisdom of God. There is a double mystery regarding Christians: in the eyes of the world the mystery about Christians is our foolishness, but in our own eyes the mystery is our union with Christ.

The Foolishness of Christians

As Paul wrote to the Corinthians,

> For consider your calling, brothers: not many of you were wise according to worldly standards, not many were powerful, not many were of noble birth. But God chose what is foolish in the world to shame the wise; God chose what is weak in the world to shame the strong; God chose what is low and despised in the world, even things that are not, to bring to nothing things that are, so that no human being might boast in the presence of God.

> And because of him you are in Christ Jesus, who became to us wisdom from God, righteousness and sanctification and redemption, so that, as it is written: "Let the one who boasts, boast in the Lord." (1 Cor 1:26–31)

I suppose that those who advocate protecting everybody's self-esteem would fault Paul for his unflattering description of Christians: foolish, weak, lowly, despised. But Paul was right: this is how the world sees us. Recall Isaiah's description of the Messiah as unattractive and undesirable (Isa 53:2); so Christians are already Christlike—just not in the way we may have desired! We also seem unattractive just as Jesus seemed unattractive. We are part of the same mystery: God's mystery, God's wisdom.

Paul said that there is a good reason for God to choose the lowly and despised people as those to be redeemed: it is so that we cannot boast that we saved ourselves by our own strength, intelligence, or righteousness. The mystery of Christianity is that Christians are not qualified to be Christians! Therefore, we cannot boast about ourselves. We can only boast in the Lord who chose us and saved us.

Unity with Christ

Paul also wrote about the other side to God's mystery regarding Christians: our union with Christ.

> The mystery that has been kept hidden for ages and generations, but is now disclosed to the Lord's people. To them God has chosen to make known among the Gentiles the glorious riches of this mystery, which is Christ in you, the hope of glory. (Col 1:26–27 NIV)

The other mystery is "Christ in you, the hope of glory." Salvation means more than forgiveness of sins; it is union with Christ. The New Testament describes the Christian life as being "in Christ" and having "Christ in me" or "with me."

> I have been crucified with Christ. It is no longer I who live, but Christ who lives in me. And the life I now live in the flesh I live by faith in the Son of God, who loved me and gave himself for me. (Gal 2:20)

"It is no longer I who live, but Christ who lives in me ..." This phrase does not mean that I am no longer me; it means that I am no longer only me. Becoming one with Christ is probably the most important and most overlooked part of salvation.

The good news (gospel) of Jesus Christ is that salvation was not completed at the cross or the empty tomb. Salvation is complete when we are united with Christ. His life becomes my life / your life. His death becomes my death / your death. His resurrection becomes my resurrection / your resurrection. His righteousness becomes my righteousness / your righteousness. His wisdom becomes my wisdom / your wisdom. And his future glory becomes our future glory. Salvation is not a get-out-of-hell-free card that sinners can hang on to until we need it. Salvation is becoming united with Christ with all of his perfections. That is what qualifies Christians to be Christians! And we gain all of that at the moment we believe.

Christlikeness

But there is even more to our salvation than this. Jesus did not just die for our forgiveness and then step aside to let redemption happen. Understanding Christ as God's Wisdom incarnate is critical to a Christian's development of Christlikeness. But the indwelling Spirit enables Christians to live wisely (Eph 5:15–17). By the Spirit, a Christian's Christlikeness is more than being forgiven or renewed, it is the power and wisdom to live as Christ did. But living wisely is not automatic. Paul had to encourage Christians to walk by the Spirit who now lived within them (Gal 5:16–25).

Paul wrote to a group of new Christians in the city of Colossae that his goal for them was

> that their hearts may be encouraged, being knit together in love, to reach all the riches of full assurance of understanding and the knowledge of God's mystery, which is Christ, in whom are hidden all the treasures of wisdom and knowledge. (Col 2:2–3)

This brief passage is packed full of statements identifying the benefits of being a Christian:

- Unity in love
- Full understanding
- Knowing the mystery of God
- Knowing Christ

- All the treasures of wisdom and knowledge

At the logical center of this complex sentence is "God's mystery, which is Christ." Everything else in these verses hinges on knowing Christ who is the mystery of God. Because of Christ, Christians can be united in love and gain wisdom, knowledge, and understanding!

What does this mean for how Christians live our daily lives? The hymn in Phil 2 about Christ humbling himself was introduced by these words:

> Have this mind among yourselves, which is yours in Christ Jesus ... (Phil 2:5)

In other words, as Christians we are to follow the example of Jesus: to empty ourselves, to humble ourselves, and to become servants of one another. For now, we join the parade of the meek, the humble, and the faithful, waiting for God to exalt us in his time.

But there is one more level to this mystery: the church.

MYSTERY THREE: THE CHURCH

The Manifold Wisdom of God

As we have seen, God used a basic pattern for how he revealed his wisdom. Before the Messiah came, God's wisdom was kept hidden, but when he came, God's wisdom was disclosed in unexpected ways. In the eyes of the world, God's wisdom seemed unappealing, even foolish! It could only be perceived by those with childlike faith. Now, that same pattern is seen in the church.

When Christians think about the purpose of the church, I suspect that we most often think of a weekly gathering of the saved for the purpose of worship, prayer, discipleship, instruction, evangelism, service to one another, and ministry to the world—and indeed, all of those things are very important. But do we ever think of the church as God's object lesson, displaying grace and unity to the world and even to the angels? In this sense the church is a mystery, unforeseen even by the Old Testament saints.

The church represents the end of mankind's tribalisms and nationalisms! God does not play favorites among the peoples and the nations. Imagine if you will—and it isn't imaginary—Christians in all nations around the world, all languages, all peoples, all races, singing, "The Church's *One*

Foundation,"[5] each in their own tongue but united in a single chorus. It is God's wisdom, revealed first in Jesus, now expressing itself in the church for the world and the angels to marvel at. This unity began with the joining of Jews and gentiles as brothers and sisters in the church.

> This mystery is that the Gentiles are fellow heirs, members of the same body, and partakers of the promise in Christ Jesus through the gospel. (Eph 3:6)

To Christians who read this verse today, almost two thousand years after the apostle Paul wrote it, it will seem strange, even contradictory to our experiences of church. Today it is no longer a mystery that gentiles are members of the church—in fact it may seem more surprising that Jews are described as equal participants! But the church two thousand years ago consisted exclusively of Jewish converts to the faith, and the idea that gentiles would be allowed in was heretical! In that world, the verse above was indeed shocking. Jews and gentiles were oil and water: God's chosen people worshiping together with foreigners who were outsiders to God's people—unthinkable! In the first days of the church, before Peter and Paul began to evangelize gentiles and the Jerusalem Council endorsed this action, the only path to faith for gentiles was to convert first to Judaism and then to Christianity. But Paul said that his ministry as a missionary to the gentiles was part of God's eternal plan,

> the plan of the mystery hidden for ages in God, who created all things, so that through the church the manifold wisdom of God might now be made known. (Eph 3:9-10)

The church is the "manifold wisdom of God." I suspect that this statement appears as puzzling to people today as it did in Paul's time.

What is so wise about the church? Paul knew better than anyone else that churches were not perfect. The church is not smarter, better, or more immune to problems than other institutions. Nevertheless, Paul declared the church with all its flaws to be a demonstration of the wisdom of God. In Eph 3:1-12 Paul identified two characteristics that comprise the unforeseen mystery of the church: grace and unity. Let's consider these two characteristics.

---

5. S. J. Stone, "The Church's One Foundation Is Jesus Christ Her Lord" (1866).

The Church Is an Act of Grace

God chose to bring the gentiles through faith into the fold of his chosen people. Christians are accustomed to thinking of our personal salvation as being "by grace" (Eph 2:8), but do we understand the church as a work of grace? This means much more than saying that the church is a gathering of sinners saved by grace. Grace permeates the church—into its very DNA. By his grace the church is Christ's body, singing God's praises, serving one another, and ministering to the world. The church is his bride, being prepared for a wedding feast when he returns. Everything about the church is—or should be—a result of God's grace.

And like individual Christians, the church is a work of his grace in progress, so no church can boast. For any church to consider itself as inherently better than any other church would be as foolish as for any Christian to consider himself or herself as inherently better than other Christians—though that is a poor illustration since both of those foolish attitudes happen all the time. "By grace" negates all forms of human pride.

The very existence of the church is evidence of God's purpose and of his love, mercy, and grace. Therefore, the attitude of the church towards insiders and outsiders should always be one of grace. How can we whose access to God is solely based on his grace not extend that grace to others? Churches should be showcases of grace: grace received and grace given by all and to all.

The Church Is a Place of Unity

The second fundamental characteristic of the church is unity. The church is more than a social club that happens to hold meetings once a week. Unity is a major theme of Paul's description of the church. Baptized into one body together are Jews and gentiles, slaves and free, males and females—all one in Christ (Gal 3:28). God's wisdom is described as "multifaceted" (Eph 3:10 HCSB), meaning many-sided, diversified. God in his wisdom designed the church to include believers from the whole world.[6] Within a few decades after Pentecost, Christianity became the first global religion, found throughout the known world. This was something new and unforeseen. Today, the church fills the entire known world, found in

---

6. See Isa 45:22; Dan 7:14; Acts 10:34–36; Matt 28:18; Luke 24:46–47; John 4:42; and Rev 5:9. The kingdom of God is a multinational happening!

every country and within every people group.[7] The worldwide church is part of God's mystery!

The world prior to the gospel's arrival was a world divided into tribes and nations who lived in enmity with one another: country against country, ethnic group against ethnic group, religious group against religious group. Judaism was one such ethnic group. Israel saw itself as distinct from and superior to everyone else. But Israel was itself divided into subgroups such as the priests and Levites, Sanhedrin and Sadducees, scribes and Pharisees, Zealots, people of the earth, tax collectors, and "sinners." These Jewish subgroups also felt superior to one another, judged one another, and showed little love or compassion for one another's needs.

Paul insisted that tribal disunity must not become true of the church. The unity of the church is intended to be a manifestation of the love, grace, and wisdom of God. The gospel is not just something we preach; it is something we must live out together:

Live the unity.

We cannot read this passage without being struck both by the emphasis on the unity of the church and the failure of the modern church in precisely this area.... Already we know what is required: We are to live unity. We are not asked to like other Christians, to be like them, or agree with them, but to recognize that we are one with them and share the same Lord and the same benefits.

We may not write people off any more than one part of the body can dismiss another part. What this text underscores is that unity is not some nonessential, some afterthought, or some by-product of the faith, but it is at the heart of Christianity. The revelation that came in Christ was a revelation about unity. If we do not proclaim unity, we have not proclaimed the gospel. If we do not live unity, we have missed the gospel's impact. The attitude we have toward others is foundational.

Do our churches exhibit grace and receptivity so that people know they are valued as equals, or do we implicitly communicate arrogance and an attitude of superiority? The application of this text to racial problems is obvious and needed, but other kinds of divisions exist as well. Many people entering a strange church (or even a familiar one) do not feel unity. What do churches communicate that silences unity? Do we convey by language or attitude a spiritual elitism or a cultural tone that

---

7. The growth of the church has been remarkable—but there is still much missionary work needed.

creates obstacles for unity? . . . Differences in culture, race, music style, or traditions will be obvious, but what should be more obvious is the unity that exists in Christ. Groups may form around various interests or styles, but undergirding the groups must be a genuine unity drawn from a common commitment to Christ.[8]

It is tragic that just as we still see modern societies divided along tribal lines, we also see such divisions in churches. It is not new for churches to choose sides culturally or politically—churches have done that for centuries—but such divisions were and are a violation of the gospel. The church must display the manifold wisdom of God!

The world may view the church as foolish. God did not create churches to be perfect, but he did intend for the church to showcase love and unity that the tribalized world could never have imagined. Jesus said, "By this everyone will know that you are my disciples, if you love one another" (John 13:35). In its grace and unity, the church is part of the mystery that God was revealing then and is revealing now.

But there is more! Let's complete the verse we started above:

> The plan of the mystery hidden for ages in God, who created all things, so that through the church the manifold[9] wisdom of God might now be made known to the rulers and authorities in the heavenly places. This was according to his eternal purpose that he has realized in Christ Jesus our Lord. (Eph 3:9–11)

Who's Watching the Church?

God did not intend to reveal the mystery of the church solely for a worldly audience but also for a heavenly one: the rulers and authorities in the heavens, all watching to see the grace and the unity of the church. The phrase "rulers and authorities" usually refers to the realm of fallen angels, though this is not clear in this text. What is clear is that angels are watching us in church.[10]

> While we must exercise appropriate theological modesty in the face of such claims, Ephesians 3 certainly suggests that there is

---

8. Snodgrass, *Ephesians*, 172–73.
9. The HCSB translates "manifold" as "multifaceted."
10. This idea of angels watching God's work in salvation is also suggested in 1 Pet 1:12.

a dispute among heavenly powers regarding the wisdom of God and the mystery of his way in the world. This passage also tells us that God has an answer up his sleeve; a tour-de-force argument to silence his opponents. What is that answer? In short, the answer is us. The mystery of God—his plan of redemption for the world by which his wisdom as creator will be vindicated—turns out to be a people; his church. God is staking this all (as he did in the book of Job) on the frail foundation of human faith. To do such a thing looks foolish, and it absolutely would be foolish were it not for the brilliant centerpiece of God's strategy: the person of Jesus Christ. . . . In solidarity with him, we as God's people are the vindication of his wisdom.[11]

Do we in the church see ourselves as a vindication of God's wisdom? The church is God's showpiece for the heavenly beings! What they are seeing is his "multifaceted wisdom," meaning unity formed out of human diversity—a work of his grace. This is God's eternal plan, the mystery that nobody saw coming, the mystery of the church.

I wonder if the angels ever look down at the church with all its flaws and wonder if God was wrong after all. Was God naïve to use the weak things to defeat the strong things and the foolish things to defeat the wise things? This secret plan of sending his Messiah in the form of a servant, of crucifying him as an atonement for sin, of investing in sinners to become saints, of gathering them into churches known for grace and unity, was it not a foolish plan? Was God humbling himself the wrong strategy?

Or will it turn out that God's investment in meekness, service, humility, mercy, kindness, and love will, in the end, be the winning strategy? Jesus invested his life in carrying out God's plan to redeem the world through love, service, and sacrifice. And he invested his ministry in a ragtag group of followers whom he commissioned to go and do likewise.

How the Church Is Supposed to Look

One of my favorite movies is *Places in the Heart*, starring Sally Field.[12] The story takes place in 1935, during the Great Depression, in a small Texas town. The story begins with Royce Spalding, the town sheriff, being accidentally shot and killed by Wylie, a drunken black youth. Wylie is quickly lynched by a white mob. Edna, the sheriff's widow, is left with

---

11. Carpenter, *Scandalous People*, loc. 1538.
12. Benton, *Places in the Heart*.

two children and a cotton farm, which is deeply in debt to the bank. The banker warns her she will lose the farm. With no help available from the community, she hires a black drifter named Moses. He promises to run the farm for her and at harvest time he recruits local black workers to pick the cotton. Their hard work saves the farm, but Moses's success as a black man in the segregated South leads to a violent attack by the local Ku Klux Klan, forcing Moses to leave town.

The plot highlights the indifference of Edna's white friends and the help of the black community to save her farm. This contrast became the setting for the movie's final scene, which takes place in the town's small, whites-only church. After hearing a sermon on 1 Cor 13—the love chapter—the church celebrates communion, in which the men serving the elements are all members of the KKK who had attacked Moses. But in this powerful concluding scene, the movie turns to symbolism: Edna is seated on her church pew alongside the people who had earned a place in her heart: Royce, her deceased husband, sits next to Wylie, the black youth who had killed him, who sits next to Moses, the black man who had risked his life to save her farm. Side by side, they celebrate the Lord's Supper as brothers and sisters.

This final scene of taking communion, an act of God's forgiveness, portrays a stark contrast between the church as it was and as it ought to be. The sad reality was a church that was segregated, concealing hatred and unforgiveness. But in Edna's heart, the church became a place of grace and unity—as God intended. In this final scene, movie viewers get to see the church as God intends, a portrayal of God's secret wisdom, the "mystery" of the church.

My wife and I showed this movie on one of our movie nights while teaching in China. The difficulty with showing this movie in China was that we had to explain the historical and cultural context of racial prejudice and segregation. I had not even thought of *Places in the Heart* as a Christian movie, but the day after the showing one of the university students who came to the movie night told us that she had believed in Christ as a result of watching that movie. What moved her to faith was the images of forgiveness portrayed in the movie. That is how the world—and the angels—ought to see the church.

GOD'S WISDOM REVEALED

God's three unforeseen mysteries are Christ, Christians, and the church. Each of these mysteries, while foolish in the eyes of the world, reveal the hidden wisdom of God. Is God's plan foolishness—as the world believes, as the church sometimes seems to believe—or is it God's ultimate wisdom?

The opposite of human wisdom is not foolishness, it is a higher wisdom. That higher wisdom, formerly a mystery, has been revealed in the gospel.

41

James and the Prayer for Wisdom

THE BOOK OF JAMES will be our final book study. James wrote about wisdom twice in his brief letter to the young churches. These two passages reveal continuity with earlier wisdom writings, especially Proverbs and Job, while introducing a new perspective on wisdom not found in the earlier books. That new perspective is the best answer to the questions raised about wisdom: Is wisdom really up to solving the problems we face globally? James's answer is It depends.

THE BOOK OF JAMES

The identity of the author of the book of James is debated. Possibly the author was the apostle James, or the Lord's half-brother James, or some other James whose identity is otherwise unknown. The traditional view that Jesus' half-brother is the author seems most likely. The book was addressed to the "twelve tribes scattered among the nations" (1:1), probably a reference to the Jewish Christians who were living in the diaspora—the gentile cities of the Roman world. The date of writing is uncertain, but the content seems to indicate an early date, perhaps around AD 50.

James's purpose in writing was practical rather than theoretical. He was not writing a systematic theology regarding Christology or the way of salvation. He was concerned that some of the same sinful practices that had led Israel astray in the Old Testament and that were still present in the Judaism of his day were emerging in the young churches. Christians, in their search for a comfortable lifestyle, had compromised the ethical standards of the Old Testament Scriptures and the teachings of Jesus. When James wrote about the need for wisdom among Christians, he framed that lesson as a specific response to the sins he saw developing in the church.

Because James wrote to Jewish Christians he often depended on references to the Old Testament to make his points. The practical lessons he was making are equally applicable to all Christians, then and now. We can see his dependence on Old Testament wisdom writings by comparing his writings with those of Proverbs.

James and Proverbs

In many ways, the book of James resembles the book of Proverbs, the book where we started our studies on wisdom. Our studies of biblical wisdom have come full cycle. Here are some of the similarities between Proverbs and James:

- Both Proverbs and James provide the reader with practical applications of ethical monotheism: if you believe in God, this is how you ought to live. They both agree that God is the sovereign ruler of his world, that he is good, and that he expects his people to be good.

- Both books view humanity as divided into two camps. In Proverbs the two camps are the wise and foolish: the wise fear the Lord and follow his ways, but the foolish choose to make their own path in life. In James the two groups are those who trust God to care for their needs and those whose desires for wealth and pleasure lead them into all kinds of sin. For James this second group includes some Christians and Christian teachers whose selfish desires were corrupting the church.

- Both books emphasize the importance of good character. Proverbs defines good character based on receiving wisdom into one's heart and walking the straight path of righteousness. James defines good character as good deeds and meekness, culminating in a harvest of righteousness.

- Both books teach about wisdom. Proverbs teaches about wisdom as a single thing all people ought to seek. Proverbs contrasts the wise with those who are wise in their own eyes—otherwise known as fools. James divides wisdom into two camps: wisdom from above and earthly wisdom, which is selfish, unspiritual, and even demonic (3:15).

- Both books teach that access to wisdom comes by asking God who gives it generously to those who ask (Prov 2:1–6; Jas 1:5).
- James quotes Prov 3:34, a verse that expresses a key lesson for both books: "God opposes the proud but gives grace to the humble" (Jas 4:6).

THE PRAYER FOR WISDOM

There are two passages in the book of James that teach about wisdom. James's first mention of wisdom occurs in one of the most quoted verses about wisdom in the Bible: the promise that God will always answer the prayer for wisdom. Throughout the Old Testament wisdom is described as a gift God gives to those who ask. This was true for young King Solomon, and he wrote it into the book of Proverbs. God answered prayers for wisdom by Old Testament heroes, including Daniel and Jehoshaphat.

The version of the prayer for wisdom in James is simple and straightforward: If you lack wisdom, ask for it. God promises to give it generously to anyone:

> If any of you lacks wisdom, let him ask God, who gives generously to all without reproach, and it will be given him. (Jas 1:5)

This may be the only place in Scripture where God promises to answer a prayer for anyone who asks. By definition, biblical wisdom is truth applied to life; therefore, the wise will ask God for wisdom. Those who are wise recognize that they are not wise enough. It takes wisdom to ask for wisdom!

My experience of praying with other believers is that we frequently rely on this prayer, perhaps if we are facing difficulties, or if we are asking for moral clarity or for guidance: Should I do this or that? Or should my friend or family member do this or that? Or should my boss, or pastor, or our president do this or that? These are prayers for guidance.

Notice that a proper prayer for guidance doesn't first tell God what to do: "God, tell so and so that they should do this"—thus instructing God. We often hear Christians giving "wise" counsel to God based on their own beliefs—and, in my opinion, their advice is often wrong. Recall the theme we have seen in the wisdom literature: nobody understands God's plans and purposes, and only fools think that they do. As the apostle Paul taught the church in Rome:

> Oh, the depth of the riches and wisdom and knowledge of God! How unsearchable are his judgments and inscrutable his ways! "For who has known the mind of the Lord? Or who has been his counselor?" (Rom 11:33–34)

Paul asks a rhetorical question: Who can counsel God? His implied answer is "nobody." Nobody knows the mind of the Lord, and nobody qualifies to be his counselor. So asking God for guidance shouldn't include counseling him as to what we think he ought to do. Asking God for wisdom means asking for his counsel. That is the prayer God has promised to answer.

Prayer plus Faith

James added one additional condition to the prayer for wisdom: belief without doubt:

> But let him ask in faith, with no doubting, for the one who doubts is like a wave of the sea that is driven and tossed by the wind. For that person must not suppose that he will receive anything from the Lord. (1:6–7)

The requirement of faith reminds us of Jesus' own teaching about prayer:

> Therefore I tell you, whatever you ask in prayer, believe that you have received it, and it will be yours. (Mark 11:24)

The prayer of faith is at the very heart of the worldview of monotheism: prayer requires believing in the God to whom we pray. It requires trusting God to be God.

Throughout the Bible, in both testaments, the meaning of faith is turning from oneself, one's own strength, and one's own righteousness to rely on God to do for us what we can't do for ourselves. Perhaps turning from trusting oneself to trusting God is the hardest part of faith! As Jesus said, and it is at the heart of James's prayer for wisdom, if we ask God for something, then we need to allow the all-wise God to act as he has promised.

Wisdom When Facing Trials

> Count it all joy, my brothers, when you meet trials of various kinds, for you know that the testing of your faith produces steadfastness. And let steadfastness have its full effect, that you may be perfect and complete, lacking in nothing. (Jas 1:2–4)

Though James said that a mature Christian will be lacking nothing, he immediately added that they might still be lacking one thing: wisdom to face their trials. It was in this context that he promised God would give wisdom to those who ask in faith. In the face of sufferings, some Christians lacked wisdom about how to respond to those persecuting them. James assured them that if they ask God for such wisdom, God will give it.[1] The wisdom that James promised was knowing how to respond to persecution being faced for Jesus' sake. And this wisdom provides what may be lacking in their maturity. It takes wisdom to become a complete Christian! So, any believer who wants to become mature should pray for God's wisdom.

Trials are God's curriculum for making our faith complete—just add wisdom. James laid out a four-step model of maturing:

> trials → testing of faith → perseverance → maturity and completeness[2]

On the one hand, Christians should greatly rejoice because those sufferings are God's way of bringing them to maturity—lacking nothing. This idea of testing leading them to maturity is similar to the theology of the book of Job. The testings he faced led to a more complete understanding of God. James made reference to the perseverance of Job and other prophets facing suffering (5:10–11).

James begins the letter with a similar thought:

---

1. See Mark 13:9–13, where Jesus made a similar promise.
2. Romans 5:3–5 lays out a similar model of growing in faith:
   suffering → perseverance → character → hope → without shame.

> Blessed is the man who remains steadfast under trial, for when he has stood the test, he will receive the crown of life, which God has promised to those who love him. (1:12)

The result of successfully facing trials is God's reward, the crown of life. So wisdom in the midst of testings completes a Christian's faith, bringing them to maturity to receive God's reward.

Wisdom completes the Christian's faith! Therefore "get wisdom"!

42

James and the Two Wisdoms

JAMES SAID THAT THERE are two kinds of wisdom: the good and the bad.

Bad wisdom happens when wisdom becomes corrupted by sin! The result of wisdom gone bad will be backbiting and strife within the church. Tragically, James saw this happening in the young churches of his day. He wrote about such wisdom gone bad as contributing to the problems facing the churches, but he offered a remedy for those problems: rely on the right kind of wisdom.

This passage about two wisdoms (3:13–18) presents the most thorough exposition of wisdom found in the New Testament, but it needs to be understood within its context. In the sections before and after his lesson on wisdom James discussed his concerns regarding the sins he saw developing inside the churches. He believed that if Christians and Christian teachers would seek the right kind of wisdom, their churches would be filled with righteousness and peace rather than backbiting and strife.

Here is a partial outline of the book of James showing how his second lesson on wisdom fits within its context:

- Context before: sins of the tongue (3:1–12)
- Lesson on two wisdoms (3:13–18)
- Context after: interpersonal conflicts (4:1–12)

In this outline the lesson on wisdom is located between passages dealing with sins that were troubling the early church: sins of the tongue and sins of interpersonal conflict. Running through these three passages is a thread that connects those sins to worldly wisdom. The problems in the churches were not due to a lack of wisdom but to corrupted wisdom.

We will begin our study of wisdom by looking at the two contexts.

THE CONTEXT BEFORE: SINS OF THE TONGUE

In Jas 3:1–12, James addressed Christians wanting to become teachers in the church. He cautioned them that not many should become teachers because teachers will be subject to stricter judgment. A qualification to become a Christian teacher was to have learned to control one's tongue—that is, one's speech. While every Christian needs to control their speech, this is especially important for teachers in the church. They are entrusted with teaching biblical truth, and with offering praise to God, yet if they see teaching as an opportunity to boast, or to judge others, they are mixing proper and improper uses of the tongue! And if their tongue is not under control, then their lives will also be out of control, and their life will contradict their teaching!

James called the tongue a restless evil and a world of unrighteousness. Though humans can tame all kinds of animals, we are incapable of taming ourselves, and, in particular, nobody can tame their own tongue. What are the sins of the tongue? We might expect that what James meant was dishonesty or hypocrisy, but neither of those sins was his focus in this passage. Rather, he warned about the misuse of speech for boasting and for cursing people made in the image of God. In the next chapter he also included judging others. Boasting, insulting, and judging are using the tongue to extol our own goodness and to denigrate others. The result of these misuses of the tongue is the destruction of one's own life and the lives of others. An untamed tongue is a tool used by worldly wisdom.

James may well have been thinking about Jesus' teaching regarding the misuse of words:

> For out of the abundance of the heart the mouth speaks. The good person out of his good treasure brings forth good, and the evil person out of his evil treasure brings forth evil. I tell you on the day of judgment, people will give account for every careless word they speak, for by your words you will be justified, and by your words you will be condemned. (Matt 12:34–37)

When Jesus said that evil people bring forth evil from their hearts, he was referring to their words. He taught that our words reveal our character and that our words will be judged. James extended Jesus' warning about careless words to the broader idea that controlling one's speech is the first step in controlling the whole body:

> For we all stumble in many ways. And if anyone does not stumble in what he says, he is a perfect man, able also to bridle his whole body. (Jas 3:2)

In other words, self-control begins with controlling one's speech. As Guy Woods wrote,

> It is utterly impossible to measure, in this life, the harm which grows out of the slander, the profanity, the falsehood, the blasphemy and the scandal of which it [the tongue] is capable. History is replete with instances of wars, strifes, alienations resulting from its evil work...
>
> A slanderer eventually exhibits the effects of his sin in his whole personality. His outlook on life becomes polluted, his confidence in his fellows vanishes, and his spiritual life dwarfs and dies. A mechanic may be capable of doing excellent work; but if we catch him lying to us, we immediately regard his work as untrustworthy. It is an ancient and true adage that one is no better than his word.[1]

After James listed the misuses of the tongue, he exclaimed,

> My brothers and sisters, this should not be. Can both fresh water and salt water flow from the same spring? My brothers and sisters, can a fig tree bear olives, or a grapevine bear figs? Neither can a salt spring produce fresh water. (3:10-12 NIV)

Christians, especially teachers, need integrity in how they speak. Mixing boasting or insults with praise for God is hypocrisy.

Perhaps nowadays Christians use words to boast, to insult, and to judge others so frequently that we are not as offended by them as was James. Without tongue control there can be no self-control! And without tongue control there can be no harvest of righteousness sown in peace by those who make peace (3:18)!

James linked his lesson about the sins of the tongue to his lesson on wisdom by asking, "Who is wise and understanding among you?" (3:13).

---

1. Woods, *James*, 164-65.

Perhaps he assumed that most people who want to become teachers consider themselves to be wise and understanding, so he asked about this directly. By this question he was challenging their self-confident attitude, and he was introducing the topic of what wisdom is really like. We will return to that question after looking at the context following the wisdom lesson.

THE CONTEXT AFTER: CONFLICT WITHIN THE CHURCH

Immediately after his lesson on wisdom, James raised another concern about the sins he saw in the young churches of his day: "What causes fights and quarrels among you?" (4:1a). James saw worldly wisdom as the source of "disorder and every sort of evil" (3:16). In other words, wisdom was complicit in the quarrels *in the church*!

> What causes quarrels and what causes fights among you? Is it not this, that your passions are at war within you? You desire and do not have, so you murder. You covet and cannot obtain, so you fight and quarrel. You do not have because you do not ask. You ask and do not receive, because you ask wrongly, to spend it on your passions. (4:1–3)

James listed three sources for quarrels and fighting: unfulfilled desires (coveting), pursuing personal pleasures (passions), and pride. These motivations are rooted in human self-centeredness. In his commentary on James, Tasker wrote,

> There are indeed few evils in human life that cannot be traced to covetousness and envy in the sense that we find these words used in this verse. Covetousness does not always lead to possession, envy does not always attain to the position of its rivals—and the inevitable result is conflict and strife.[2]

Conflict arises when we don't get what we want. We often see quarreling, fighting, and even killing[3] in our daily news, but we might not associate them with the sins of coveting and pride, as James did. When we have desires, we should pray and trust God to meet our needs. But unfortunately, when our desires are rooted in selfishness, God does not answer

---

2. Tasker, *James*, 87.

3. At first I thought James's reference to killing was an exaggeration or metaphor until I compared it to Jas 5:6. He was being literal!

those prayers. And so our unfulfilled desires lead us into conflict with one another.

This evidence for conflict rooted in selfish desires and pride is found throughout Scripture, starting in the garden of Eden and Cain's murder of his brother. James's analysis of the sources of interpersonal conflict is similar to the description of foolishness and wickedness found in Proverbs—as Solomon said, there is indeed nothing new under the sun! And James's warning for Christians then still applies to Christians today.

But interpersonal conflict is not the worst outcome of human self-centeredness: such desires also disrupt our relationship with God! Coveting, immoral pleasures, and pride result in unanswered prayer, spiritual adultery, enmity, and the loss of God's favor. And James was not writing to unbelievers but to Christians!

> You adulterous people! Do you not know that friendship with the world is enmity with God? Therefore, whoever wishes to be a friend of the world makes himself an enemy of God. Or do you suppose it is to no purpose that the Scripture says, "He yearns jealously over the spirit that he has made to dwell in us"? But he gives more grace. Therefore it says, "God opposes the proud but gives grace to the humble." (Jas 4:4–6)

Christians often blame non-Christians or the surrounding culture for the evil and divisiveness in society, but James was not letting us off the hook: "You adulterous people!" His reference to adultery could have been a literal reference to sexual sin happening in the church. This would fit with the reference to "passions" (4:1), a word which can also mean "lusts." But most likely, James was referring to spiritual adultery, a reference back to the Old Testament prophets who condemned Israel's unfaithfulness to God as adultery. In the Old Testament, Israel had been chosen by God to be his covenant people, a commitment akin to marriage. Therefore, idolatry was akin to marital unfaithfulness.[4] Christians are also bound by covenant with God through Christ, and James calls Christians who violate this covenant adulterers. He was not writing about idolatry in the literal sense of worshiping graven images of foreign gods, rather he was talking about idolatry in the spiritual sense of pushing God aside in order to pursue earthly desires. Both Jesus and Paul called greed a form of idolatry (Matt 6:19–24; Eph 5:5). James calls friendship with the world

---

4. Hos 2:1–13; Jer 3:6–13; Ezek 23:35–39.

enmity with God. Christians need to take seriously the exclusivity of our commitment to God.

While Christians may sing about God as our friend, we need to be aware that he may also be our enemy if we are committing spiritual adultery through greed, lust, pleasure seeking, and pride. The words James uses are strong, but he was trying to get the attention of Christians who had slid back into the friendships they had before they were "married" to Christ.

The condition given by James in this passage is that we all need God's grace! Quoting Prov 3:34, James wrote, "God opposes the proud but gives grace to the humble" (4:6).

We often describe salvation as being by grace through faith—which is good theology—but James says that God gives grace (or "shows favor," NIV) to the humble. Pride is the opposite of true faith. Humbling oneself before God is at the heart of belief. This verse could be considered the theme verse for both Proverbs and James.

A few verses later James identified another source of conflict within the church: slandering and judging one another.

> Do not speak evil against one another, brothers. The one who speaks against a brother or judges his brother, speaks evil against the law and judges the law. But if you judge the law, you are not a doer of the law but a judge. There is only one lawgiver and judge, he who is able to save and to destroy. But who are you to judge your neighbor? (4:11–12)

James argued that only God is above the law and therefore only God is qualified to judge others. We who are under the law and are judged by it are not qualified to act as judges. For us to judge a brother or sister is to play God over them. Judging others is another sin resulting from worldly wisdom.

The context before James's lesson about wisdom deals with the sins of the tongue. The context afterward deals with quarrels, fighting, and judging. James linked these passages together by the thread of worldly wisdom. In this context, we see that worldly wisdom is complicit in the disruption of society and of the church. We can diagram these passages like this:

sins of the tongue → worldly wisdom → conflict among believers

All three of these passages refer to personal selfishness resulting in every kind of evil (3:16). No wonder James was so concerned about the sins he was seeing in the new churches!

THE TWO WISDOMS

James began his lesson on wisdom with a brief question introducing the topic:

> Who is wise and understanding among you? By his good conduct let him show his works in the meekness of wisdom. (3:13)

The good kind of wisdom is associated with good deeds and meekness (or humility or gentleness). It has been suggested that James chose good deeds and meekness as evidence of good wisdom because they described his half-brother Jesus, the incarnation of Wisdom. Here are two descriptions of Jesus' ministry. The apostle Peter summarized the ministry of Jesus as follows:

> He went about doing good and healing all who were oppressed by the devil, for God was with him. (Acts 10:38)

The apostle Paul wrote,

> I, Paul, entreat you, by the meekness and gentleness of Christ ... (2 Cor 10:1)

The view that James considered Jesus to be the role model for living wisely means that good deeds and humility are to be the standards for all Christians as well. In this lesson on wisdom James used good deeds and meekness to introduce the wisdom that comes from above. When we pray the prayer for wisdom (1:5), we can expect God to answer by telling us to do good deeds and to be humble and meek.

But James did not see wisdom as always positive. It has a dark side.

Worldly Wisdom

James's lesson on wisdom continued by contrasting the two wisdoms: worldly wisdom and heavenly wisdom. The "bad" kind of wisdom, wisdom corrupted by sin, is very different than the good wisdom James had just written about.

> But if you have bitter jealousy and selfish ambition in your hearts, do not boast and be false to the truth. This is not the wisdom that comes down from above, but is earthly, unspiritual, demonic. For where jealousy and selfish ambition exist, there will be disorder and every vile practice. (3:14–16)

As Grant Osborne described it,

> In contrast to this heavenly wisdom is the earthly wisdom which is typified by bitter jealousy, selfish ambition, boasting, and falsehood. Such wisdom is unspiritual and even demonic. The result of such attitudes is disorder and every vile practice.
> Bitter jealousy and selfish ambition are the antithesis of true wisdom as characterized by meekness. "Selfish ambition" is a divisive willingness to split the group in order to achieve personal power and prestige (it is translated "rivalry" in Gal 5:20; Phil 1:17; 2:3).[5]

Selfish ambition results in earthly wisdom. We may read examples of such "wisdom" on social media and find it in self-help podcasts: Look out for number one. Follow your dreams. Never settle for less than you deserve. Humility is for the humble. Such self-centered ideas are the basis for social discord and division.

James actually blames such corrupted wisdom for the disorder in the world and in the church! Why do neighbors argue and fight? Because of worldly wisdom consisting of self-centeredness, covetousness, and pride. Why do Christians divide their churches over personality or politics? Worldly wisdom. We often see this worldly, demonic "wisdom" today, and it is still responsible for much of the social disorder and evil around us. Worldly wisdom is actually dangerous!

James is not saying that there are actually two opposite kinds of wisdom. Rather wisdom, which is good, can be corrupted by sin. Envy and selfish ambition change a good thing into a disaster for the world. (This is similar to the virtue of love, which is the "greatest of these" [1 Cor 13:13] but when corrupted by selfishness, love becomes lust and coveting—the source of many of the troubles in the world.)

---

5. Osborne, notes on *James*, 2396.

The Wisdom from Above

Heavenly wisdom is a great good, which James described using a list of ten virtues beginning with purity and ending with peace. His list is similar to other lists of virtues given in the New Testament—for example, Jesus' teaching in the Beatitudes and the fruit of the Spirit, as illustrated in the following chart:

The Wisdom from Above Jas 3:13–18	The Beatitudes Matt 5:3–12	The Fruit of the Spirit Gal 5:22–23
Pure	Poor in Spirit	Love
Peaceable	Those who mourn	Joy
Gentle	Meek	Peace
Open to reason	Hunger and thirst for righteousness	Patience
Full of mercy		Kindness
Good fruit	Merciful	Goodness
Impartial	Pure in heart	Faithfulness
Sincere	Peacemakers	Gentleness
Righteousness	Persecuted	Self-control
Peacemakers		

The three lists are similar and present a consistent picture of godliness. Combining the lists we see five clusters of virtues:

- Purity, goodness, righteousness, purity in heart
- Humility, meekness, gentleness, mercy
- Peaceable, peacemaking, kind
- Impartiality
- Loving, faithfulness, sincerity

Comparing these lists shows that godliness consists of the inner attitudes of purity and humility and the outer acts of kindness and mercy. We see that James's description of wisdom is very similar to the fruit (traits) imparted by the Spirit, which is very similar to the ethics of the kingdom. Godliness in all three lists becomes visible in personal character and in how we treat one another. This is the kind of wisdom God approves.

The actions and attitude that led Jesus to humble himself, to empty himself, and to become a servant and a sacrifice should be the attitude and the character of each Christian as well. But these virtues described here are not inborn traits which some may come by naturally. They are not natural; they are supernatural, the wisdom God gives. The virtues of purity, peace loving, and the others are not rules to be obeyed in human strength. They are gifts to be received from God.

GOOD WISDOM AND BAD WISDOM TODAY

In chapter 4 I said that I pray for wisdom for our nation's leaders who have to deal with numerous sizable problems facing our planet, our country, and our lives today. Perhaps I should be more specific in that prayer request: I should pray for them to have good wisdom.

James cautioned that what is often called wisdom is actually dangerous! Bad wisdom is complicit in creating the problems we see in the world and in the church today. If our leaders use their tongues for boasting and criticizing, then they have the wrong kind of wisdom. If our leaders demonstrate selfish ambition and envy resulting in disorder and strife, they have the wrong kind of wisdom. If our leaders are filled with covetousness and lustful desires, resulting in fights and quarrels, they have the wrong kind of wisdom. What is bad wisdom? It is wisdom corrupted by sin, by selfishness, by ambition, by envy, by lust, by covetousness, and by pride.

James told us to seek the good kind of wisdom, the evidence of which will be our good deeds and humility. If our interpretation is correct, James was referring to the life of his brother Jesus as the model of heavenly wisdom; thus, to be Christlike requires good deeds and humility.

Throughout the New Testament good deeds are considered to be a mark of a Christian:

> Let your light shine before others, so that they may see your good works and give glory to your Father who is in heaven. (Matt 5:16)

> [Christ] gave himself for us to redeem us from all lawlessness and to purify for himself a people for his own possession who are zealous for good works. (Titus 2:14)

> Keep your conduct among the Gentiles honorable, so that when they speak against you as evildoers, they may see your good deeds and glorify God on the day of visitation. (1 Pet 2:12)

In a vision an angel told Cornelius,

> Your prayers and gifts to the poor have come up as a memorial offering before God. (Acts 10:4 NIV)

Just as Peter could summarize the ministry of Jesus as going about doing good (Acts 10:38), so this ought also to describe those with wisdom from above. Such good deeds include prayer, charity for the poor, healing the sick, considering others as more important than oneself, loving your neighbor as yourself, and doing all this in an attitude of humility (or meekness). Good deeds done with a humble attitude are the evidence of the good kind of wisdom.

This lesson by James is a close parallel to Paul's description of the attitude that should describe Christians:

> Do nothing from selfish ambition or conceit, but in humility count others more significant than yourselves. Let each of you look not only to his own interests, but also to the interests of others. Have this mind among yourselves, which is yours in Christ Jesus. (Phil 2:3–5)

We should pray for our national and church leaders to have the good kind of wisdom, which is evident in meekness and good deeds, purity and peace loving, mercy and kindness, and righteousness. That sort of wisdom can begin to heal our land.

PART SEVEN

Refining Wisdom

In our search for wisdom, how far have we come?

43

Truth Applied to Life

REDEFINING WISDOM

IN EVERY CULTURE AROUND the world people seek wisdom, the insight and foresight they need to understand the uncertainties of their lives and to seek a path forward to success. Theists also seek this kind of wisdom in order to improve our lives. At this basic level, generic wisdom and biblical wisdom are very similar, they both seek to apply truth to life.

But, as we have also seen, monotheism has its own variety of wisdom, and it is not always what people expect or want. It will not solve all of our problems or give error-free guidance for the path ahead, but it will prepare us to become the right person to walk that path. Biblical wisdom is more about hearts than smarts.

Perhaps no passage better encapsulates monotheism's view of wisdom than this doxology, written by the apostle Paul:

> Oh, the depth of the riches and wisdom and knowledge of God!
> How unsearchable are his judgments and inscrutable his ways!
>
> "For who has known the mind of the Lord,
>   or who has been his counselor?"
> "Or who has given a gift to him
>   that he might be repaid?"

> For from him and through him and to him are all things. To him be glory forever! Amen. (Rom 11:33–36)

God is all wise, and no human is wise enough to understand his purposes or to give him advice. Whatever wisdom we may have—and hopefully we all have some—is derived from God having placed wisdom in each person's heart. That startup portion of wisdom can be enhanced though learning: learning from the teachings of the wise, learning from observing the successes and failures of others, and learning from the word of God. For believers the best source of wisdom is the Spirit who lives within us and gives us the mind of Christ.

Our studies of biblical wisdom can be summarized in four words: practical, moral, character, and relationships.

Biblical Wisdom Is Practical

Wisdom applies truth—that is, understanding and knowledge—to real life situations. Biblical wisdom starts with the fear of the Lord. Wisdom teaches us how to live for God on the streets, when we are not in church. It will be evident in the daily choices we make in every area of life.

Biblical Wisdom Is Moral

Within the wisdom literature, wisdom's partner is righteousness. Wisdom plus righteousness enables one to choose good paths. Proverbs defined the good path as the trio of righteousness, justice, and fairness: three virtues derived from the character of God and expected within the character of all men and women. Moral wisdom is more than shunning evil. Moral wisdom is seen in how we treat others, especially in how we treat the poor, the vulnerable, and the strangers among us.

Biblical Wisdom Is About Character Transformation

Character counts! Character is an expression of the values that have been internalized in each person's heart, acting as a moral compass. This process begins with wise choices and good behavior. Prominent traits of good character are humility, honesty, generosity, and faithfulness.

Biblical Wisdom Is Relational

One purpose of wisdom is to make each person into a better person. Better people will have better relationships within their marriages, their families, their neighborhoods, their nations, and their churches. Just as righteousness exalts a nation, so wisdom improves every relationship, even how we treat our enemies and our animals.

All four of these aspects of wisdom are grounded both in the fear of the Lord—letting God be God—and in humility, resulting in submission to God and service to others. Humility requires a realistic view of oneself, without being wise in one's own eyes. As Proverbs, James, and Peter teach,

> Toward the scorners he [the Lord] is scornful, but to the humble he gives favor. (Prov 3:34)

> It says, "God opposes the proud but gives grace to the humble." (Jas 4:6)

> "God opposes the proud but gives grace to the humble." Humble yourselves, therefore, under the mighty hand of God so that at the proper time he may exalt you. (1 Pet 5:5–6)

That repeated verse is at the heart of the wisdom of monotheism.

REVIEWING THE WISDOM LITERATURE

Each of the book studies and topical studies in the previous chapters has presented a different perspective on wisdom. Let's review the major contributions of these studies to our understanding of wisdom.

Proverbs

The book of Proverbs comes the closest to being a systematic theology of wisdom, though it consists primarily of practical theology, not abstract theology. The individual proverbs in Proverbs, taken together, are a presentation of the worldview of wisdom: what it is, how to acquire it, and how it works in daily life. It is ethical monotheism in practice. Many of the proverbs are brief case studies in living wisely and living morally.

Proverbs affirms the reality of God and the reality of good. God is not mentioned in every verse, but his activity is clearly behind every verse. God is the chief actor in Proverbs but not the sole actor. Human life is likened to an interactive game in which each person is a player, freely making choices that God judges and either blesses or rejects. His blessings include success, prosperity, and long life. His curses are the opposite of those blessings. But Proverbs also makes clear that people can't understand his purposes in their own lives. If the outcome of our plans and choices is in the hands of God, then wisdom begins with fearing him.

According to Proverbs, the choices we make today shape our character tomorrow: whether we become wise or foolish, upright or wicked. The choice is ours.

Ecclesiastes

This book, written by Qoheleth (probably Solomon) whom I called the teacher, explores the same territory as Proverbs, asking, What is the good life? But Ecclesiastes approaches this question from a very different vantage point: Solomon did research to answer this question. After investigating the paths that supposedly lead to a good life: wealth, accomplishments, pleasure, a good job, and even his personal favorite—that is, wisdom—the teacher concluded that all of them are vanity, meaning they are at best a shallow happiness that lasts about as long as a soap bubble.

The teacher identified three major reasons for his conclusion that everything is vanity: (1) the fact that bad things happen to good people (and vice versa), (2) the many uncertainties of life resulting in our inability to know which events will happen and why, and (3) the one absolute certainty, death, which looms over us all; whether rich or poor, whether righteous or unrighteous, whether human or animal, we will all die. And, as the saying goes, we can't take it with us, so the accomplishments we had in this life won't accompany us to the grave. And once we die, we will soon be forgotten, and our legacy will be enjoyed by others, perhaps by fools.

However, the teacher was not entirely pessimistic. He identified two aspects of the good life that everyone, rich or poor, can enjoy: the ordinary pleasures of eating and drinking with family and friends, and his final conclusion that everyone's duty is to trust and obey, to fear God and keep his commandments. In its conclusion, the book of Ecclesiastes sounds like Proverbs after all.

The Book of Job

Job dared to question the one thing that Ecclesiastes never did: the justice of God. Is he trustworthy? Throughout human history many skeptics have questioned the goodness of God, but Job was not such a skeptic; he was a sincere believer with "perfect integrity," who, nevertheless, dared to ask hard questions about his faith. Ironically, his doubts about God's goodness were actually an expression of his faith: because he had always trusted God to be good, he could not understand why God suddenly seemed to be acting out of character.

The book of Job tells a single story consisting of two meetings in heaven, a series of lengthy debates on earth, a pair of Q and A sessions with a windstorm, and finally a climax in which God announced the winner and losers of the debate—without ever revealing what was really going on. And every part of this drama focuses on the man Job. In this story, Job's righteousness was clearly on trial, but God's justice was also on trial, and actually wisdom was being challenged as well: Was the wisdom of the wisest men of that day, including Job, up to explaining the circumstances of Job's life? It was not. The failure of human wisdom to explain Job's sufferings set the stage for a new definition of wisdom to be revealed in the book.

The score card for the actors in the drama was as follows:

- Satan lost his wager with God. Job did not curse God.
- Job's friends made false accusations against Job, and despite their pious words, they also spoke falsely about God.
- Job was declared the victor, not based on having better arguments but based on his unshakable faith.
- God "won" as his trust in Job's integrity was upheld—though God did have to teach Job a lesson about how he administers his world according to a plan.
- Wisdom, which could not explain Job's problems, survived in a new form: as fearing God and shunning evil—which was how God had described Job at the beginning of the story.

In retrospect, Job became a model for all of us who also suffer without knowing why.

The Gospels

The unanimous conclusion of the Old Testament wisdom writers was that nobody knew God's wisdom. It was inaccessible and inscrutable and not even "the wise" could understand God's purposes and plans. That conclusion was reversed when the Messiah arrived. He knew the very thoughts of God.

Jesus redefined wisdom at every level. He was more clever than the theologians of the day and could answer their challenging questions. His claim to wisdom, however, went much deeper. He not only knew God's plans, which had been concealed from the beginning of time, but he was co-wise with God. But beyond this, he was God's wisdom in the flesh, the *Logos*, the incarnation of Wisdom. And to some he revealed God's wisdom—if they came to him as humble as a child.

So, when the Messiah came and lived among us, wisdom also came and lived among us. In Jesus his followers could learn wisdom from his teachings, and they could see wisdom in practice by watching how he lived.

The Writings of Paul

The apostle Paul took the idea of Jesus as Wisdom incarnate and ran with it. Paul wrote that Christ is God's Power and Wisdom (1 Cor 1:24), he is both Creator and Redeemer, transforming the lives of those who are united with him by faith, and bringing about a new gathering of all the people of God, including Jews and gentiles, now together as one body. It may surprise those of us, who see the church with all its flaws, that Paul called the church a manifestation of the wisdom of God and that he saw it as God's showcase of unity and grace, a testimony to the world and to the angels.

Paul described the gospel message as a mystery revealing God's wisdom, a message those alleged to be wise had not foreseen and did not recognize when it appeared. Just as Jesus said that his Father did not reveal truth to the educated men of his day, Paul now preached a "foolish" message to the weak and the foolish. But any who believe this message receive the mind of Christ and the Spirit who enables them/us to live wisely and godly now. This is a very different sort of wisdom and a far better one than the wisdom this world offers.

The Book of James

James offered two lessons about wisdom. The first was that wisdom is available to anyone who will ask God to provide it—if they ask with faith and without doubt. This gift of wisdom has the ability to complete what may be lacking in a person's faith.

In his second lesson, James took our understanding of wisdom to a deeper level by dividing it into two camps: earthly wisdom and heavenly wisdom. The first type is wisdom corrupted by sin: the sins of pride, boasting, lying, envy, selfish ambition, fighting, pleasure seeking, and judging one another. James saw this earthly wisdom as responsible for the conflict and corruption in the churches of his day.

On the other hand, the wisdom God gives is marked by good deeds and meekness—like the wisdom of Jesus. Heavenly wisdom is humble, pure, merciful, peaceable, and righteous. As we have repeatedly said, wisdom is best seen in good character.

James's division of wisdom into two camps and his observation that wisdom can be corrupted by sin leading to every sort of evil might cause us to question whether wisdom is what the world needs now. If wisdom is complicit in bringing about the conflict and corruption in the churches of our day, then we all need to reexamine our hearts, our words, and our relationships to be sure that we have the right sort of wisdom. In particular, Christian teachers need to control their tongues (their speech) if they are to display the sort of wisdom typified by good deeds and meekness. This is the wisdom that the church—and the world—needs now!

44

The Inauspicious Record of Wisdom

THE SURVEY OF THE wisdom books in the previous chapter concluded with a discouraging realization: wisdom can be corrupted by sin. As we shall see in this chapter, that thought is not new. It is as old as the garden of Eden! This chapter will look at two sources of confusion that have clouded our understanding of wisdom: moral confusion and cultural diversity.

MORAL CONFUSION

Lady Eve

The search for wisdom goes way back. Wisdom was something that Eve wanted. But as she grasped for it, she lost it. The irony of her desire for wisdom was that the serpent's offer of a god-like knowledge of good and evil had the opposite effect. Her taste test of the forbidden fruit took Eve, Adam, and the rest of us down the wrong road leading to moral confusion.

Here is a retelling of that first temptation from Gen 3:

> Eve had a good life in the Garden. She and Adam were simple (naïve and inexperienced), but they were content. They had everything they needed to live and be happy. But, as we all know, having everything we need is never enough. There was one thing

Eve lacked: wisdom—that is the knowledge of good and evil. But she wasn't aware of that lack until someone told her that she lacked it. Suddenly she wanted it. Suddenly she needed it.

Now, the wisdom literature tells us what to do when we lack wisdom, we ask God for it. But that simple answer didn't occur to Eve because the individual who told her she lacked wisdom also told her that the knowledge she wanted was readily available for the taking. That tempter, the Serpent, invited Eve to come and eat, and reassured her that she would become as wise as God, and there would be no negative consequences: she would not die.

Eve was deceived. She ate. She died. We died.

How ironic that humanity's moral confusion sprang out of an attempt to gain wisdom and moral understanding! What is good? What is evil? It seems we still don't know.

Lady Folly

This inauspicious beginning of the search for wisdom has been repeated countless times throughout history. Eve's quest for wisdom apart from God has become the template used ever since to gain wisdom—with the same results.

In Prov 9 we read about another tempter—we have called her Lady Folly. She makes a similar offer:

> The woman Folly is loud;
>   she is seductive and knows nothing.
> She sits at the door of her house;
>   she takes a seat on the highest places of the town,
> calling to those who pass by,
>   who are going straight on their way,
> "Whoever is simple, let him turn in here!"
>   And to him who lacks sense she says,
> "Stolen water is sweet,
>   and bread eaten in secret is pleasant!" (Prov 9:13–17)

Lady Folly knows that the children of Eve are still simple and she appeals to their naïveté: "Come and eat. Forbidden foods taste the best! There won't be any consequences for eating at my feast." However, she conceals the ultimate consequence of eating her food is death: "the dead are there" (9:18).

These two stories are repeated daily in every town, in every period throughout history: "Come and eat." And the forbidden food these tempters offer is delicious not because one is hungry but just because it is forbidden. Stolen water is desirable because it is stolen. Secret bread is more tempting because it is eaten in secret.

We hear echoes of Lady Folly's voice in almost every novel, movie, TV show, advertisement, and internet post. Her voice is still heard on street corners as well as in the most prominent places in town; and the simple still respond. Tragically, it is not just the simple who respond to her invitation to "come and eat" but also the "wise," who should have known better. They write academic essays defending their crookedness. And those who read their "wisdom" end up more confused and more confusing to others. The world is awash with fools who have dined at Lady Folly's buffet.

The book of James gives us additional insight about those who choose Lady Folly's feast. It seems that we don't even need to be invited to "come and eat":

> Each person is tempted when he is lured and enticed by his own desire. Then desire when it is conceived gives birth to sin, and sin when it is fully grown brings forth death. (Jas 1:14–15)

In other words, we yield to temptations because we want to. That is the ultimate foolishness!

Worldly Wisdom

The problem of wisdom goes much deeper than good people being tempted to stray from good paths. The Bible in both testaments says that human wisdom is incapable of discerning God's wisdom. Solomon said that not even the wise can comprehend it. Jesus praised his Father for concealing truth from the wise and understanding and revealing it to little children. The apostle Paul said that God in his wisdom had made the wisdom of men foolish: "For the foolishness of God is wiser than men, and the weakness of God is stronger than men" (1 Cor 1:25). God's plan to bring salvation and his kingdom was not just beyond the reach of human wisdom, it contradicted it! Possessing human wisdom was counterproductive in understanding what God had been doing.

James took these thoughts one step further by giving us a new analysis of how bad human wisdom can be:

> If you have bitter jealousy and selfish ambition in your hearts, do not boast and be false to the truth. This is not the wisdom that comes down from above, but is earthly, unspiritual, demonic. For where jealousy and selfish ambition exist, there will be disorder and every vile practice. (3:14–15)

Worldly wisdom may seem attractive, but it is deceptive. The result of worldly wisdom is disorder and every vile practice—the end of which is death.

Of course, the greater tragedy in this historical record of wisdom gone bad is that James was not describing the sins of the pagan world as he warned about worldly wisdom; he was writing about the churches of his day. Was he also writing about churches of our day? Do jealousy and selfish ambition describe churches which, according to the mystery of God, were supposed to be places of grace and unity?

Would James have to ask us, "Who is wise and understanding among you?" (Jas 3:13).

Would James feel the need to remind our churches, "God opposes the proud but gives grace to the humble"? (Jas 4:6).

The Human Heart

Perhaps we are all tempted by fruit that is "good for food and a delight to the eyes" or by "stolen water" or by "selfish ambition"; but the result of worldly wisdom is always the same: disorder and death. The temptations differ, but the result is the same.

The irony of this history of wisdom's failures is that Eve already had enough wisdom to have avoided the temptation by which the serpent enticed her. She already knew the one rule she was supposed to follow—she even quoted it—but then she chose not to follow it. She knew better but she disobeyed. By definition, any temptation has to involve some prior knowledge of right and wrong. So, when tempted, every sinner knows better. As James described it, every sinner gets dragged away by evil desires, which lead them into sin. So, every sinner knows better. The book of Proverbs suggests that every fool also knows better.

Jesus taught that evil desires are present in every heart. He reframed the Old Testament teaching about uncleanness by saying that the source of human uncleanness is not our environment—so we should stop blaming our environment for making us do what we secretly wanted to do;

the problem, according to Jesus, is that our heart is already full of evil thoughts and intentions (Mark 7:14–23). Human evil is the disease for which Proverbs said wisdom is the cure. But to effectively treat the disease, wisdom must be internalized and guarded within one's heart, or we will continue to stray. As the teacher of Ecclesiastes wrote, "This only have I found: God created mankind upright, but they have gone in search of many schemes" (Eccl 7:29). We actually search for wicked schemes.

Even Solomon's wisdom did not keep him from making foolish choices in his own life. It seems that not even biblical wisdom is an adequate treatment for the flaw found in every human heart. As long as we secretly desire "stolen water," not even wisdom can help us. That is why we need more than wisdom. We need a Savior.

CULTURAL DIVERSITY

If the first challenge to our gaining wisdom is moral confusion, a second challenge is cultural diversity. Around the world in different countries and cultures there are thousands of local forms of wisdom that differ from one another.

Let me say upfront that I like cultural diversity. As a former missionary I have enjoyed the various cultures where my wife and I have lived, and I have learned better approaches to life in each place. Learning from others is one path to gaining wisdom and that is most obviously true when living in another culture. But this diversity also creates problems for living wisely.

A definition of wisdom given in chapter 6 is "understanding how the world works and choosing courses of action that will work accordingly." To be wise requires an understanding of basic reality and knowledge of how to live successfully within that reality. But this definition raises the question as to whether any of the world's cultures really understand how the world works. Every culture and every worldview has its own variety of wisdom teachings that reflect its assumptions about reality. Cultural diversity has produced wisdom diversity, and that diversity has both strengths and weaknesses.

Wisdom diversity can be a strength because within each culture the local wisdom is relevant and practical. Because it is aligned with the local cultural assumptions about reality, the advice offered by local wisdom makes sense, and it often "works" within that system. For example, in a society that believes in spiritism,[1] a witchdoctor or fortune teller may prescribe animal sacrifices, magic rituals, or amulets to cure sickness. Magic is a kind of wisdom that makes sense and is believed to work within a spiritist culture. However, in a culture based on the assumptions of naturalism, a worldview that denies any spiritual or supernatural reality, a doctor or a counselor might prescribe surgery, pills, or talk therapy—treatments that make sense and are believed to be effective within the assumptions of that culture. To a naturalist, the amulet used by a witchdoctor seems to be silly superstition. To the animist, the pill prescribed by the medical doctor may seem to work by magic. Both of these examples show how the treatment for sickness prescribed by wisdom professionals will be believed to be effective according to the assumptions of their own worldview. And people who share that worldview will follow their advice because it makes sense to them.

In each culture, the local wisdom seemingly works because it relates to the local worldview. But being relevant to a particular culture is also a weakness because no form of wisdom can rise higher than its host culture. Local wisdom will always share the flaws of the local worldview and belief systems.

I agree with Albert Einstein's assessment of common sense: "Common sense is actually nothing more than a deposit of prejudices laid down in the mind prior to the age of eighteen."[2] But I would paraphrase Einstein to say that "wisdom is the collection of cultural prejudices acquired by age eighteen." Cultural diversity has brought forth thousands of wisdoms around the world. Each is a collection of the cultural blinders and biases through which people view life. The result is a wisdom relativism in which the local wisdom will make sense while other wisdoms won't. No variety of wisdom works everywhere—which negates the whole idea of wisdom.

My wife and I have experienced wisdom relativism as we have lived in several other countries with their own cultures and their own ideas of wisdom. Even as we have moved from state to state within the United States, we have been surprised at the degree of cultural diversity between states. American regions can differ as greatly as do other countries! Every place has its own biases and blinders. And those biases always influence the local views of common sense, of wisdom, of morality, of values, of

---

1. Spiritism is also called by other names—for example, animism or tribalism.
2. Einstein, quoted by Barnett, *Universe and Dr. Einstein*, 52.

priorities, and even of how to practice the Christian faith. To live as a Christian in Oklahoma is different than how to live as a Christian in Minnesota or in India! And, like Job's friends, everyone everywhere seems to think that they have God all figured out. But are any of them actually wise?

As I said above, I enjoy cultural diversity. One of my joys in visiting foreign lands is attending churches where the preaching and singing are in a language I can't speak or understand. It reminds me of what heaven will be like. But as I travel, I have not found the people in any place to be wiser than in any other place. Perhaps the people who attend the local church where Jean and I now attend would be offended that I don't consider America to be the epitome of wisdom. I feel certain that some of the members of our church think of America as the greatest country in the world.[3] But, as a citizen born and raised in the United States, I know it well enough that I can see both its virtues and its follies intertwined. Sometimes its virtues are also its follies. And such a mixture of virtues and follies is found in every country and culture.

Cultural diversity is good because it enables us to see life through different lenses and learn from them. But cultural diversity is also a weakness because every culture has its own set of biases and blinders, which cloud its wisdom. Not only does each culture have its own kind of wisdom, it also has its own kind of foolishness. Wherever we go around the world, we find both.

The question remains: Is there any wisdom that rises above its local roots? Is there a super-cultural wisdom to seek? As a Christian I want to believe that biblical wisdom is that supra-cultural wisdom. But perhaps that is just my own biases speaking.

---

3. On a recent trip to Australia, I picked up a gospel tract in a local church that showed an Australian flag on one side and stated "we all know that Australia is the greatest country in the world" on the other. I smiled and kept the tract to show to my American friends.

45

No One Is Smart Enough to Be Wise

ANOTHER PROBLEM IN OUR search for wisdom is the observation that wisdom often doesn't "work" because nobody is that smart. We have repeatedly said that being wise is not the same as being smart, but wisdom does require some basic intellectual skills such as knowledge, understanding, and discernment. Perfect wisdom would require perfect knowledge and intelligence, and nobody is that smart.

LOST IN A MAZE

In his book *Knowing God*, J. I. Packer gave an illustration of the problem of human wisdom.[1] He described a large railway station in which tracks from different cities converged into a central rail yard. There they crossed, merged, and diverged in what appeared as confusion to passengers trying to watch it all from one of the platforms. From the passengers' perspective, the paths followed by the trains were confusing. But Packer suggested, if these passengers could gain access to the control tower with its diagram showing all the tracks, they could understand the pattern. But without such access, everybody is lost in the tangle.

Since I have almost no experience in large railway stations, I offer a different illustration that makes the same point: Suppose someone is trying to find their way through a corn maze (a maize maze?). At various

---

1. Packer, *Knowing God*, 92.

points in the maze, they come to an intersection of paths where they have to decide whether to turn right or left. Which path will lead them to the finish and which one will leave them further lost in the maze? From their vantage point inside the maze they can't tell, but if they had a link to a drone with a camera flying overhead, they could see which option was best. People imagine that wisdom is like having such a drone.

These illustrations suggest that our lives are often like being lost in a maze without a drone. None of us have the top-down perspective or the necessary knowledge to understand all that is going on. Nobody sees the big picture with its multiple variables, and nobody knows the future. None of us are smart enough to be wise.

The flip side of that illustration is the true story told in chapter 1 of the time my wife and I were guided by a GPS to take a single-lane road atop a levee. It was the wrong road, and we were forced to drive backwards for a mile between steep slopes on both sides. Reversing the GPS's error was frightening! My conclusion from that story was that GPSs are very useful except when they're wrong—and they often are wrong. It seems we can get lost with guidance or without it! Wisdom is like that.

Packer said that nobody is smart enough to be wise, but it seems many people feel confident that they are smart enough. Sometimes their self-confidence is simple foolishness, the narcissistic belief that one is smarter than everyone else. We see such self-confidence all around us—and we even encourage it in our children. While children need support, self-esteem can be overdone.

Perhaps, however, a few people really are smarter or more skilled and therefore wiser than others—at least in regard to some specialty. Their self-confidence is based on their personal experience or training, and those of us who lack their expertise trust them for guidance when we face problems or opportunities relating to their specialty. But even experts make mistakes. And comparing the advice of expert to expert shows how different their answers can be. Expert advice is good but not perfect.

Advisors are our GPSs to navigate through life. Whether we are facing smaller daily questions or the bigger questions that can shape our career, even our GPSs can be wrong. And if we are facing life and death kinds of decisions, or worldview-level questions—such as, What's really real? Or how can we discern truth? Or is there a God and what does he think about my life?—those gigantic questions are beyond everyone's level of expertise!

A wise person recognizes what they know and don't know. This requires honesty and humility, two traits which are at the heart of true wisdom. When anyone has confidence beyond the limits of their own knowledge, we call their confidence hubris. Such overconfidence, while common, can create worse problems than just getting lost on the way to a visitor's center—imagine getting lost on the way to heaven!

OVERCONFIDENCE AND CONFIRMATION BIAS

Research on the topic of overconfidence has shown that there is often an inverse relationship between confidence and competence. I found this correlation in the research for my doctoral dissertation.[2] I questioned college students doing intercultural ministry regarding how effective they considered themselves, and then I compared this with their supervisor's ratings of their effectiveness. Higher levels of self-confidence among students correlated with lower effectiveness ratings by their supervisors. In other words, confidence and competence were inversely related.

In his book *Think Again: The Power of Knowing What You Don't Know*, Adam Grant summarized research findings on the limitations of self-confidence and on the dangers of confirmation bias that cause us to think our knowledge is better than it is. Grant said, "If knowledge is power, knowing what we don't know is wisdom."[3]

The teacher of Ecclesiastes ran into this problem as he did his research—only the failure of wisdom he found was his own:

> All this I have tested by wisdom. I said, "I will be wise," but it was far from me. That which has been is far off, and deep, very deep; who can find it out? (7:23–24)

Ultimately the teacher concluded that nobody, not even "the wise"—not even he himself—understands what happens under the sun (8:17).

This negative assessment of the lack of understanding for the so-called wise may remind us of Socrates, the Greek philosopher, who conducted an investigation seeking individuals who were truly wise within the city of Athens. Socrates' dismissal of the claim of wisdom by these so-called wise men led to his arrest and execution for daring to question the status quo.

---

2. Giles, "Intercultural Competence," 180.
3. Grant, *Think Again*, 28.

In their two different investigations searching for wisdom among real people, both Solomon and Socrates reached identical conclusions: there is no wisdom anywhere. Nevertheless, many people, then and now, profess to be wise. In response to this, the book of Proverbs warns that to be wise in one's own eyes leaves one worse off than a fool (Prov 26:12).

There is an exception to Packer's principle that nobody is smart enough to be wise, or Grant's warning that self-confidence is usually overconfidence—the exception being that God, who is smart enough and who alone is truly wise, can reveal his knowledge to us. He has spoken in Scripture and through his Son with whom he is co-wise. It is by revelation, not intellect, that wisdom is found. And the Bible's wisdom writers all agree that such knowledge begins with the fear of the Lord.

Our investigation into wisdom have taken us from Eden, to Jerusalem, to Athens, and into modern cultures around the world, finding in each place that the search for wisdom has been a series of false starts and dead-end roads. Human wisdom has repeatedly failed to live up to its billing, leaving humanity ever more confused and leaving us with no certain answers for the many problems we face.

The next chapter will begin to restore wisdom to its status as the most desirable of all the virtues.

46

Restoring Wisdom

IF WISDOM SEEMS TO be just a bunch of cultural biases and empty deceits, is there nothing left from our study of wisdom worth holding onto? As I approach the conclusion of my study, I want to build an understanding of wisdom that will enable us to apply truth to our lives wisely. Let's rebuild a foundation for wisdom from the ground up.

Restoring wisdom will involve a three-part process labeled the beginning, the middle, and the end of wisdom. Taken together, these three phases must each be applied in this order for us to become wise. Each of the following sections will conclude with a practical application applying its truth to life.

THE BEGINNING OF WISDOM IS IGNORANCE

For each of us, wisdom begins with acknowledging that we lack it. Acknowledging our ignorance is the first real step to overcoming it. When God in a dream offered to give young King Solomon anything he would choose, he requested wisdom to rule his people well (1 Kgs 3:7–9). But the first part of his request was an acknowledgment of his lack of such wisdom. Throughout the biblical wisdom writings we saw that the only place to start in acquiring wisdom is humility, the humility to admit that we lack wisdom.

Perhaps it is surprising to consider ignorance as a virtue, but it may be humanity's best feature. Ignorance is not a virtue in itself, but it plays two pivotal roles in the search for wisdom: a negative role and a positive role.

Avoiding Being Wise in Our Own Eyes

Let's first consider the negative role. Claiming to be wise is the mark of a fool; therefore, acknowledging ignorance is avoiding foolishness. A fool doesn't know that he or she is a fool. They imagine themselves as smarter and wiser than others.

> Be not wise in your own eyes;
> fear the Lord, and turn away from evil. (Prov 3:7)

> The way of a fool is right in his own eyes,
> but a wise man listens to advice. (12:15)

> A fool takes no pleasure in understanding,
> but only in expressing his opinion. (18:2)

> Even a fool who keeps silent is considered wise;
> when he closes his lips, he is deemed intelligent. (17:28)

Fools display overconfidence in their intelligence and ability. As we saw in the previous chapter, confidence and competence are often inversely related. The fool's arrogance leads him or her to boast about themselves and to demean others. James called such boasting a denial of the truth. Being wise in one's own eyes is a sham and a scam because it hurts oneself and others, and because it prevents one from fearing the Lord. Fools would be wiser to admit their ignorance.

Continuous Learning

Now, consider the positive effects of acknowledging one's ignorance. The wisdom books, especially Proverbs, give several reasons to start our search for wisdom by admitting we lack it.

First, nobody is born wise. Proverbs calls the wisdom novice "simple" or "naïve." There is hope for the simple to become wise—if they listen to instruction and avoid temptation—but they are very vulnerable because Lady Folly is always beckoning them. They need to learn prudence (foresight and shrewdness) before it is too late.

A second reason found in Proverbs and Ecclesiastes is that even the wise are still learning (Prov 1:5; 9:9; Eccl 1:17). There is no shame in staying "in school." The best path to wisdom is by continuing to learn from others.

Ecclesiastes gave another reason for admitting our ignorance: life is filled with many uncertainties, including the weather, the uncertainty of who will win in sporting events or in battles, the timing of life events, which come at us unexpectedly, and the day of our death—which is the big unknown. Such uncertainties make life unpredictable, which greatly limits the possibility of giving wise advice. It is as if the teacher's lengthy search for the meaning of life ended up with a bunch of "God only knows"—but meant literally.

Perhaps the main reason for admitting one's ignorance is the fact that we are ignorant. In the conclusion of the book of Job, after being interrogated by the Lord, Job finally confessed his ignorant words regarding God's administration of God's world. He had finally learned that God has a plan, a reasonable purpose for all that he does, but Job hadn't even known there was such a plan. The smartest thing Job said in the whole book was to admit his own ignorance.

The poem "Ode to Wisdom" (Job 28) describes how miners dig deep into the earth to find valuable minerals but nobody knows where to find wisdom, which is even more valuable. Neither the ocean, the sky, or even Sheol know where to find wisdom. In the search for wisdom, everyone and everything is ignorant.

In the New Testament we learn one more reason to value ignorance: human wisdom has been counterproductive in understanding God's plan for humanity, which was a mystery until revealed in Christ. For the scholars, philosophers, and world leaders of those days (and still today), admitting their ignorance about things they knew little about would have been appropriate and a mark of true wisdom.

In the search for wisdom, it is important to recognize the difference between ignorance and stupidity. To be stupid is to not know and not know that we don't know, so we act like we know—which is foolishness. But to be ignorant is to not know and to acknowledge we don't know but are willing to learn. This combination of honesty *and* humility *is the beginning of wisdom.* The beginning of wisdom is admitting we lack it.

This Truth Applied to Life

How can we recognize someone who is wise? First, they are not wise in their own eyes; they are still learning; they know what they know and what they don't know, and they are willing to admit what they don't know. The truly wise are not known for boasting about their wisdom.

In my experience, a good way to learn about one's ignorance is to become a foreign missionary. Some missionaries arrive in another country ready to teach, confident (overconfident) in their ability to adapt to the local culture, and with a know-it-all attitude toward religion. But wise missionaries arrive aware of their ignorance, willing to learn, and willing to make mistakes and then laugh at themselves. It is humbling to walk down the street of a foreign town and know that every two-year-old child speaks the local language and understands the culture better than you do! But that exercise in humility is a first step to wisdom—and it can also be the first step to learning the new culture!

Perhaps for those of us who won't become foreign missionaries and may never travel abroad, we can learn from their attitude. A humble approach to life and a desire to learn from others is the beginning of wisdom for anyone.

THE MIDDLE OF WISDOM IS THE FEAR OF THE LORD

According to the worldview of monotheism, God is at the very center of everything that happens. This is the viewpoint revealed throughout Scripture: God is the King, Lord, Creator, Judge, and Redeemer. And God's rule extends far beyond the brief history of the world recorded in Scripture or in our world history textbooks. God is the Creator not just of our planet but of an entire universe, defined by a timeline extending from eternity to eternity including the "time" before creation (whatever that means) and the "time" after the eschaton (whatever that means). The created cosmos is defined from top to bottom by the realm of the heavens, the earth, and the nether regions, including the stars, the sky, the land and seas with all the inhabitants of each sphere: angels, powers, birds, fish, plants, animals, and humanity—with its race of narcissistic people who, though they were made in God's image, have always imagined themselves to be his superior. God's sovereign power controls the heavens, the weather, the seasons, the mighty sea creatures, diseases, kings, and kingdoms, and he determines the outcomes of each person's plans and choices. And, at one time, God even controlled the path of a "star" to guide some gentile astrologers to find the Jewish Messiah. God's vast knowledge encompasses what reaches beyond mankind's best telescopes or our most powerful microscopes and even includes knowing about each sparrow falling from its tree, knowing the number of hairs on each head, and knowing the secrets of each person's heart. But God's own secrets, his own plans and purposes, are shrouded in mystery. This is our God.

Even these descriptions of the God who lives in what we call infinity barely scratch the surface of his ways. The biblical writers all assert the mystery of God's wisdom. They believe that God rules his universe and his people according to a plan, but they also assert that his plan is unknown and unknowable. Humanity's smartest scholars offer their best guesses as to the principles that guide reality and history, but their guesses are speculations. Unless God reveals his plans and purposes through his prophets or through his Son, we all remain clueless. Biblical wisdom requires revelation, and it requires trusting God rather than relying on one's own understanding.

So, what have we learned about God's wisdom?

1. He has had an eternal plan to reconcile the world to himself through Jesus Christ, a plan that was hidden throughout history until the time of Christ's appearing. Christmas is not just a happy holiday, it is a turning point in time, scheduled before creation itself.

2. God determines the events of history: the rise and fall of kings and kingdoms; the winners and losers of battles and of elections; he determines disasters, hurricanes, tornadoes, floods, droughts, and plagues of many kinds. How God uses these events to accomplish his eternal purpose is always a mystery. Though many books claim to explain God's reasons for historical disasters, the truth, according to Ecclesiastes, is that of the making of such books there is no end. And, another truth, also according to Ecclesiastes, is nobody, no matter how smart, understands God's reasons—not even the wise! When it comes to interpreting history, if God is silent, then the wisest thing anyone can do is to remain silent.

3. God also determines the events of individual lives. Referencing Ecclesiastes again, the poem "A Time for Everything" (Eccl 3:1–8) describes every life with a list of paired life events, ranging from

positive to negative events, happy to unhappy times, each of which may happen to each of us at the "proper time" as determined by God. God has even scheduled the wicked for a day of trouble (Prov 16:4). God schedules the day of our death—though, it seems, we might hasten this day through foolishness (Eccl 7:17; 9:12). Each person has been allotted a time to live, work to be accomplished, and even good times to be enjoyed along the way. It is wisdom for each of us to accept his plans, to be content, and to enjoy the life that God has allotted for us. We gain nothing by resisting the content or timing of the plans God has set.

4. Though the wisdom literature acknowledges God and his sovereign rule as at the center of how the world works, human freedom and responsibility are not downplayed. We each can choose our paths, our plans, and our actions, and he judges our choices—usually doing so silently from the background. Proverbs, Ecclesiastes, Job, and James emphasize the importance of making wise choices and warn about the dangerous and even deadly consequences of making poor choices. Proverbs calls bad choices foolish or wicked. Ecclesiastes calls them stupid or mad. James calls them sinful and enmity with God.

So how does God's sovereignty fit together with human responsibility? Konkel wrote,

> God fashions the thoughts of all people.... He determines the limits of their freedom. The Lord who stretched out the heavens and founded the earth, formed the spirit (or breath) within humankind and he will fulfill his purposes for his people.[1]

The sovereign God allows all of us a limited degree of freedom, but he never stops seeking his own purpose for the world and for each life.

The Wisdom of Monotheism

As we said earlier, every worldview has its own variety of wisdom. For monotheism wisdom is grounded in God having created the world to be an orderly place. Wisdom only "works" if there is a degree of predictability allowing for the wise to choose the best path forward. But what does wisdom mean if the primary actor in the world is all knowing, all powerful, and yet all mysterious? What does wisdom mean if in fact

---

1. Konkel, "יצר," 504.

nobody really understands God's plans? A central question of the wisdom literature is, How can anyone make wise decisions when God's ways are inscrutable and unpredictable? Job's answer to that question, his hope which Satan was unable to topple, was to continue trusting God even when he didn't understand God's reasons.

Throughout Job's long debate with his friends, Job was already wise—though he didn't understand that he was. In the poem "Ode to Wisdom" (Job 28), wisdom is defined:

> And he [God] said to man, "Behold, the fear of the Lord, that is wisdom, and to turn away from evil is understanding." (Job 28:28)

The fear of the Lord is the only reasonable answer to the question as to how Job or any of us can live wisely when God's ways are unknown. Though Job's questions at times bordered on doubting his faith, he never lost it. He held on to his hope that God was still good, still just, and still trustworthy. And that thread of hope was what enabled him to keep his faith. At the end of Job's story, God revealed himself as sufficient to administer the universe and therefore as trustworthy to handle Job's life. God's revelation of himself, whether through his questions, his lectures, or through the power of a windstorm, was all the wisdom Job needed—though he never got answers to his question, "Why me?"

Because God is sovereign and because his purposes and plans are unknown and unknowable, the only wise choice is to fear and trust him! The sovereign God is trustworthy, which is why "the fear of the Lord" is the beginning of wisdom (Prov 9:10).

Does the fear of the Lord still define wisdom in the New Testament? On the one hand, the New Testament did not change the basic understanding of wisdom. God's ways are still greater than our ways and his thoughts are greater than our thoughts, and therefore the essence of wisdom is still to fear him. Christians acknowledge this continuity by keeping Prov 3:5-6—"Trust in the Lord with all your heart and lean not on your own understanding"—as one of the most memorized verses from Scripture.

God's inscrutable plans for administering the world, human history, and the redemption of his people became visible in the most unlikely of places: in a poor, homeless, itinerant rabbi named Jesus. He revealed his Father's wisdom both in his teachings and in his life. James reframed the definition of wisdom as good deeds and meekness, and he did this based on his personal experiences with Jesus.

The apostle Paul redefined wisdom as being found in Christ who embodied God's power and wisdom. And for those who believed in him, as foolish as that belief seemed to the world's so-called intelligensia, they received the mind of Christ—a better kind of wisdom.

This Truth Applied to Life

Monotheism has its own variety of wisdom, and it is not what we expect or desire. Many times, Christians are too much like Job's friends, believing in a simple God who acts predictably and in a small God who fits neatly into our little theological boxes. The wisdom literature universally affirms that God is neither simple nor predictable, and he is not limited to our miniaturized ideas about him.

For Christians, the highest form of wisdom is having the mind of Christ, but this will not enable us to solve every problem, big or small. Biblical wisdom has never been primarily about problem solving. Instead, biblical wisdom teaches us to walk the straight path in the way that Jesus did, with good deeds and meekness. Biblical wisdom is about caring for one another and caring for the grass being trampled by the elephant wars all around us—even the wars in our churches.

In both the Old and New Testaments, fearing God is the starting point toward making moral choices, which are also based on following the instructions we learned from parents, teachers, and wise advisors; and along the way we accept God's corrections and discipline to keep us on the straight path. God has promised straight paths to those who trust in him. The wise let God be God, and they accept his sovereign—but unknown—plans and timing as gifts. Rather than resisting God's paths, the wise practice contentment and enjoyment for the brief lifetime God has allotted each of us.

What will wisdom look like in our hearts and lives? I suggest integrity.

THE END OF WISDOM IS INTEGRITY

What is God's plan for the lives of his people? The answer found throughout the wisdom literature is good character. In the Old Testament such character was based on wisdom and righteousness, traits that can be internalized and kept in the heart. In the New Testament good character was defined by the life of Jesus the Messiah. For his followers, good character was/is Christlikeness.

Biblical terms that describe good character are an obedient heart, walking the straight path, godliness, being upright, faithful, honest, and humble. We could add many other desirable traits to this list, but, in my opinion, the most important character trait is integrity.

The English word "integrity" is part of a cluster of related words meaning "oneness" or "wholeness," with related English words like integer, integrated, entire, unit, and unity. The implied meaning is of one single thing or, perhaps, a composite thing. In terms of human character, the word "integrity" suggests consistency between a person's core beliefs and habitual behaviors. Integrity requires honesty, and so we often use "integrity" and "honesty" as synonyms. The English antonyms for integrity are duplicity and hypocrisy. In simple terms, integrity means "real," and its antonym is "fake." In terms of character, for those with integrity, the outer appearance of good character is real. For those lacking integrity, the appearance of good character is a show.

In the Hebrew language, there is a slightly different cluster of words translated as "integrity": perfection, without blemish, moral goodness, and blamelessness.[2] Just as animals for sacrifice had to be without blemish, so a person, to be holy, should be without moral blemish, blameless. The Hebrew sense of integrity is character based on the character of God. God always displays integrity in his dealings with humankind.

> God's integrity is defined by the basic credo of the OT, "The Lord our God, the Lord is one" (Deut 6:4), in the sense that God is always the one and the same God, true to himself; hence always trustworthy and utterly dependable, because there exists complete harmony between his being and deeds. Humanity's integrity is but a reflection of this oneness, and consequently there is a correspondence between intention and action, faith and deeds, dogma and ethos. It implies a wholesome life in the presence of the Lord, as of one who is blameless in the cult, reliable under all circumstances, trustworthy in business dealings, and living in harmony with one's neighbor, always compassionate and serving the cause of justice and peace. Integrity means soundness of character and adherence to the moral principles of

---

2. Olivier, "תמם," 306–8.

uprightness and honesty exemplified by David (1 Kgs 9:4) and Job (Job 2:3, 9; 27:5).[3]

Thus, integrity implies the perfection of God in terms of his consistency between inner intentions and outer behaviors. Perhaps this sense of perfection as consistency is what Jesus meant when he said that people must be "perfect, as your Heavenly Father is perfect" (Matt 5:48). While believers may never achieve sinlessness, our goal is to develop consistency, always being the same person, including in both character and behavior.

We could envision two opposite kinds of integrity: a consistency based on godliness or one based on ungodliness. A devil may have consistency between an evil heart and evil actions, a negative integrity. Sadly, this negative form may be easier for us humans to achieve. It is easier to be all bad than all good. But in Scripture the references to integrity always mean integrity in the positive sense: a consistency of good character with both godly attitudes and godly behaviors. Such consistency will include loving others, including both our neighbors and our enemies, because we value the image of God in all people; honesty in words and in business practices, because we value truth more than status or wealth; fleeing adultery, because we hold on to faithfulness to commitments made; and serving others—rather than desiring to be served by others—because we value humility and equality. Integrity is about consistency inside and outside in all circumstances and in all relationships. Integrity unifies the traits of righteousness into one trait, which is the capstone of the character of the wise.

Though integrity does not require sinlessness, it "guides the upright" (Prov 11:3), in contrast with the perversity of the treacherous. In a world of multiple temptations to crookedness, integrity can keep the upright on straight paths.

The book of Job highlights Job's integrity (Job 1:1; translated as "perfect integrity" in the HCSB; see also 1:8; 2:3, 9; 27:5; 31:6). Job's integrity included both high-quality morality and unshakable loyalty to God. Job's goodness was not just an outer show; his goodness manifested what was in his heart.

Throughout the book of Job, it was his integrity that was on trial. When Satan accused him and assaulted him, when his friends falsely accused him, Job's integrity protected him from sin. Ironically his accusation that God was treating him unjustly was actually a statement of his

---

3. Olivier, "כן," 664.

faith: God had always been good, and Job believed that he still was. Job continued to trust God because he had always known him to be trustworthy. And, amazingly, God also trusted Job because he had also known him to be trustworthy. God had integrity; Job had integrity.

This Truth Applied to Life

It is unfortunate that the importance of character is being downplayed by some Christian writers today. The gospel of prosperity, the gospel of popularity, and the gospel of political influence have led some Christians into choosing friendship with the world over allegiance to God. Without character in the church, integrity will also be lacking. Sadly, integrity is rare. Businesspeople, politicians, even friends and family often say one thing and mean the opposite. When such duplicity happens among religious people, we call it hypocrisy.

Integrity, a consistent morality between one's thoughts, one's words, and one's deeds, between commitments made and commitments kept, is at the heart of good character and of wisdom. A key word in applying integrity to life is trustworthiness. I hope we are all blessed to know a few people that we feel confident we can rely on when we need them because they are always the same person and their words reveal their thoughts. People with integrity can be trusted!

But the biggest question for each of us is, Am I a person with consistent character who can be trusted? If we lack integrity, we lack wisdom.

47

Wisdom for the Rest of Us

THE PROBLEM WITH THE picture of restored wisdom in the last chapter is that it is too perfect. None of us is a Jesus or even a Job.

The same criticism has often been made of the picture of wisdom (or of foolishness) in the book of Proverbs: either it is too good (or too bad) to be true. We said in our study of Proverbs that the book presents an ideal to which people should aspire. Proverbs teaches that every choice that anyone makes shapes their character and points them along a straight path or a crooked one, which will further shape their character. These ideals may seem too good to be true in any person's life, but the lessons these ideals teach are very real.

The last chapter described an ideal wisdom for which we can ask God. The promise is that righteousness and wisdom will keep us from stumbling. But our daily reality may sometimes feel more like this:

> The righteous falls seven times and rises again. (Prov 24:16)

Neither wisdom nor righteousness is foolproof—pun intended. We all may stumble, many times. Or, to paraphrase Jesus, though a righteous person falls seven times seventy times, they will get up—again and again! That is realistic.

In the final analysis, wisdom is not an abstract concept to be discussed in philosophy courses, self-help books, or in Bible study groups, it is a way of life to be lived out by real people in their homes, their businesses, their neighborhoods, their nation, and their churches. On the one hand, wisdom is expertise in living well. The principles of wisdom and righteousness are available to all, and they usually work. The purpose of those practical tips is to make each of us into a better person who treats others better, resulting in better families, better communities, and a better world for everyone. And though we sometimes slip or fall, wisdom, as seen in good character, can bring us back to the good path.

But beyond offering tips for the good life, the wisdom literature teaches that there is one certainty in the midst of life's many uncertainties: God is our Creator, our Teacher, our Judge, and our Redeemer. Though his ways may be beyond our understanding, and he may be silent when we ask him why, we can still trust him and enjoy the life he has allotted to us.

Bibliography

Adams, Douglas. *The Ultimate Hitchhiker's Guide to the Galaxy.* New York: Del Rey, 2002.
Aitken, Kenneth. "זקן." In *NIDOTTE* 1:1137–39.
Arndt, W. F., and F. W. Gingrich, eds. *A Greek-English Lexicon of the New Testament and Other Early Christian Literature.* Chicago: University of Chicago Press, 1957.
Baer, D. A., and R. P. Gordon. "חסד." In *NIDOTTE* 2:211–18.
Barnett, Lincoln. *The Universe and Dr. Einstein.* Foreword by Albert Einstein. New York: William Sloane, 1948.
Baker, David W. "רעע." In *NIDOTTE* 3:1154–59.
Benton, Robert, writ. and dir. *Places in the Heart.* Culver City, CA: Tri-Star Pictures, 1984.
Brown, Colin. "Mystery Religions." In *NIDNTT* 1:64.
Campolo, Tony. *Let Me Tell You a Story.* Nashville: Thomas Nelson, 2000.
Carpenter, Eugene. "עשה." In *NIDOTTE* 3:546–52.
Carpenter, Eugene, and Michael Grisanti. "רשע." In *NIDOTTE* 3:1201–4.
Carpenter, Micah. *A Scandalous People: Ephesians on the Meaning of Christian Faith and Human Life.* Eugene, OR: Wipf & Stock, 2020. Kindle.
Chan, Kam-Yao Alan, et al. "רפא." In *NIDOTTE* 3:1162–73.
Chisholm, Robert B. "בשר." In *NIDOTTE* 1:777–79.
———. "שהד." In *NIDOTTE* 3:1220.
David, Hal, lyricist. "What the World Needs Now Is Love." Composed by Burt Bacharach. Recorded by Jackie DeShannon. Hollywood: Imperial Records, 1965.
Domeris, W. R. "רוש." In *NIDOTTE* 3:1085–87.
Doyle, Arthur Conan. "The Adventure of the Final Problem." *The Strand Magazine*, London, Dec. 1983.
Dumbrell, W. J. "ענו." In *NIDOTTE* 3:454–64.
Dutra, Julian. "What Did Socrates, Plato, and Aristotle Think About Wisdom?" *The Collector*, June 12, 2022. https://www.thecollector.com/socrates-plato-aristotle-wisdom/.
Eib, Lynn. *50 Days of Hope: Daily Inspiration for Your Journey Through Cancer.* Carol Stream, IL: Tyndale Momentum, 2012.
Finkenrath, Günter. "Secret, Mystery, μυστήριον." In *NIDNTT* 3:501–6.
France, R. T. "Jesus Christ, Life and Teaching of." In *NBD* 563–75.

Franklin, Benjamin. *Wit and Wisdom from Poor Richard's Almanack.* Garden City, NY: Courier Dover Publications, 1999.

Giles, Greg. "The Relationship of Intercultural Competence to Ministry Effectiveness in the Christian College Context." PhD diss., Trinity Evangelical Divinity School, 1998.

Grant, Adam. *Think Again: The Power of Knowing What You Don't Know.* New York: Viking, 2021.

Grisanti, Michael A. "שמח." In *NIDOTTE* 3:1251–54.

Harman, Allan. "עין." In *NIDOTTE* 3:385–90.

Harnick, Sheldon, lyricist. "Tradition." Composed by Jerry Bock. *Fiddler on the Roof.* New York: Broadway, 1964.

———. "Sunrise, Sunset." Composed by Jerry Bock. *Fiddler on the Roof.* New York: Broadway, 1964.

Hartley, John E. "Job, Theology of." In *NIDOTTE* 4:780–96.

Horton, Geoff. "St. Teresa of Ávila: 'If This Is How You Treat Your Friends . . .'" *Fauxtations* (blog), Oct. 3, 2016. fauxtations.wordpress.com/2016/10/03/st-teresa-of-avila-if-this-is-how-you-treat-your-friends/.

Howley, G. C. D. "Evil." In *NBD* 348–49.

Hubbard, David A. "Proverbs, Book of." In *NBD* 977–79.

———. "Wisdom." In *NBD* 1244–45.

———. "Wisdom Literature." In *NBD* 1245–46.

Konkel, A.H., "יצר." In *NIDOTTE* 2:503–6.

Ladd, George Eldon. *A Theology of the New Testament.* Grand Rapids: Eerdmans, 1974.

Lewis, C. S. *The Last Battle.* New York: Macmillan, 1956.

———. *The Lion, the Witch, and the Wardrobe.* New York: Macmillan, 1956.

———. *Mere Christianity.* New York: Macmillan, 1960.

Martin, Frederic M. "Donald Trump and the Question of Character." Unpublished article, last modified 2019. Microsoft Word file.

Milne, B. A. "Righteousness." In *NBD* 1020–21.

Olivier, J. P. J. "כן." In *NIDOTTE* 2:664–65.

———. "תמם." In *NIDOTTE* 4:306–8.

Ortlund, Raymond C., Jr. *Proverbs: Wisdom That Works.* Wheaton, IL: Crossway, 2012.

Osborne, Grant R. Notes on *James.* In *The ESV Study Bible.* Wheaton, IL: Crossway, 2008.

O'Toole, James. *The Executive's Compass: Business and the Good Society.* Oxford: Oxford University Press, 1993.

Packer, J. I. *Knowing God.* Downers Grove, IL: InterVarsity, 1973.

———. "Revelation." In *NBD* 1014–16.

Peck, M. Scott, ed. *Abounding Grace: An Anthology of Wisdom.* Kansas City: Ariel, 2000.

Scott, R. B. Y. *Proverbs, Ecclesiastes.* Anchor Bible 18. New York: Doubleday, 1965.

Seeger, Pete. "Turn! Turn! Turn! (To Everything There Is a Season)." Track A6 on *The Bitter and the Sweet.* Columbia Records, 1959.

———. "Where Have All the Flowers Gone." Track 1 on *Where Have All the Flowers Gone: The Songs of Pete Seeger.* Columbia Records, 1967.

Shelley, Bruce L. *Church History in Plain Language.* 2nd ed. Nashville: Thomas Nelson, 1995.

Smith, Gary V., and Victor Hamilton. "גאה." In *NIDOTTE* 1:786–89.

Snodgrass, Klyne. *Ephesians*. NIV Application Commentary. Grand Rapids: Zondervan, 1996. Kindle.
Tasker, R. V. G. *The General Epistle of James*. Tyndale New Testament Commentaries. Grand Rapids: Eerdmans, 1977.
Thomas á Kempis. *The Imitation of Christ*. English translation 1901. https:en.wikisource.org/wiki/Of_the_Imitation_of_Christ.
Tomasino, Anthony. "ערד." In *NIDOTTE* 3:563–67.
Tongue, D. H. "Pride." In *NBD* 955–56.
Tucker, Ruth A. *Women in the Maze: Questions and Answers on Biblical Equality*. Downers Grove, IL: InterVarsity, 1992.
Wakely, Robin. "הרר." In *NIDOTTE* 2:288–95.
Waltke, Bruce K. "Proverbs, Theology of." In *NIDOTTE* 4:1079–94.
Ward, Ted. *Values Begin at Home*. Wheaton, IL: Victor, 1979.
Wegner, Paul D. "זקן." In *NIDOTTE* 1:1134–37.
Wikipedia. "Arthur Conan Doyle." https://en.wikipedia.org/wiki/Arthur_Conan_Doyle.
Wilson, Gerald H. "Wisdom." In *NIDOTTE* 4:1276–85.
Wood, Gordon S. *The American Revolution: A History*. New York: Modern Library, 2002.
Woods, Guy N. *A Commentary on the Epistle of James*. Nashville: Gospel Advocate, 1964.
Yancey, Philip. *The Bible Jesus Read*. Grand Rapids: Zondervan, 1999.

www.ingramcontent.com/pod-product-compliance
Lightning Source LLC
Chambersburg PA
CBHW071227230426
43668CB00011B/1340